5, 16. 00

For Katrina Clark,
    with warn regards,
    Pericles

MODERNISM, NATIONALISM, AND THE NOVEL

In *Modernism, Nationalism, and the Novel* Pericles Lewis shows how political debates over the sources and nature of "national character" prompted radical experiments in narrative form amongst modernist writers. Though critics have accused the modern novel of shunning the external world, Lewis suggests that, far from abandoning nineteenth-century realists' concern with politics, the modernists used this emphasis on individual consciousness to address the distinctively political ways in which the modern nation-state shapes the psyche of its subjects. Tracing this theme through Joyce, Proust, and Conrad, amongst others, Lewis claims that modern novelists gave life to a whole generation of narrators who forged new social realities in their own images. Their literary techniques – multiple narrators, transcriptions of consciousness, involuntary memory, and arcane symbolism – focused attention on the shaping of the individual by the nation and on the potential of the individual, in time of crisis, to redeem the nation.

PERICLES LEWIS is Assistant Professor of English and Comparative Literature at Yale University. He has published articles on Joseph Conrad, James Joyce, Bram Stoker, Walter Benjamin, and Giambattista Vico. This is his first book.

Modernism, Nationalism, and the Novel

PERICLES LEWIS

CAMBRIDGE
UNIVERSITY PRESS

PUBLISHED BY THE PRESS SYNDICATE OF THE UNIVERSITY OF CAMBRIDGE
The Pitt Building, Trumpington Street, Cambridge, United Kingdom

CAMBRIDGE UNIVERSITY PRESS
The Edinburgh Building, Cambridge CB2 2RU, UK http://www.cup.cam.ac.uk
40 West 20th Street, New York, NY 10011-4211, USA http://www.cup.org
10 Stamford Road, Oakleigh, Melbourne 3166, Australia
Ruiz de Alarcón 13, 28014 Madrid, Spain

First published 2000

Printed in the United Kingdom at the University Press, Cambridge

Typeface Monotype Baskerville 11/12½ pt.   *System* QuarkXPress™ [SE]

A catalogue record for this book is available from the British Library

Library of Congress cataloguing in publication data

Lewis, Pericles.
Modernism, nationalism, and the novel / Pericles Lewis.
p. cm.
ISBN 0 521 66111 0 (hardback)
1. Fiction – 20th century – History and criticism.   2. Nationalism
and literature – History – 20th century.   3. Modernism (Literature)
PN3503.L39   2000
809.3′9358 – dc21 00-31372 CIP

ISBN 0 521 66111 0 hardback

Contents

Acknowledgments

Financial support that enabled me to write this book came from the Department of Comparative Literature, the Stanford Humanities Center, the Center for European Studies, and the Institute for International Studies at Stanford University, from the Whiting Foundation, and from the Post-Doctoral Fellowship Program of the Social Sciences and Humanities Research Council of Canada. I wrote much of the book as a visiting fellow in the Department of English at the University of California at Berkeley and have completed the manuscript as an Assistant Professor in the departments of Comparative Literature and English at Yale University. I wish to thank each of these institutions and the people at them for their support. Parts of chapter 1 appeared in *Joyce Through the Ages*, edited by Michael Patrick Gillespie (Gainesville: University Press of Florida, 1999) and are reprinted by permission of the University Press of Florida. Parts of chapter 3 appeared in *Nineteenth-Century Literature* and are reprinted by permission of the University of California Press.

While I was first planning this project, I attended two very stimulating seminars: Hans Ulrich (Sepp) Gumbrecht's "How Realistic was European Literary Realism?" and Michael Tratner's "The Politics of Modernism." Both Sepp and Michael have read and commented on many drafts since then, and their very different but perhaps complementary approaches have shaped my own. I am also grateful to Jeffrey Schnapp, who encouraged my research from the beginning and read and commented on an earlier draft of this work. Catherine Gallagher not only commented on much of the manuscript but also sponsored my extended visit to Berkeley and helped to make my postdoctoral research productive. Judith Butler, George Dekker, Morris Kaplan, Niva Lorenzini, Ramón Saldívar, and Ian Watt discussed the work in progress with me, and their various intellectual influences can be seen throughout. A dedicated friend, Barbara Fuchs collaborated with me on thoughts about nationalism in the early stages and offered thorough comments on the next-to-last draft. Without offering an entire remembrance of things past of my own, I would like to mention that many people have contributed to my thinking about the modernist novel in ways that footnotes cannot adequately document. Here, I will just thank a few friends who have stayed with me ever since the beginning: Sara Beam, Melissa Goldman, David Hensley, Harriet Nowell-Smith, David Porter, Corvin Russell, and Deanne Williams. Mariangela Calubini and Elena Ledda welcomed me to the d'Annunzio archives at the Vittoriale degli Italiani and facilitated my research there. Anston Bosman, Duncan Chesney, and Fernanda Moore assisted me with some of the final research. I would like to thank Abdul JanMohammed for taking an interest in this book and Ray Ryan of Cambridge University Press for facilitating its publication. I am indebted to the anonymous reviewers of the manuscript for their useful suggestions.

Sheila Hayre gave me valuable advice at each stage of the project, detailed responses to the various drafts, and all other kinds of support as well. Our discussions of the dynamics of cultural difference challenged some of my universalistic assumptions. Finally, I wish to thank our families for their constant encouragement. My parents, in naming me, gave me no choice but to become a democrat, and my perspective on nationalism thus reflects a sort of predestination. The social-democratic and multicultural tradition in which I was raised involved a rather particular, but still not uncommon, variety of liberal Canadian nationalism; and the ongoing crisis of the Canadian confederation has certainly influenced my reflections. My own experience of living in, and becoming a permanent resident of, the United States, and the much longer migrations of my family and in-laws brought the questions of citizenship and nationality to the forefront of my consciousness, as did the loss of my grandparents, three of whom died while I was away from home, working on this project. I dedicate this book to the memory of Andrew and Peggy Brewin and Sara and Martin Lewis.

Note on texts

Most quotations are in English only. I have included the original language or a reference to a text in the original language only where the English is insufficient to illustrate my point. I have sometimes silently modified translations. Unless otherwise noted, translations from French or Italian are my own. References to *Nocturne* are to the Rosenthal translation listed below; references to *Notturno* are to the Ferrata edition, and these translations are my own. The following abbreviations have been used:

Alatri   Paolo Alatri, *Gabriele D'Annunzio*, Turin: Unione Tipografico-Editrice Torinese, 1983.

HD   Joseph Conrad, *Heart of Darkness* (1899), ed. Robert Kimbrough, 3rd edition, New York: W. W. Norton & Co., 1988.

IP   Honoré de Balzac, *Illusions perdues* (1837–1843), vol. v of *La Comédie humaine*, Paris: Gallimard, 1976–1977.

LI   Honoré de Balzac, *Lost Illusions*, trans. Herbert Hunt, Harmondsworth: Penguin, 1971.

Notturno   Gabriele d'Annunzio, *Notturno* (1921), ed. Giansiro Ferrata, Milan: Mondadori, 1983.

Nocturne   Gabriele d'Annunzio, *Nocturne and Five Tales of Love and Death*, trans. Raymond Rosenthal, Marlboro, Vermont: Marlboro Press, 1988.

Origins   Hannah Arendt, *The Origins of Totalitarianism* (1951), new edition, San Diego: Harcourt Brace, 1979.

Portrait   James Joyce, *A Portrait of the Artist as a Young Man* (1916), corrected by Chester G. Anderson and ed. Richard Ellmann, New York: Viking, 1964.

Recherche   Marcel Proust, *A la recherche du temps perdu* (1913–1927). 4 volumes. New Pléiade edition. Ed. Jean-Yves Tadié *et al.* Paris: Gallimard, 1987.

Remembrance   Marcel Proust, *Remembrance of Things Past*, trans. C. K.
Scott Moncrieff, Terence Kilmartin, and Andreas
Mayor, Harmondsworth: Penguin, 1983.

CHAPTER ONE

The modern novelist as redeemer of the nation

James Joyce's Stephen Dedalus, in *A Portrait of the Artist as a Young Man*, ends his diary entry for April 26 with a declaration that could stand as a motto for many of the novelists of his day: "Welcome, O life! I go to encounter for the millionth time the reality of experience and to forge in the smithy of my soul the uncreated conscience of my race."[1] The conjunction "and" in this little manifesto suggests the close but oblique relationship between the two goals the aspiring novelist has set for himself. The encounter with experience seems a deeply personal goal, while the forging of the conscience of the race has important political implications. Stephen links the personal and political goals by claiming that the forging will take place in the smithy of his soul. The problem that has faced many literary critics in interpreting Stephen's goal, as in understanding modernism more generally, has been that the quest for an authentic form of a pure, inner experience seems at variance with the desire to transform the race. If Stephen really wants to serve his race, then why does he leave Ireland and bury himself in books? Why not join the nationalist movement and fight for political independence? Or why not, at least, write a work that will rouse other Irishmen and women to political action?

Stephen's answer to these questions depends on a rather odd form of theology in which the idea of the "race" takes the place reserved in the Catholic tradition for the idea of God, the only "uncreated" being. The actual living members of the Irish nation become the Church of this new religion. Stephen himself plays the role of Christ in a new nation-alist theology, redeeming his nation by reshaping the conscience of his race. This theology places an emphasis on the role of the race in shaping the individual's experience that Joyce's critics have often ignored. Stephen's use of the expression "uncreated" has often been taken to imply that Stephen plans to create a brand new racial conscience from nothing (to "forge" in the sense of "inventing"). Most critics assume that

Stephen wishes to break free from Irish tradition and to invent something entirely new, in a Godlike *creatio ex nihilo*. Seamus Deane, for example, writes of the passage: "Endlessly repeated experience is going to be made into something that has so far remained 'uncreated,' . . . [as Stephen produces] a writing that is not embedded in or reducible to the categories of previous Irish experience."[2] The original and most common meaning of "uncreated" suggests precisely the opposite interpretation, however. In Christian dogma, "uncreated" refers to the Creator, who is "of a self-existent or eternal nature," precedes Creation, and is the source of the entire created world.[3] By calling the racial conscience "uncreated," Stephen suggests not that this collective soul remains to be invented, but rather that it is itself the source of all experience. In forging the uncreated conscience of his race, then, Stephen will not be inventing something entirely new, but re-enacting and thus reshaping an eternal substance that precedes and conditions all his personal experiences. Stephen's experience, like the flames of the smithy, will give a new form to this substance, which he has inherited and which inhabits his soul. The racial conscience is the source of all Stephen's experiences, but, as a great soul, Stephen in turn transforms the racial conscience. Thus the individual, unique encounter with reality that Stephen plans for himself in Paris has not only a personal but a racial, and national, significance. Contrary to much of the Joycean critical tradition, Stephen imagines not an absolutely original creation but a transformation of the ideal racial conscience he embodies through yet another encounter with the reality of experience.

The racial conscience is a sort of god that Stephen plans to serve through his writing and his personal experience. Stephen proposes to do rather more in his writing, however, than simply justify the ways of God to Irishmen. In Christianity, the only "uncreated" being is God. In Stephen's theology, it is "the conscience of [the] race" that is uncreated, and Stephen himself is its prophet, or perhaps its redeemer. Just as Christ stands for all humanity in his death on the cross, Stephen plans to become a Christ-figure, redeeming his "Godforsaken" race by symbolically standing for the Irish nation as a whole (p. 37). This image of the modernist novelist as redeemer of the nation contributed to Joyce's reworking of a literary archetype of nineteenth-century realism, the novel of disillusionment. The heroic narrator-protagonist became, in Joyce's vision, the focus for a reawakening of national consciousness centered on the awareness that individuals are both subjects and objects of historical processes. The sovereign nation-state was, for Stephen

Dedalus as for many of his contemporaries, the social unit that could allow individuals who shared nothing but a common cultural heritage to grasp the fact of their conditioning by historical circumstances and to come to consciousness of their collective ability to shape their own destinies. This awakening of national consciousness from the nightmare of history was a primary concern of the novelists who undertook the literary experiments we have come to label "modernist."

THE MODERNIST NOVEL AND THE CRISIS OF LIBERAL NATIONALISM

In linking the novelist's personal lived experience with the forging of a national consciousness, Stephen epitomizes an attitude that influenced the development of modernism in the European novel around the turn of the century. This study addresses the role of the modernists' experiments with the form of the novel in their attempts to rethink the values and institutions associated with the sovereign nation-state. In various ways, the novelists considered here (Joyce, Conrad, Proust, and d'Annunzio) used their own experience as a model of the national situation. They shared Stephen Dedalus's interest in a mystical relationship between the novelist-hero and his people (the novelist-hero in these cases is nearly always male; clearly, the discourse is "gendered"). The modernists represented this relationship through an account of the vagaries of the novelist-hero's consciousness of the nation-race rather than through a chronicle of the external social and political events of their era. They frequently concerned themselves with what Louis Althusser would later identify as the subject's "interpellation" by society and the state, that is, with the processes whereby an individual comes to inhabit a particular set of beliefs (an ideology) and to "live, move, and have [his] being" within that set of beliefs, as Althusser says, quoting St. Paul.[4] The aspect of this interpellation that seemed most fundamental to many of them was the individual's belonging to a particular nationality. Today, we might refer to this shaping of the individual by the nation as an effect of "culture," but each of the modernists considered here described nationality in terms of "race." Like Stephen, these novelists tended to use the word "race" to refer to the complex amalgam of biological and cultural factors that made up their conception of the nation, although each used the term in a way conditioned by his particular political and intellectual heritage.

Many critics have interpreted the modernists' concern with psychology, with the subjective experience of time, and with the form of the novel itself as a sign of "introversion"[5] or of a lack of political commitment, corresponding to a rejection of the "external reality" that concerned nineteenth-century realist novelists. Yet, as Stephen's diary entry suggests, the modernist novel does not reject external reality entirely; rather, it concerns itself with the relationship between the individual consciousness and the external reality that it confronts. Perceiving a gap between the meaningful inner life of the individual consciousness and an outer world that shapes that inner life but seems in itself devoid of spiritual meaning, the modernists sought a means to bridge that gap, to glean a meaning from that apparently senseless outer world. Famously, they found in art itself the means of transforming the contingencies of everyday life into a meaningful formal structure. Yet many novelists of the modernist period found another, less often noted means of mediating between the apparently hostile and meaningless social world and the meaningful but powerless consciousness of the individual novelist-hero. They found it in the idea of a national consciousness, which lent an apparently eternal, if not universal, significance to their isolated experiences and offered a matrix through which to interpret events that otherwise appeared to lack any internal logic.

Many of the characteristic formal concerns of the modernist novel first found expression in the works of novelists who reached maturity in the 1890s. The use of multiple and highly subjective narrators, attempts to transcribe the "stream of consciousness," the non-linear representation of time, poetic prose, self-consciousness about the form of the novel, and reliance on myth, private symbolism, the leitmotiv, and literary allusion all arose from the reaction against realism and naturalism during the last decades of the nineteenth century. Each of the main formal elements of modernism had appeared separately by the time that the fictional Stephen proposed, around 1902, to forge in the smithy of his soul the uncreated conscience of his race. It was in the period leading up to the First World War that they began to coalesce in the forms that, after the war, would characterize "high" modernism. In the novel, these formal experiments were linked by a rethinking of the relationship between the objective, omniscient narrator and individual characters with limited, subjective perspectives.

The novel, as a genre, had always depended on – and played with – this relationship.[6] Stories had been told by unreliable first-person narrators since Defoe and Richardson. Sterne's *Tristram Shandy* called attention to the artificiality of realistic narrative conventions. What distinguished the first generation of modernists, however, was their

shared concern to work out, in novelistic form, the implications of perspectivism, the notion that no purely objective account of the external
world is possible – that any such account would necessarily be the
product of a particular consciousness and perspective. The solution of
this philosophical problem was a primary concern of Kant's *Critique of
Pure Reason*, and the problem itself was already latent in Descartes's
Meditations. It was Nietzsche, however, who pushed the implications of
perspectivism furthest, for example in his statement that "everything has
become: there are *no eternal facts*, just as there are no absolute truths."[7]
The modernists differed from earlier novelists not in recognizing the fact
that our perceptions of reality are always mediated by language and by
consciousness – that recognition was at the root of the very form of the
novel in general. Rather, the modernists were remarkable for investigat-
ing in a concerted way the possibility that the mediated nature of our
consciousness might preclude our ever arriving, by rational means, at a
consensus as to the nature of external reality. Modernist experiments
implied that our perceptions of the outside world and of each other are
so tainted by culturally specific or individually idiosyncratic values that
there might be no way of arbitrating fairly between the competing
claims of various individuals or groups – no eternal facts, no absolute
truth, hence no absolute justice.

One typical response to the problems of perspectivism raised in
Nietzsche's thought was a turn to an organic conception of the nation
as the source of all values. The old God was dead, but in the nation many
intellectuals and popular movements found a new God. Ernest Gellner
has observed: "Durkheim taught that in religious worship society adores
its own camouflaged image. In a nationalist age, societies worship themselves brazenly and openly, spurning the camouflage."[8] The last decades
of the nineteenth century witnessed a dramatic increase in the influence
of the organicist conception of the nation-state. Nationalism had, from
the French revolution to 1848, largely been associated with political liberalism, with which it shared the principle of the self-determination of
peoples. As Eric Hobsbawm has noted, however, a "sharp shift to the
political right of nation and flag" occurred after 1870, partly as a result
of attempts by authoritarian governments to make use of nationalist
sentiment for their own ends and partly because the apparent triumph
of liberal nationalism in Western Europe had failed to secure in a meaningful way the long-awaited goals of liberty, equality, and fraternity.[9]
From the 1870s onward, the United Kingdom, France, and Italy were
ruled by liberal political systems that included representative bodies such

as parliaments. In the period preceding the first world war, national liberation movements gained in strength throughout Europe and emerged in the rest of the world. Liberal nationalism seemed to triumph in 1919 in the Treaty of Versailles, by which the victorious powers redrew the map of Europe along national lines, enshrining the "principle of nationality" in international law.

Yet, during this same period, the principles of nationalism and liberalism were increasingly at odds. New, "organic" conceptions of the nation-state undermined the traditional politics of nineteenth-century liberal nationalism. The institutions of the liberal nation-state, newly established in much of Europe, were under attack from the authoritarian right. In Great Britain, the term "imperialism" was given its modern use to describe nationalist propaganda in support of overseas adventures. The imperialist conception of the national interest conflicted with that of traditional British liberalism, and the British Liberal Party split in two over the question of Home Rule for Ireland. In Ireland itself, after Parnell's death in 1891, a new, "cultural" nationalist movement subscribed to a theory of the "Celtic Race" and excluded Protestants from its definition of the Irish nation.[10] In France, the nationalist side in the Dreyfus affair questioned the liberal principle that all citizens should be equal before the law. A racial conception of "Jewishness" contributed to a uniquely modern form of anti-semitism in which Jews were represented as incapable, for reasons of racial heredity, of being assimilated into the French nation. Right- and left-wing opposition in Italy led to a continual crisis of the liberal parliamentary system there from the late 1890s onward. Radicals and ultra-conservatives formed a strange alliance in 1910 in the "Nationalist" party, which would agitate in favor of intervention in the First World War and eventually ally itself with the Fascist party. Prefiguring Fascist ideology, the Italian Nationalists demanded expansionist foreign policies and a corporatist economic system.[11] In various ways, then, most of the countries of Western Europe experienced the growth of modern forms of nationalism as a threat to the established (and often very recently established) liberal political order.

These conflicts between liberalism and organic nationalism all pointed to the problem of whether the nation should be understood as a legal and political unit, defined by the voluntary membership in it of individual citizens, or as an ethnic and social unit, defined by the shared culture, history, and (perhaps) biological inheritance that was thrust upon individuals, not chosen by them. The newer, organicist forms of

nationalism depended on a definition of the nation as ethnically and linguistically homogeneous. Often drawing for their intellectual justification on forms of Darwinism, they claimed that the ethnic group, rather
than the individual, was the basic unit of society. The individual was primarily an emanation of the national "character." According to organicist theology, national destiny, rather than individual qualities or choices,
determined the individual's actions. The legal, formal equality of citizenship in the liberal state was insignificant next to what the organicists
considered the real brotherhood arising from shared blood and a shared
linguistic or cultural heritage. Organic nationalists found the existence
of ethnic minorities within the borders of European states intolerable,
since it meant that citizens of a given state might not share the same
nationality, while people who shared a nationality might not have access
to a common state. As Hannah Arendt has observed, in organic nationalism, the state was transformed "from an instrument of the law into an
instrument of the nation."[12] Instead of representing justice in the
abstract, the state was to represent the interests of the nation understood
as a homogeneous ethnic group.

These transformations in the political significance of the nation-state
were a source of concern for many novelists around the turn of the
century. Stephen Dedalus exemplifies their obsession with problems of
national identity. One of the motives of modernist formal experiments
was, as Michael Tratner has shown, to gain access to the collective myths
through which individuals interpreted the world.[13] Tratner argues that
the dawning of the age of mass politics and the perceived replacement
of nineteenth-century individualism by twentieth-century collectivism
inspired much modernist experimentation. A particular form of collective myth that strongly influenced the modernists was the desire to tap
into a national unconscious. The modernists' concern with the nature of
consciousness in language, in particular, points to the sense that the
nation shapes the individual through the national language. The modernists typically responded to the organic theory of the nation in two
related ways. Sometimes, as in the case of d'Annunzio, they embraced
it wholeheartedly and sought to serve it. More frequently, however, they
treated the influence of "national character" on the individual as a fundamental existential fact and developed a heightened sense of irony that
allowed them to investigate the shaping effects of nationality on the individual's destiny. Thus, if an unmediated objectivity was impossible, they
attempted to offer at least a sort of objectivity-through-subjectivity, a
joyful or anguished acceptance of the limited perspective bestowed on

each individual by her or his belonging to a given culture, to a given nation. Stephen Dedalus accepts his condition joyfully, but his creator, James Joyce, expresses more anxiety about it. Conrad, drawing on the traditions of English utilitarian liberalism and Darwinism, expresses a nostalgia for an English character he imagines to be on the verge of extinction. Proust, drawing on the voluntarist conception of the nation-state derived from the French revolution, eagerly deconstructs the idea of a French "racial" identity, but still finds in the nation-state one key to the possibility of human freedom. In all of these cases, the conventional critical wisdom that associates modernism with individualism, cosmo-politanism, or a rejection of society seems inadequate. The modernists' encounters with organic theories of the nation suggest, on the contrary, an abiding concern with the social and its impact on the individual, and a vision of the novelist's role as central to the national life.

The modernists' reworking of the techniques of the realist novel involved a rethinking of the political and epistemological theories on which realism had drawn. The techniques by which the nineteenth-century realist novel had represented the relationship between individ-uals and society reflected assumptions about human nature, knowledge, and history that realist novelists shared with contemporary liberal polit-ical theorists. As exemplified by such mid-nineteenth-century thinkers as Alexis de Tocqueville and John Stuart Mill, liberal theory held that indi-viduals, by nature, pursue their own private interests, which the liberal tradition had defined primarily in economic terms. Left to pursue these interests without outside interference, individuals would find the most efficient means of achieving their ends, thus leading to increased pro-ductivity and the growth of civil society – the process of "civilization." According to classical liberal theory, society progresses according to its own immanent laws, which are not immediately evident to individual social actors. The role of the state is to facilitate this progress by avoid-ing any undue interference in it while ensuring that no member of society infringes on the rights of another. The state may also encourage patriotic sentiments and forms of sociability, but ultimately it is the aggregate welfare of the individuals in society that measures the success of a liberal political system.

The conception of society in canonical realist novels, such as those of Balzac, resembles that of early nineteenth-century liberalism in several respects: autonomous individuals pursue their own interests, motivated by the desire for material gain and for social esteem; they share a common human nature, although the circumstances of their birth and upbringing shape their characters in diverse ways; the shared social reality in which they interact is governed by immanent laws of its own that are not in themselves evident to the individuals who make up society. The formal techniques of the realist novel reflect this conception of society. Individual characters have only limited perspectives, and their perceptions of reality often reflect their selfish interests and their inability to see their own cases objectively; in the words of liberal theory, "no man is a fit Arbitrator in his own cause."[14] The dialogic character of the novel, the fact that it represents the many perspectives taken to this shared reality by individuals from different backgrounds, resembles the liberal model of society in that it acknowledges the extent to which differing interests shape the various perceptions members of society have of the world and of each other. The functioning of the novelistic universe depends on the narrator's role as a neutral arbiter. He stands aloof from the characters and disentangles their competing claims and perceptions. Like the state in liberal political thought, he acts as the guarantor of the shared, social reality. Just as the liberal state is the instrument of a neutral law and justice, so in the realist novel the narrator is the instrument of objectivity and truth in a world in which the competing claims of individuals threaten to undermine social harmony. Even when he speaks against the vices of "society," the narrator is the voice of a shared reality within which the characters interact and to which they must adapt themselves. The realist novel, then, represents a parliamentary, rather than an absolutist, conception of reality and truth. The shared world of "society" exists independently of any single one of its members, but it also embodies the consensus among these members.

The crisis of liberal nationalism at the end of the nineteenth century revealed the extent to which liberal values and institutions depended on the shared assumptions of a national culture and in particular on the idea that the interests of the nation-state could be identified with the common good of all the individuals in a given society. The idea of the sovereign nation, whose individual members all shared common interests and cultural assumptions, underlay much of the actual working of liberal political systems. To the extent that some inhabitants of a given territory did not share, or were not seen to share, these common national interests and assumptions, liberalism increasingly came to seem incapable of reconciling their needs and interests with those of the national majority. This obstacle appeared even more insurmountable when such interests came to be associated with biological inheritance. A cultural minority, or a given class of citizens, might easily be assimilated into the national mainstream, but it appeared to many political thinkers that a minority or a colonized people, when identified by putatively inherited racial characteristics, could never share the cultural and other assumptions of the nation as a whole. Thus the Irish, Africans, and Indians appeared to many English liberals incapable of national self-government, and many French thought the Jews incapable of full French citizenship.

The modernists' reworking of the techniques of realism responded to the contemporary crisis in the institutions associated with the nation-state and the liberal conception of society. According to organic nationalist theorists, the basic unit of society was not the individual but the ethnic group (variously labeled the "nation" or the "race"). Individuals, then, rather than being autonomous, rational agents who pursue their own interests, were projections of an underlying ethnic identity, unconsciously pursuing the interests of the group. Their membership in the national community molded their consciousness. The sense, in modernist novels, that consciousness is always overdetermined by what T. S. Eliot called "vast impersonal forces" reflects the growth of a conception of individuals as the playthings of such collective identities as national wills. This study complements earlier approaches to the rise of those "vast impersonal forces" by focusing on the centrality of the problem of the nation-state to the crisis of liberalism and by directly relating the modernists' formal experiments to their active political concerns. I hope that the comparative nature of this study will underline the common problems facing novelists in four very different Western European political contexts as well as the unique intellectual and political concerns each of these major contributors to literary modernism brought to his work. I focus in particular on the increasingly problematic role of the narrator in modernist novels, which exemplifies the changing conception of the nation-state around the turn of the century. The objective, omniscient narrator, correlate of the liberal state, disappears in modernism. What takes over the storytelling is either a projection of the consciousness of an individual protagonist (as in *A Portrait of the Artist as a Young Man, A la recherche du temps perdu*, or *Heart of Darkness*) or a more generalized projection of a collective consciousness (as in *Ulysses* or the novels of Virginia Woolf; this technique is also foreshadowed in the last novels of Henry James). Either form of representation reflects a conception of objectivity as always shaped by the mediating forces of culture and consciousness. The narrator is no longer the instrument of justice, divine or earthly; he has become a sort of super-ego, a figment of the collective imagination.

By describing the highly subjective experiences of their protagonists, the modernists demonstrated the inevitable lack of an Archimedean point from which to judge the world. Far from abandoning realism's concern with politics, they used these experiments to examine the shaping of knowledge by nationality and the limitations of "realistic" and liberal conceptions of society. These experiments all drew attention to the crisis of the liberal nation-state, although the solutions to this crisis envisioned by the various modernists differed widely. The modernists scrutinized the distinction between an objective narrator and subjective characters with limited perspectives, and gave life to a whole generation of narrator-heroes who forged social realities in their own images. They sought to demonstrate the power of national myths to shape even apparently "objective" perceptions of reality. Whereas realism accepted the liberal bifurcation between private, ethical life and public, socially assigned roles, the modernists sought through their experiments to achieve a unified, public morality that would overcome the ironic structure of life in a society constantly being transformed by history. Their various attempts to unify the first- and third-person perspectives served this goal and led them to describe a "dialectic of enlightenment," which revealed the dependence of the enlightened ideals of liberty and equality on the myth of national fraternity. Conrad's multiple narrators, Joyce's transcriptions of consciousness, Proust's appeals to involuntary memory, and d'Annunzio's intermingling of lyric and narrative all focused attention on the shaping of the individual by the nation and on the potential for the individual in turn to redeem the nation in time of war or crisis. While these authors appear today as great canonical figures of their respective national literatures, I hope to call attention also to their marginality, the fact that modernism was largely a creation, as Terry Eagleton has noted, of "exiles and émigrés."[15] Although these figures are not always seen as political novelists, I hope to demonstrate their engagement with the crisis of the nation-state and their explorations of the possibilities and limits of liberalism. The literary works are, of course, not simply coded philosophical messages, but the attempt to place them in the context of debates about contemporary politics should reveal that they were complex attempts to grapple with political, epistemological, and existential problems that remain crucial to contemporary cultural and social thought.

While I treat the development of discourses about the nation-state in a historical perspective, I also attempt to uncover the systematic underpinnings of liberal theories of the nation-state. These underpinnings developed, of course, out of a particular historical context. As well as embodying a rather broad set of doctrines about the nature of human relations, liberalism is a historical phenomenon. Perhaps, as Robert Denoon Cumming has suggested, liberalism has even more of a tendency than most belief systems to undergo crises, for liberalism is "at once a *tradition* and an attempt to go beyond the *limitations* of that tradition which its *crisis* exposes."[16] In other words, liberalism is not simply a specific set of doctrines – for example, rule by law, equality of legal condition, freedom of conscience, speech, and association, the right to private property, popular sovereignty, limitation of state power – but a tradition of developing solutions to political problems by a reasonable overcoming of differences and a faith in the capacity for self-improvement (within limits) of human beings. In particular, as John Burrow has shown, liberalism has often sought to reconcile the participant's and the observer's (or the ethical and the sociological) perspectives on human nature, or rather not to reconcile the two perspectives so much as to find in the duality of human nature the conditions of possibility for moral and political progress.[17] The nation presented itself for a time as the site of identification at which the ethical self and the sociological self could find peace with one another, but ultimately liberalism seems to demand a distinction between the realms of ethics and sociology, of freedom and necessity, at odds with the nationalist urge toward *Sittlichkeit* or moral unity.[18]

Even more than most other institutions or ideas, the nation is both a "product" of and a contributor to the processes of history, because of its powerful emotional and intellectual appeal and its role in the development of the modern state. Like a fetish, the product of people's work that they worship as a god, the nation has stirred people's admiration and affected their actions. Like a fetish, too, it continues to have great power no matter how much "clear-sighted analysis" explains away its imagined magical powers.[19] Yet the nation-state is a very complex fetish, complete with heads of state and government, ministries, literary and philosophical traditions, territory and citizens. Max Weber showed that ideas can be more than mere epiphenomena produced by inevitable historical forces and capable simply of serving one set of social forces or another. They can also influence action in unpredictable ways. As Weber argued, "Magical and religious forces, and the ethical ideas of duty based upon them, have in the past always been among the most important formative influences on conduct."[20] I am concerned here with one such magical and religious force, the idea of the nation.

JOYCE, BALZAC, AND THE DYNAMIC OF DISILLUSIONMENT

This magical force held James Joyce in its thrall. Joyce's Stephen Dedalus, and by extension Joyce himself, have gained a reputation among some literary critics as apolitical "individualists" because Stephen rejects overtly nationalistic art. Yet, even as he refuses to learn Irish or to endorse the program of the Gaelic League, Stephen affirms the importance of his nationality to his art: "This race and this country and this life produced me . . . I shall express myself as I am" (p. 203). This budding artist proposes to use the fact that he himself is a product of a particular race and country as a means of achieving a new sort of freedom. This freedom will consist in using his experience and his self-expression to embody the fate of the race that has created him. In *A Portrait of the Artist as a Young Man*, although Stephen does not endorse the nationalist political program, he does set himself the typically nationalistic goal of reviving his nation-race. He hopes to do so, however, not through traditionally political activity but by searching within his own soul to make his writing embody the fate of his race and thus to afford his race an opportunity for rebirth. Joyce's narrative technique emphasizes the close relationship between Stephen and the Irish race. In revising the traditional plot structure of the novel of disillusionment, Joyce attempts to overcome the radical distinction between the objective viewpoint of the omniscient narrator and the limited perspective of the individual character. It is through the fusion of these two perspectives at the end of the novel, with Stephen's ascension to the role of narrator, that Joyce inaugurates a radical revision of the novelistic tradition. At the same moment, Stephen attempts to overcome his own subjectivity by merging it in the larger fate of his nation. The overcoming of the bifurcated perspective of novelistic realism embodies in literary form Stephen's longed-for synthesis with the conscience of his race.

A Portrait tells the story of Stephen's emergence into consciousness as an emergence into Irish history. Political events that play a crucial role in Stephen's conception of his place in history, such as the fall of Parnell, precede Stephen's conscious understanding of Irish politics, and Stephen's attempts to understand such events are part of the novel's drama. From the first page of the novel, references to the Irish historical and political situation fill Stephen's growing mind. Dante's two brushes – a maroon one for the radical Michael Davitt and a green one for the moderate Parnell – color his childhood perceptions before he even knows what the colors may signify. As a child, Stephen cannot solve the problems that theology and politics raise for him: "It pained him that he did not know well what politics meant and that he did not know where the universe ended. He felt small and weak" (p. 17). Stephen is conscious of growing up in a world in which politics and history weigh upon the brains of the living. He is surrounded by discussions of Irish politics and particularly of Parnell's campaign for Home Rule. Without being able to articulate the reasons for his fate, the young hero feels himself to be growing up as part of what his father calls a "Godforsaken priestridden race" (p. 37). Stephen's entrapment in the nightmare of Irish history and his living out of its logic make him the potential author of an Irish national epic. In his epic, however, the artist himself will play the role of redeeming hero who, by his mystical union with the conscience of the race, helps to transform the Irish people.

A Portrait exemplifies the heightened attention to the conflict between objective and subjective modes of narration that marked the modernist transformation of realist literary techniques. Joyce's experiments with narrative technique contribute to his reworking of the disillusionment plot, which, in Georg Lukács's description, portrayed the fate of the individual whose soul was "wider and larger than the destinies which life [had] to offer it" in a world "abandoned by God."[21] Honoré de Balzac's *Lost Illusions* was the model for the novel of disillusionment, which formed an important sub-genre of the nineteenth-century realist novel. Joyce's Stephen Dedalus resembles in many respects Lucien de Rubempré, the hero of *Lost Illusions*. Like Lucien, Stephen is a young, naïve, provincial genius who hopes to become a great author in Paris. Joyce seems to have based Stephen's motto "silence, exile, cunning" on Lucien's "Fuge, late, tace" ("Flee, lurk, be silent").[22] *A Portrait of the Artist as a Young Man* also suggests a more fundamental similarity between Stephen and Lucien by using the language and archetypes of the many nineteenth-century novels of disillusionment: the obscure young man from an impoverished but respectable country family, closely identified with the author, who wants to become his country's national novelist; his admiration for Napoleon and the romantic poets; his scorn for the "mob" and for liberal or democratic politics; his loss of innocence; his disappointment in romantic love and his subsequent turn to prostitutes; his prodigality at his devoted family's expense; his attempted return to the fold of family and church; the novel's conclusion with his apparent, but suspect, arrival at maturity. Yet, whereas the events of *Lost Illusions* take place in Paris, and Paris represents for Lucien the "reality of experience" that will shatter his illusions, the events of *A Portrait of the Artist* take place in Stephen's childhood, before he has even formulated his plan to go to Paris. For Balzac, the encounter with the disagreeable realities of life begins when the young provincial leaves for Paris and ends in defeat and return to the provinces; for Joyce, the encounter starts soon after birth, and the projected trip to Paris is only the millionth manifestation of a process which will continue unto death. This difference between the two novels points to the rethinking of the metaphysics of disillusionment that underlies Stephen's conception of himself as a Christ-figure for the Irish nation and his plan to "forge in the smithy of [his] soul the uncreated conscience of [his] race." Joyce's reworking of Balzacian themes and techniques owes much, of course, to Flaubert and to what Lukács has described as the "crisis of bourgeois realism" after 1848, but I focus here on the two novels, *Lost Illusions* and *A Portrait*, as models, respectively, of realism and modernism, which demonstrate the radical change in the conception of the individual's relationship to the nation-state that contributed to the development of modernism in the novel.[23]

Balzac's novel depends on a sharp distinction between the inner world of his heroes' personal fantasies and illusions and the outer world of a hostile, conventional society. The protagonists must adapt their fantasies to the unchangeable outer world or die. The role of their perceptions and their consciousness is to make them aware of a reality outside themselves to which they must conform. "Disillusionment" is the process of the individual's learning his (or her) proper relationship to society as a whole and to the nation in particular. (The typical hero of a novel of disillusionment is male, but there are some interesting female examples, especially Emma Bovary and to a certain extent George Eliot's Maggie Tulliver. A major obstacle to a woman's encountering society at large was of course the fact that the woman was expected to stay home, not to venture out into the hostile external world. Even the slightest attempt to leave home ends in disaster for most nineteenth-century heroines.) Upon arriving in Paris, Lucien confronts the conventions of society as "a foreigner ignorant of the language" (*LI*, p. 174). In order to support himself, he writes for the newspapers. His friend Etienne Lousteau explains to him that the newspaper "accepts as truth [*vrai*] anything that is plausible [*probable*] . . . We start from that assumption." The world of journalism stands in the novel for the conventionality of society in general, with its interest in mere appearance rather than spiritual essence (p. 350). Having failed to make his way in society, Lucien at the end of the novel reaches the point of disillusionment and contemplates suicide. Balzac writes: "The day when a man despises himself, the day when he sees that others despise him, the moment when the reality of life is at variance with his hopes, he kills himself and thus pays homage to society, refusing to stand before it stripped of his virtues or his splendour" (p. 633). For Balzac, the "illusions" or fantasies of the individual soul are in a sense truer than the artificial "reality" of society at large. Yet, in *Lost Illusions*, the "reality of life" triumphs. The illusions of youth are beautiful, necessary, and destined for defeat.

Lost Illusions confronts the hero with a hostile external world that seems to offer sterile ground for the fulfillment of his developing personality. Like later novels of disillusionment, it describes a world in which the hero is condemned to an apparently permanent state of "transcendental homelessness."[24] In order to fulfill his destiny, Lucien must leave behind his literal and spiritual home. He must go out into the world in order to grow and to make his life meaningful, but – to his surprise and disappointment – he encounters a world that is dominated not by spiritual truth or a meaningful structure but merely by social convention. The novel thus opposes the empirical "reality" of "society," which appears to the hero to be purely arbitrary and to lack any internal logic, to the inner truths of the hero's soul. Balzac uses language with a political valence to describe Lucien's failed attempt to master that social reality. At the beginning of the novel, before Lucien leaves Angoulême for Paris, Balzac attributes to him "the normal tendency a man has to view everything in terms of himself. We all say, more or less, like Louis XIV: 'I am the state'" (p. 71). Lucien must learn that, unlike an absolutist king, he is not the state. Rather, the state represents a society that, while made up of people more or less like himself, is indifferent to him personally. Lucien manages, with the help of some journalist friends, to rise fairly high in society, but as he approaches his inevitable downfall, Balzac writes of him: "To every man who is not born rich comes what we must call his fateful week. For Napoleon it was the week of the retreat from Moscow" (p. 448). Like Napoleon, Lucien has overreached himself. The comparison of the hero to Napoleon points to the inevitable collapse of the illusion that one person can come to embody the state, to create reality in his own image.

In the novels of Balzac, each character is born effectively outside society and must, in order to pursue the goals of profit and honor, or more generally to fulfill his or her individuality, enter into society, abandoning some freedom and independence in exchange for the recognition of other characters. In *Lost Illusions*, the narrative voice offers on the one hand a third-person account of the external events of the plot and records on the other hand the subjective impressions of individual characters, including their ambitions and emotions. What the novel treats as objective "reality" is the world governed by the conventions of society. The narrator typically offers the reader two types of information: the impressions of individual characters, which he reports through indirect discourse or direct quotation, and the general social knowledge which is at the same time the property of everyone and of no one in particular. The "omniscient" narrator, so often compared to God, in fact embodies not God's perspective but that of society in general. He reports general social knowledge in tones approximating those of a tour guide, a gossip columnist, or a university professor, depending on the exact object of social knowledge at hand. In *Lost Illusions*, social knowledge of this sort includes knowledge of paper-manufacturing processes, fashion, and the politics of the Restoration period.[25] It is to this world that Lousteau's remark about newspapers is apposite: it "accepts as truth [*vrai*] anything that is plausible [*probable*]."

With social knowledge of this sort, there is no possibility of absolute, mathematical certainty; there can be only a knowledge of the highly probable, that which is generally accepted. No *a priori* judgments apply; only *a posteriori* judgments, based on experience, are possible, and those judgments are problematic because one can never know for certain that things are what they seem. One condition of the novel form is that human understanding (of external reality and of other humans) be imagined as radically limited. Despite the common understanding of realism as accepting uncritically the transparent referentiality of language, Balzac does not treat knowledge of external reality and of society as unproblematic.[26] If knowledge of the world around us were immediate and unproblematic, it would not be possible to maintain illusions. It is the fact that knowledge must be gained through experience that constitutes the possibility of the disillusionment plot, and it is the fact that the knowledge so gained is not of eternal truths or of things in themselves but only of phenomena or appearances that makes a novel interesting. (The "omniscient" narrator does not in general make claims about things in themselves or about anything in what Kant called the "supersensible" realm.) However, the realist novel does admit the possibility of achieving at least a relatively adequate understanding of phenomena or appearances, and it is the narrator who embodies this relatively adequate knowledge.

The conflict between the objective account of events offered by the narrator and the subjective impressions of individual characters creates irony, the sense that the reader understands the character's position better than the character does. In Balzac's novel, these two perspectives are effectively isolated from one another. The narrator offers the external, objective account, while each character relies on his or her own limited, subjective perceptions, which the narrator conveys primarily through direct quotation. Most sentences record either a purely objective happening or a purely subjective impression. Even when the narrator is relating Lucien's impressions through a form of free indirect discourse, without the use of quotation marks, Balzac "labels" the subjective sentences by using such phrases as *"Lucien trouva"* ("Lucien thought" or "it seemed to Lucien that"). He thus tends to establish a distance between the narrator's account of events and Lucien's, as in the following sentence: "The queenly lady did not get up, but she very graciously twisted round in her seat, smiling at the poet, who was much impressed by this serpentine contortion, which he thought distinguished" ["La reine ne se leva point, elle se tortilla fort agréablement sur son siège, en souriant au poète, que ce trémoussement serpentin émut beaucoup, il le trouva distingué."].[27] In a sentence such as this, one of the relatively few in which the perspective of the narrator and that of the character are intermingled, the narrator clearly suggests that Madame de Bargeton's gesture is not as distinguished as Lucien believes. The words *"reine"* and *"agréablement"* suggest a confusion of the two perspectives, since it is not immediately evident whether the narrator feels, as Lucien obviously does, that these words are appropriate in a description of Madame de Bargeton. Yet, the introduction of Lucien's impressions through the clauses beginning "who was much impressed" [*"que ce trémoussement serpentin . . ."*] and "which he thought" [*"il le trouva"*] leads the way to a resolution of the potential ambiguity of the sentence. The narrator has ironically presented the lady as a queen, and it is only Lucien who finds distinction in her serpentine contortions. Such moments of potential ambiguity, while they are frequent and in fact create much of the pleasure of reading the novel, usually resolve themselves fairly quickly. Balzac often uses the technique of the rhetorical question to call attention to potential ambiguity, but he usually answers the rhetorical question almost immediately. The narrator continually informs the reader of social conventions that Lucien does not understand, thus ensuring that the reader will understand them: *"Lucien n'avait pas encore deviné que . . ."* ("Lucien had not yet divined that . . .").[28] Unlike *Père Goriot* or "Sarrasine," *Lost Illusions* depends for its plot structure on no crucial hidden fact awaiting discovery. The "mystery" of the novel is how Lucien's career will develop over time, but the general outlines are clear enough in advance to any given reader. Secondary characters, such as David Séchard or the Baron Sixte du Châtelet, predict Lucien's fate with considerable accuracy in "asides" or "interior monologues" right from the beginning of the novel, thus giving even a reader totally unfamiliar with novelistic conventions and Parisian society a good sense of what to expect.

As it appears in Balzac, the disillusionment plot structure suggests an almost tragic conception of the relationship between the individual and society. Society measures individuals by two ultimately interchangeable criteria: status and wealth. Because society is a realm dominated by arbitrary convention, it is impossible for the individual to find a truly meaningful fulfillment of his (or her) ambitions in it. Yet, for Balzac, the individual is preeminently human only in his interactions with others, that is, in his entrance into the very conventional society which appears so hostile and foreign to him. The result of disillusionment, for Lucien, is the sudden recognition that he has nothing inside himself that can counterbalance the judgments of society as a whole, that he cannot stand before society "stripped of his virtues or his splendour." The individual has a natural sense of freedom and independence, but he can exist only in a world of artificial conventions. The disillusionment plot structure draws attention precisely to the fact that any attempt to stand entirely outside society is futile and meaningless. The life of the individual is by nature embedded in the life of society. This recognition of the embeddedness of every individual life in the general fabric of society and history is a defining feature of the novel as a genre, and Balzac presents it as an inevitable and painful contradiction of the hero's natural sense of independence.

Balzac does, however, present an alternative to Lucien's suicidal response to the situation in the fate of David Séchard, Lucien's brother-in-law and childhood friend. In their youth, the two men are "two poets."[29] Lucien wants literally to write poetry, while David dreams of making a fortune out of the method for manufacturing paper that he has invented. While Lucien contemplates suicide and eventually sells himself into the power of the diabolical Vautrin, David accepts his fate with better grace. Forced to sell his invention to his rivals the Cointets, he tells his wife Eve that they will have to be content with a peaceful life in a village, but he observes that at least his paper-making process will profit France as a whole: "after all what do I matter in comparison with my country? . . . I'm only one man. If everybody profits from my invention, well, I am content" (p. 664). David finds within his own household and in his relationship with his wife Eve a fulfillment that is sheltered from the conventionality and competitive dynamics of society in general. Eve gives him the recognition which Lucien had sought in society at large. On the one hand, the intimate sphere of personal relations is the site of David's fulfillment of his own individuality. On the other hand, the idea of his country, which implies here his brotherhood with other men, compensates him for his failure to realize his fantasies of greatness.

The protagonists of *Lost Illusions* have two significant options: to abandon their attempt to realize their illusions and thus to accept a humble, provincial fate, like David; or to fail repeatedly in the attempt to fulfill their imagined destinies, running up against the indifference of society until eventually society defeats them and leads them to the brink of suicide, like Lucien himself. The alternative to a continual Faustian striving is to "cultivate one's own garden," like Candide. Another literary comparison seems to have been more on Balzac's mind. The title, "*Illusions perdues*," echoes that of Milton's *Paradise Lost* (in French "*Paradis perdu*"). The disillusionment plot is a secularized form of the story of the Fall. In the fallen world, the possibilities are to try to be like God (as Lucien does) or to accept one's place in the world abandoned by God (like David). From Milton on, the married state is part of the acceptance of the fallen nature of this world. It is rejected or seen as inadequate by all the Faustian heroes of the novels of disillusionment. David Séchard resembles Adam; hand in hand with his own Eve, he takes his solitary way. David shows that he sees himself as a second Adam when he comments on Eve's first name: "Your very name has been a symbol of my love for you. Eve was once the only woman in the world, and what was literally true for Adam is a spiritual truth for me" (p. 106). For David, the social realm can be reduced essentially to the pursuit of profit. He condemns it by claiming that he and Eve are not greedy enough to succeed in it. Lucien, on the other hand, resembles the fallen Satan, and belongs entirely to the fallen social realm. His name even echoes that of Satan before his exile from Heaven, Lucifer. Lucien seeks his sexual fulfillment with great ladies or with prostitutes, both types of women who belong to the social rather than the intimate, domestic sphere.

Balzac makes one direct reference to Milton in *Lost Illusions*, when Vautrin talks about the fear of moral solitude and the possibility of writing a poem about man's primordial desire to have an accomplice or a companion ("*complice*") in his destiny. Vautrin hopes to overcome this solitude by adopting Lucien as his "*complice*," whereas David's "*complice*" is Eve. Vautrin suggests that a poem on this subject could accompany *Paradise Lost*, which he describes as an "apologia for rebellion" ("*une apologie pour la révolte*").[30] The homoerotic undertone of the complicity between Lucien and Vautrin is notable. It will recur in most of the novels being considered in this study. David seems to put into practice a sort of Protestant ethic, although he is of course a Catholic. Lucien, on the other hand, is Catholic through and through, and a dedicated royalist, as he himself declares frequently, not least in describing the conflict between Protestants and Catholics in his own novel, *L'Archer de Charles IX*. He allies himself with the forces of reaction, and eventually, in the sequel *Splendeurs et misères des courtisanes*, he commits suicide just as Restoration monarchy to which he had attached himself collapses. Immediately after Lucien's death, the July 1830 revolution ushers in the age of liberal politics during which Balzac himself wrote *Lost Illusions*. Although Balzac would continually express nostalgia for the strong absolutist state, his novels demonstrate that he knew he lived in a world in which that possible ordering of society was an anachronism. In the *Human Comedy*, as in *Paradise Lost*, but in contrast to the *Divine Comedy*, the world is an irretrievably fallen space in which the individual is condemned to be judged by the meaningless categories of society; the greatest wisdom available on this earth comes from resigning oneself to this fate. The best one can do is to accept one's fallen state and attempt to live righteously.

DISILLUSIONMENT AND THE POSSIBILITY OF LIBERAL POLITICS

Balzac's secularized version of the narrative of the Fall calls attention to certain epistemological and political assumptions of literary realism. The narrator of *Lost Illusions* presents the fallen world of society as ruled by mere convention. The only form of freedom available to the characters is to withdraw into a private realm of authentic values. It is the family that affirms the eternal values of loyalty, truthfulness, and love, while the social sphere affirms the mutable conventions, mores (*mœurs*), that Balzac makes his particular object of study. Erich Auerbach and others have noted that Balzac's generation contributed to literary realism "an instinctive historical insight," that human nature, or at least its manifestations, varies over time. Balzac "conceives the present as history – the present is something in the process of resulting from history."[31] Balzac himself writes in his preface to the *Human Comedy*:

The Social state has uncertainties and accidents which Nature does not permit itself, for it is Nature *plus* Society. . . . [although] the mores [*mœurs*] of animals are interesting, to our eyes at least the habits of each [species of] animal remain perpetually the same; whereas the habits, clothing, methods of speech, the abodes of princes, bankers, artists, citizens, priests, and paupers, are all widely dissimilar, and change with the wishes of civilizations.[32]

Lost Illusions calls attention to this mutability of social conventions by treating "Society" as the fallen form of human nature. For human nature to vary so radically is a sign of our belonging to a temporal realm, fallen away from the spiritual realm of eternal truths. In our world, as the arch-criminal Vautrin, in painting his materialist conception of history, tells Lucien: "There are no longer any laws, merely conventions" ("Il n'y a plus des lois; il n'y a que des mœurs").[33]

While the conventions of society are mutable, however, they are not random. Another crucial element of Balzac's historicism was his suggestion that society (or what political theorists call "civil society") develops according to its own immanent laws, which are the product neither of a super-human agency nor of conscious choice on the part of human beings. Rather, they result from a vast number of smaller choices made by individuals pursuing their own goals. Balzac presents himself as a social historian who will chronicle the resulting developments: "French society was to be the historian; I was to be nothing but the secretary . . . I give to continual, everyday occurrences, secret and manifest, and to the actions of individual life, to their causes and their motives, as much importance as historians have until now bestowed on the events of the public life of nations."[34] Balzac, then, emphasizes the development of great social forces out of the actions of individuals. He claims that the minor facts that constitute social mores justify his attention because they motivate historical development, and implies that the "public life of nations," the traditional preserve of historians, is a mere super-structure built upon the true forces of history, which are the "continual, everyday occurrences" in the lives of seemingly insignificant individuals. Auerbach has noted that Balzac's innovation in this respect is to give serious literary treatment to the lives of relatively obscure and, as it were, "random" individuals, rather than heroic or princely figures. In this respect, Balzac resembles many liberal political theorists of the nineteenth century, who argued that the underlying forces of history belonged to the social realm and that the task of the state was to accommodate itself to the level of development which society had reached. Thus Tocqueville studied the influence of customs on political institutions and argued that "The laws contribute more to the maintenance of the democratic republic in the United States than the physical circumstances of the country, and the customs [*mœurs*] contribute more than the laws."[35] Similarly, John Stuart Mill argued, against much of the previous utilitarian tradition, that "the proper functions of a government are not a fixed thing, but differ in different states of society," and that a major task of politics was to find the appropriate form of government for the stage of progress reached by various societies.[36]

Like contemporary liberal theorists, then, Balzac was struck by the importance of mores or customs in shaping the individual's desires and capacities. Balzac himself held reactionary and royalist political views, but his novels display a world in which the strong state for which he nostalgically yearned has become an impossibility and the omnivorous forces of civil society must be obeyed. He treats the individual as positioned within a network of social relations, rather than born into a state of nature, marooned on a desert island, or lately emerged from the Garden of Eden. Auerbach points to the origins of this historicist conception of human nature in the experience the French had after the Revolution of having their lives continually transformed by historical forces, and more generally in the social thought of Rousseau and the romantics. A crucial problem for nineteenth-century fiction was to describe how people shaped by the facts of history could still put their faith in eternal values. As Catherine Gallagher puts it, the history of the novel to the middle of the nineteenth century "established dynamic tensions between freedom and determinism, between public and private worlds, and between the representation of facts (what is) and that of values (what ought to be)."[37] Gallagher emphasizes the role of the English industrial novelists in "uncovering the tensed structure of their own form." Balzac, on the other hand, manages to present these structuring tensions within a fairly harmonious novelistic universe. More than any other single realist novelist, he provided a model of the relationship between private and public that the modernists, fifty years later, would seek to overcome.

Balzac's narrative technique establishes a framework within which people can be understood as at once rational, autonomous individuals and members of social groups conditioned by belief systems proper to those groups. Balzac's novels amount to a series of attempts to describe the ways in which people are both free and determined, sharing a common human nature but shaped so differently by circumstances that different social groups can be compared to different species. A crucial existential problem for both liberal political theory and the realist novel is the fact that, although society is made up of individuals who are presumed to make rational decisions in their own interests, the aggregate activity of these individuals seems to follow laws of its own (laws of development, social laws) that are apparently beyond the conscious control of the individuals who make up society. While earlier Enlightenment liberals, inspired by Christianity, had claimed that human beings were created "free, equal, and independent," liberals from Rousseau onward were painfully aware that individuals were actually born into a society in which they were unequal and dependent on others and in which various social forces shaped their action.[38] As Rousseau famously put the problem, "Man is born free, and is everywhere in chains."[39]

Although Balzac, like many of his contemporaries, treats human nature as radically mutable, he does not accept that the individual should derive all of his or her values from contemporary society. Indeed, it is necessary and desirable, according to Balzac, for the individual to be capable of "stand[ing] before [society] stripped of his virtues or his splendour."[40] The individual's potential to step away from the demands of a fallen, temporal society, and to establish in the intimate sphere a relationship based on higher moral considerations, is an essential factor of the disillusionment plot. The rise of historicist modes of thought, encouraged by rapid social and political change, called attention to a tension between "ethical" and "sociological" perspectives on human action, or what John Burrow has called the language and stance of the "participant" and of the "observer."[41] The ethical perspective, on the one hand, describes the point of view of the participant in society, who attempts to fulfill his or her individual goals and perhaps to live righteously on the basis of values taken to be transcendent or eternal. The sociological perspective, on the other hand, describes society from without, as an impartial observer would, and thus tends to treat the "transcendent" values affirmed by the ethical perspective simply as products of social practices and historical forces or what Edmund Burke defended as "prejudice." Much of post-Rousseauian liberalism takes the tension between these two perspectives to be constitutive of any attempt to analyze society or human nature. From the French Revolution onward, a major concern of political thought was to reconcile, or at least to explain, the tension between the two perspectives. As Burke realized, many of the values most cherished by a society seem from a rationalistic perspective to be simply products of history or custom. Burke prefigured much of the historicist liberalism of the nineteenth century by arguing that one must embrace these prejudices, which, irrational though they might appear, in fact served the immanent rationality of history.

Whereas Burke attempts to show the ultimate compatibility of the "ethical" and "sociological" viewpoints, Kant describes them as invariably in tension with one another. Kant offers the most thorough defense of what might be called the "bifurcated" perspective on human nature. As a physical being with needs and interests, the individual always acts heteronomously, that is, in a way determined by something outside the individual's will (even if this something is an element of the individual's own nature, such as hunger or sexual desire). In order to act morally, however, the individual must act autonomously, that is, independently of any determinations in the "sensible," physical world. She must therefore conceive of herself as belonging to an "intelligible" or "supersensible" world in which the will is free from all determinations. This idea of freedom, while necessary for our moral action in the world, cannot ultimately be proven through the use of speculative (pure) reason, because the free will belongs to the supersensible realm of things-in-themselves, which is inaccessible to pure reason. On the other hand, it cannot ultimately be disproven either. The sociological perspective on the individual's actions describes the individual's behavior as determined in the sensible realm, the realm of appearances. The ethical perspective is that from which the individual considers her own actions as autonomous in the realm of essence.[42] Similarly, but, like Burke, with an emphasis on the ultimate compatibility between ethical and sociological perspectives, Tocqueville attempts to maintain a tension between what he calls the aristocratic and democratic conceptions of history, and points out the need, in order to preserve a working concept of free will, to understand the individual as neither entirely "master of himself" nor completely subject "to an inflexible Providence or to some blind necessity."[43]

Each of these varieties of political liberalism – Rousseau's, Burke's, Kant's, Tocqueville's, and Mill's – drew ultimately on certain tendencies of Christian metaphysics, particularly as emphasized by Reformation theologians and particularly on the "disenchantment" of the world described by Max Weber, with its roots in the radical distinction between the fallen world, in which one must "Render unto Caesar's that which is Caesar's" and the eternal realm of undying values which Christianity associates with the intimate sphere ("The Kingdom of God is within you").[44] The disillusionment plot structure, with its secular re-enactment of the expulsion from Paradise, offers a model of life in a modern, liberal society. The duality between the characters' subjective perceptions and the narrator's objective observations affirms the radical distinction between private and public spaces. The narrator does have access even to intimate information about the characters' lives, but he necessarily approaches this information as an outsider, a kind of police spy, as Franco Moretti has remarked.[45] He speaks for society as a whole and treats the characters as products of given milieux, describing "what" they are, rather than "who" they take themselves to be, to borrow a distinction of Heidegger's and Arendt's.[46] When the characters leave home and enter society, they expose themselves to the fallen realm of conventions in which the narrator is expert. When they successfully return home and renounce the world, as David does at the end of *Lost Illusions*, they generally escape from the narrator's orbit and enter that realm of pure, spiritual values that seems to hold no interest for the narrator or the reader.

A tension persists throughout *Lost Illusions* between the ethical perspective from which individuals attempt to make decisions based on their own rationality and presumed autonomy and the sociological perspective from which individuals appear as simply determined by social class and ideology and incapable of truly autonomous decisions. On the one hand, there is an ethical, individual perspective from which a given character attempts to make sense of a position in which he or she is placed. This is the perspective of the interior monologue or of the indirect discourse by which Balzac puts himself inside his characters' minds. On the other hand, the narrator, guardian of social knowledge and "objectivity," continually offers the sociological perspective, according to which the individual's decisions are not truly free, but are the products of social class, prejudice, and other forces beyond the characters' conscious control. The narrator presents the view of society in general (not the God's-eye-view). He understands the mere conventionality of the fallen world. It is only by rejecting society's conventions and retreating into a private realm of authentic values that the characters hope to regain a measure of freedom. The realist novel, in general, like liberal political theory, presents such a bifurcation as a basic condition of the representation of social reality. Autonomous human life in society depends on a sharp division between the strictly private or intimate and the public or social: in joining civil society, the individual gives up certain freedoms to the majority of the community but maintains certain rights and freedoms that cannot be alienated. Such a bifurcation, then, was a precondition of the liberal conception of human beings as autonomous individuals whose consensus lies at the basis of the formation of society. Balzac's realism adopts this essential precondition of liberal thought.

Balzac conceived of his project as a chronicle of the realm of conventions, in all their historical mutability: to write "that history forgotten by so many historians – the history of mores . . . for France of the nineteenth century."[47] This formulation points to the importance of the nation as the sum of relevant mores or conventions according to which the characters interact in the fallen world of civil society. Benedict Anderson argues that a major force in creating the sense of belonging to a nation that might be called "national consciousness" was the rise of "print-capitalism," particularly the newspaper and the realist novel. According to Anderson, the newspaper and the novel encourage the development of the national community not only because they circulate in the national language, but because they report on (real or fictional) events from the abstract position of the national community. By describing a national landscape in which people share a common store of social knowledge, co-exist in a shared public space, and move through time or history together, these forms of communication created a shared "national imagination" among diverse readers. A typical realist plot involves the "movement of a solitary hero through a sociological landscape of a fixity [in time and space] that fuses the world inside the novel with the world outside." The novel thus places both the fictional and real worlds within a conceptual "horizon" that is "clearly bounded" by the extent of the nation.[48] In the secular, temporal world described by the newspaper or the novel, the nation replaced the religious community as the source of a sense of shared destiny among people.

Like the novels that Anderson analyzes, Balzac's *Human Comedy* describes events within a national horizon. The characters' lives revolve around two poles, Paris and the provinces. Although each of Balzac's characters knows only a handful of the others, they all share a horizon of experience defined mainly by a shared high culture in the French language and a shared set of national institutions – newspapers, the military, parliament, the state's administrative service, the business world. This shared national context is emphasized by the appearance of several characters in more than one novel of the *Human Comedy*, alternately as protagonists or as part of the supporting cast. The characters' experience of time and history shows the close relationship between their individual lives and the life of the nation as a whole. Changes in ministry or

régime lead to changes in the fortunes of characters of various political
persuasions. The nation functions in Balzac's novels, however, not as a
rallying point for a political agenda, but as a sort of backdrop against
which the lives of individuals develop. It is essentially a limit or horizon
of experience. The individual's life is influenced by events on the
"national stage," but the nation is still conceived fundamentally as the
aggregate of the individuals who compose it, an external, conventional
reality into which the individual enters upon leaving home and the provinces. The typical hero or heroine of Balzac's novels leaves for Paris in
young adulthood.

In *Lost Illusions*, then, Balzac draws on models of human nature,
human understanding, social organization, and the nation that he
shared with contemporary liberal political thinkers. The individual is
effectively autonomous, that is, capable of making rational decisions on
the basis of his or her will alone. Yet that fundamental autonomy is continually undercut by the demands of self-interest (whether self-preservation or the desire for money and esteem) and by the individual's location
within a particular, historically specific set of circumstances. Balzac
treats human knowledge of the external world, of other humans, and of
the ultimate good as fundamentally problematic. All judgment depends
ultimately on the evidence of the senses and more generally on consciousness, but both the senses and consciousness are always suspect.
Individuals do, however, manage to achieve a consensus as to the nature
of external reality, which is shared in two senses: it is literally a shared
public space; and it is governed by conventions to which all members of
society are presumed to subscribe, the mores that Balzac made his object
of study. These conventions are not immutable and are, in fact, the site
of continual contestation and struggle. No single member of society
promulgates them, and judgments about which conventions are to be
accepted or rejected depend on a complex set of social interactions. The
possibility exists that these mores, or conventions, and the laws of social
development will ultimately lead society to a world of purely material
values at the expense, not only of the older aristocratic values associated
with glory and honor, but also of the ethical values of duty, love, and
friendship. In the meantime, however, these mores, even though they are
purely social norms and not divinely ordained, manage to be recognized
by all the members of society, who ignore them at their own peril. A
certain set of conventions maintains its force, and the mouthpiece of
society, who articulates them and applies them in a neutral fashion to
each of the individuals in society, is the narrator. The limits of this

society are coextensive with those of the nation. As Balzac observed, "French society was to be the historian; I was to be nothing but the secretary" (p. x). Only the existence of this "objective," outside, social world, guaranteed by the narrator, makes possible the character's overcoming of his or her limited perspective that consists in losing the illusions of youth. There exists, however, a sphere, the intimate realm of the household, in which the laws of society are irrelevant. It is in the household that the individual is formed before confronting society as a young adult, and it is to this intimate realm that the individual is capable of retreating upon having experienced the disillusionment of life in society. The realist novel provides a model for understanding life in a liberal nation-state, for reconciling the individualistic striving for autonomy characteristic of modernity with the demand for social stability and justice. This model depends on the acceptance of a bifurcation between the realms of social behavior and ethical action.

JOYCE'S TRANSFORMATION OF THE DISILLUSIONMENT PLOT STRUCTURE

That bifurcation between social and ethical life would prove unacceptable to Joyce's Stephen Dedalus. Stephen's career in *A Portrait of the Artist as a Young Man* mirrors Lucien's in several respects, and Joyce's novel accepts many of the premises of Balzac's realism. Like Lucien, Stephen confronts a hostile external world which seems to lack any meaningful pattern of its own and to depend entirely on social convention. Stephen too experiences his encounter with this world in terms borrowed from contemporary politics. Whereas Lucien follows the model of Napoleon, Stephen imagines himself as a second Parnell. Finally, like Lucien, Stephen experiences a tension between his utter dependence on the values offered to him by the society that has produced him and his sense that these values are inadequate, that his own soul is capable of something truer. The plot of *Lost Illusions* relies on the ultimate contradiction of this sense of an ability to rise above social values. Balzac displays an almost tragic awareness of the fact that what we perceive as our own is not really our own. We are shaped by forces beyond our control. The only way to come to terms with this fact is disillusionment, which can end either in suicide, the ultimate capitulation to society, or in a "realistic" acceptance of one's place in society and an attempt to live as freely as possible within a circumscribed intimate sphere. For Joyce, however, unlike for Balzac, the recognition of the close interrelation between the

individual and society leads to a solution of the problem of disillusionment: the idea of the conscience of the race, which the individual experiences as a pure interior realm but which is also the emanation of society.

Joyce converts the disillusionment plot structure from a single,
momentous event in the life of the protagonist into an indefinite process,
coextensive with life itself. Stephen proclaims his desire to go to Paris and
"encounter for the millionth time the reality of experience" at the end,
not the beginning, of the novel, after he can already claim to have
encountered experience thousands of times before. Whereas Balzac presents the reader with fully formed young adult characters who are ready
to leave home for Paris, Joyce starts with an infant. Joyce thus presents
the formation of character itself as a product of social forces, rather than
(as in Balzac) the unique function of the intimate household. The role
of language itself in the novel emphasizes the lack of a dividing line
between the household and society at large. The novel begins with the
protagonist's first attempts to make sense, in language, of the reality of
experience, and it is through his many encounters with reality, always
mediated by language, that his consciousness develops. As Stephen
learns language, he also learns his place in history and in geography.
Thus even his nursery song about a "wild rose" blossoming on a "little
green place" leads him a little later in life to muse half-consciously on the
possibility of Irish nationhood: "you could not have a green rose. But
perhaps somewhere in the world you could" (p. 12). As Stephen remarks
to his friend Davin, "When the soul of a man is born in this country
there are nets flung at it to hold it back from flight" (p. 203). One of these
nets is language, which captures the soul in a particular way of encountering reality. Yet, Stephen transforms this consciousness of the individual's shaping by society into the material for a transfiguration of society
through the individual. Through his manipulation of language in
writing, Stephen hopes to overcome the dynamic of disillusionment and
to convert the hostile, contingent "reality of experience" into the
material of his own meaning-making process. He thus conceives of
himself as "a priest of eternal imagination, transmuting the daily bread
of experience into the radiant body of everliving life" (p. 221). What
makes this transubstantiation possible is the mystical unity of the priest-
like artist with the "conscience of the race."

Stephen's pronouncements about his relationship to his society show
an extreme form of the tension described by Tocqueville between the
attitude of aristocratic historians who imagine man to be "master of
himself" and the democratic historians' sense of being subject "to an

inflexible Providence." On the one hand, Stephen continually asserts that he can overcome his shaping by society: "You talk to me of nationality, language, religion. I shall try to fly by those nets" (p. 203). Like Lucifer, he rejects servitude: "I will not serve that in which I no longer believe whether it call itself my home, my fatherland, or my church: and I will try to express myself in some mode of life or art as freely as I can and as wholly as I can, using for my defence the only arms I allow myself to use – silence, exile, and cunning" (p. 247). These statements have contributed to the conception of Stephen as an individualist or an adherent of "art for art's sake." Yet Stephen just as often expresses an extreme fatalism, a conviction that his actions are predestined, and in particular that they are part of a teleological plan which Stephen himself can only vaguely sense. As a child, he is conscious of having been born to serve an unknown end: "in secret he began to make ready for the great part which he felt awaited him, the nature of which he only dimly apprehended" (p. 62). He frequently senses throughout the novel that his life is headed toward a predestined goal, "the end he had been born to serve yet did not see" (p. 165). Near the end of the novel, he tells Cranly that he was "someone else" in his childhood: "I was not myself as I am now, as I had to become" (p. 240). He couples this sense of destiny with a skepticism of the capacity of the human mind to act in ways that are truly new. Toward the end of the novel, Stephen tells the dean of his college that he is "sure there is no such thing as free thinking inasmuch as all thinking must be bound by its own laws" (p. 187). If the mind does obey "its own laws," it meets the formal definition of "autonomy" (self-rule), but this autonomy does not constitute a Kantian metaphysical freedom, since it involves no active will on the part of the thinker; thought is merely an automatic process, like breathing or the circulation of the blood. Stephen seems trapped in a determinism that suggests that his own thoughts can only develop in accordance with his instincts, his previous experience, and the nets in which that experience has captured him: "this race and this country and this life produced me . . . I shall express myself as I am" (p. 203). Stephen's very "illusions" are products of experience, of speaking a certain language and belonging to a certain culture. His previous experience conditions how Stephen's consciousness will perceive the outside world, but each new encounter adds to Stephen's store of experience and thus transforms his consciousness. All experience is new in as much as it does transform Stephen's mind, but it is also old in that Stephen can interpret it only in accordance with the many encounters that have already created him.

In some respects, then, *A Portrait* seems merely to intensify the dynamic of disillusionment. Stephen's sense of having been produced by his society and of being incapable of "free" thinking makes him resemble Lucien de Rubempré when, at the end of *Lost Illusions*, he realizes that he has nothing inside himself to oppose to the "reality of life" in society. Stephen seems unable to accept the Enlightenment position articulated by Kant which understands human beings as free in the supersensible realm but determined in the sensible realm. It is the intense conflict between his deterministic conception of the laws of the mind and his desire for utter freedom or autonomy that leads Stephen to seek in a dialectical conception of "experience" an escape from this central dilemma of human freedom. In order for this dialectical notion to allow Stephen a sense of meaningful freedom, Stephen must achieve a synthesis of his mind with external reality that can allow him to do something more than enact the inevitable logic of history.

Around the time that he was completing *A Portrait*, Joyce read Vico, who argues that we as humans can know our own history because we have made it ourselves.[49] He also read Marx, who argues that while humans make their own history, they do not do so under circumstances of their own choosing. In *Ulysses*, alluding to Marx, Stephen will enunciate his conception of history as "a nightmare from which I am trying to awake."[50] Already, in *A Portrait*, Stephen's awakening consists in his becoming conscious of his entrapment in the nightmare of Irish history. By recognizing that the ethical self he has now is a product of the historical forces at work in human society, that his mind is a product of human history and human history is a product of the human mind, Stephen hopes to overcome the dynamic of disillusionment. His coming to consciousness is a gradual process that culminates in the epiphanic moments of the novel's final chapter, a fulfillment of historical laws that will also lead to their transfiguration.[51] It will allow him to achieve the unity with the Irish race that raises his experience above the level of mere necessity and contingency. When he goes to the rector to complain of having been beaten by Father Dolan, he sees himself as a historical personage: "A thing like that had been done before by somebody in history, by some great person whose head was in the books of history . . . History was all about those men and what they did" (p. 53). *A Portrait* tells the story of his finding his own place in history. In order to do so, Stephen places Irish history in the context of a mythical religious pattern that culminates in his own person.

Parnell's fall from power and grace will play something like the role of original sin in Stephen's Irish eschatology. Parnell seems to have represented to Joyce, as to many of his contemporaries, the last hope for a civic, liberal Irish nationalism that would unite Protestants and Catholics. After his exposure as an adulterer and the resulting loss of support for the Irish Parliamentary Party, the very possibility of a solution to the Irish national problem in the realm of formal politics seemed to be lost. As Yeats remarked in his speech accepting the Nobel Prize in 1925, "The modern literature of Ireland, and indeed all that stir of thought which prepared for the Anglo-Irish war, began when Parnell fell from power in 1891. A disillusioned and embittered Ireland turned from parliamentary politics; an event was conceived and the race began, as I think, to be troubled by that event's long gestation."[52] Stephen first hears of Parnell on the second page of the novel. He learns of Parnell's death as he lies in the school infirmary, where he has been imagining his own death (pp. 24, 27). Later, he recalls that moment: "But he had not died then. Parnell had died. There had been no mass for the dead in the chapel and no procession" (p. 93). At the family's next Christmas dinner, Stephen struggles to understand the argument between Dante, a family friend who condemns Parnell, and Mr. Casey, a family friend who glorifies Parnell as "my dead king" (p. 39). Stephen's father sides with Mr. Casey and bemoans the fate of his "priestridden Godforsaken race" (p. 37). The morning after that Christmas dinner, Stephen attempts to write his first poem, a commemoration of Parnell (p. 70). Parnell, for Stephen, is both an Adam whose fall has terrible consequences for his entire (Irish) race and a failed Christ, who might have redeemed Ireland. Stephen imagines Parnell dying in his place, just as Christ died so that all humans might have everlasting life. Parnell inspires Stephen to write, and Stephen imagines himself as capable, through his writing, of redeeming Parnell's fall and repaying Parnell for having died in his place. At the Christmas dinner, he hears the first references in the book to the notion of the Irish race. Stephen's father observes, "we are an unfortunate priestridden race and always were and always will be until the end of the chapter" (p. 37). At the end of the novel, during the Easter season, Stephen will finally devote himself to writing as a means of redeeming his race. Through his writing, then, Stephen will offer the sacrifice of his own soul to Ireland. Just as this act of martyrdom will save the Irish, however, it will also allow Stephen to achieve unfettered freedom because, in embracing his moral unity with the Irish race, he will reconcile his ethical self with his socially constructed identity.

The religious crises that play such a central role in the novel lead

Stephen towards his conception of himself as a priest of the secular world and the race. In the first of these crises, Stephen, who has slept with prostitutes, attends a Christian retreat and contemplates Hell. He sees himself as resembling Lucifer after his fall from heaven, "plunging headlong through space" (p. 124).[53] After hearing a sermon on Hell, which gives him a number of images for his later conception of the conscience of the race, Stephen confesses his sins. He feels a sense of rebirth and imagines himself as a second Adam, with Emma as his Eve. At the end of the central third chapter, in which Stephen experiences this crisis, Joyce alludes to Milton's Adam: "How simple and beautiful life was after all. And life lay all before him" (p. 146).[54] Stephen experiences a brief spiritual regeneration, which comes to its inevitable end when the director of Belvedere College asks him to consider whether or not he has a vocation to be a priest. Stephen recalls his many "proud musings" on the subject: "He had seen himself . . . accomplishing the vague acts of the priesthood which pleased him by reason of their semblance of reality and of their distance from it . . . In vague sacrificial or sacramental acts alone his will seemed drawn to go forth to encounter reality" (pp. 158–159). Stephen realizes that he cannot become a priest and that he will again fall. His later encounter with reality, though, will involve a reworking of these images of the Catholic mass. As Stephen walks home, considering "that which he had so often thought to be his destiny," he sees Dublin, "visible to him across the timeless air," and he becomes aware of his actual destiny. He finds in his family name, Dedalus, "a prophecy of the end he had been born to serve and had been following through the mists of childhood and boyhood, a symbol of the artist forging anew in his workshop out of the sluggish matter of the earth a new soaring impalpable imperishable being" (p. 169).

In conceiving of his new destiny, as Joyce's critics have often observed, Stephen models himself in part on Lucifer. He repeats Lucifer's "*non serviam: I will not serve*" (pp. 117, 239). Milton's Satan, to whom Joyce frequently alludes, served in part as a symbol of the priesthood, in what Milton viewed as its pernicious attempt to establish itself as a mediator between man and God. Like Balzac's Vautrin and many of the romantics, Stephen invests Satan with a heroic status, and sees in his rebellion a Promethean (or Daedalian) attempt to bring heavenly inspiration to the earthly world. Like Balzac's Lucien, Stephen resembles Lucifer, who rebelled against his servitude. However, Stephen seems conscious, in his many attempts to model his life on that of Jesus, that if he were to succeed in "transmuting the daily bread of experience into the radiant body of everliving life," he would cease to be merely a priest or Lucifer and would become Christ Himself. Stephen concerns himself with the mystical unity of father, son, and Holy Ghost. As the "Scylla and Charybdis" episode of *Ulysses* with its many references back to *A Portrait* will make clear, Stephen hopes to become his own father and thus to overcome his debts to his own heritage. He seems to realize that if Lucifer had succeeded in his rebellion, he too would have become his own father – God – and would have replaced Jesus.[55] At the end of *A Portrait*, Stephen rejects his mother, noting that Jesus did the same, and puts Cranly in the role of his own John the Baptist (pp. 242–248). In college, Stephen's teacher Mr. Tate accuses him of heresy for his statement in a paper "about the Creator and the soul" that the soul should strive to imitate the perfection of the creator *"without a possibility of ever approaching nearer"* (p. 79).[56] Stephen quickly corrects himself: "I meant *without a possibility of ever reaching."* In the final chapter of the novel, Stephen finally devotes himself to an imitation of Christ that implies the opposite heretical position: that he can actually reach divine perfection, and become both God the Son and God the Father.

In order to redeem his experience, then, Stephen must move beyond either Adam or Lucifer to become Christ. That he cannot content himself with being Adam points to a central thematic difference between *A Portrait* and *Lost Illusions*: Stephen lacks a single friend who can act as a foil for him as definitively as David Séchard does for Lucien. In *Lost Illusions*, David showed the possibility of a life devoted purely to the intimate emotions of love and duty. The intimate realm of the household, however, cannot provide Stephen with a shelter from the social forces that affect life outside the home. For a number of reasons, Stephen cannot have a "room of his own." His parents keep changing houses because they cannot afford their rent, so Stephen lacks the material basis of intimacy. As the scene at the Christmas dinner table shows, too, the intimate sphere is thoroughly saturated with the tensions of the social sphere. Stephen's conception of himself as at once a product of "this race and this country and this life" and an autonomous being capable of expressing himself freely in life and art seems to result from his having grown up without experiencing a solid boundary between the intimate sphere of the household and the social sphere of the nation. At the same time, however, Stephen recognizes the intimate sphere as a possible alternative space which he himself rejects. He makes the distinction between household and nation impossible for himself by rejecting the companionship of women and the friendship of men. He thinks of his relationship to his own family as being comparable to the "mystical kinship of fosterage," akin presumably to Jesus's relationship to Joseph and Mary (p. 98). He refuses Cranly's offer to be "a friend" or "more than a friend" (p. 247). Stephen's rejection of the intimate sphere, then, while prepared for him by material circumstances, also has for him a moral significance. Stephen hopes to achieve an "unfettered freedom" by recognizing and expressing the ways in which he has been produced by his race, his country, and his life. This total devotion to the race means foregoing the possibility of a sphere outside society and history in which to pursue the purely intimate ends of love and friendship.

THE CONSCIENCE OF THE RACE AND THE MORAL UNITY OF THE NATION

Stephen's choice of the word "race" to describe the source of the identity of his ethically free and sociologically determined selves points to his concern with achieving a moral unity of the nation as the basis for the new form of freedom he hopes to achieve through his writing. Stephen has promised to fly by the "nets" of "nationality, language, religion" before dedicating himself to the "conscience of the race," leading to much critical confusion. His choice of vocabulary seems rather shocking, since to affirm "racial" ties seems to involve accepting the idea of a biological essence of the nation, as opposed to the purely legal or political notions of membership in the community implied, for example, by the term "citizenship." The biological content of Stephen's ideal does not sit well either with the older critical conception of Joyce as an apolitical individualist or with more recent attempts to find in Joyce a progressive, anti-racist critic of capitalism, patriarchy, and imperialism. Among the conceptions of Joyce's politics that emerges out of recent, politically oriented criticism is that he was a sort of ultra-individualist. This is the tenor of much of Dominic Manganiello's discussion of Joyce's interest in anarchism. For example, he argues that "For Joyce, the freeing of the individual was the main issue, indeed the only one."[57] Similarly, he asserts that "Stephen's mission of ennobling his country holds a new promise of freedom, since the artist asserts that the individual is more important than institutions such as Church and State" (p. 41). In more recent works, Emer Nolan notices Joyce's kinship with the Irish nationalist project but still sees Stephen as involved in a "resolutely individualistic self-fashioning" and, in line with most previous criticism, considers Stephen simply an aesthete.[58] Vincent Cheng considers race primarily in terms of biologist racial theory rather than in its full range of application which could include cultural as well as biological phenomena. He sees in Stephen's conception of race an overturning of an "English/Irish dialectic."[59] Yet, Joyce's attitude to race seems more complex than many progressive critics have been willing to admit. Joyce tended to associate Stephen, in particular, with anti-democratic politics, as Michael Tratner has shown. Tratner notes that in *Stephen Hero*, the first draft of *A Portrait*, Stephen speaks of uniting the Irish with the broad movement of "Aryan civilization," echoing Wagnerian and other anti-semitic fantasies.[60] By the time of *A Portrait*, however, the race that Stephen plans to serve seems more closely identified with the Irish nation. Joyce's irony towards Stephen makes it difficult to say whether the author endorses the character's political views, but several of Joyce's own critical statements draw upon a "racial" conception of the Irish similar to Stephen's, notably his reference to the Irish, in "The Day of the Rabblement," as "the most belated race in Europe."[61] What, then, does Stephen mean by "race"?

Stephen's references to "race" contain echoes not simply of modern racist tracts like Arthur de Gobineau's *The Inequality of Human Races*, but also of older, "pre-scientific" conceptions of "race" as a group sharing a common lineage and fate. It is in this latter sense that Milton's fallen angels frequently refer to the competition between their race and the race of mankind: "Shall we then live thus vile, the race of Heaven / Thus trampled, thus expelled to suffer here these / Chains and these torments?"[62] In his *Victorian Anthropology*, George Stocking has demonstrated the tendency among post-Darwinist anthropologists and philosophers to treat "race" as an amalgam of cultural and biological factors. The resulting amalgam did carry elements of the rigid biological determinism that, according to Cheng, Joyce "rejects and reverses" in his later fiction.[63] Yet the concept of "race" still had the flexibility, in the early twentieth century, to refer not just to a rigid biologism but also to the "moral" factors, such as customs and institutions, that later anthropologists would distinguish as "culture."[64] The concept "race" blurred the boundaries between the terms that the later liberal tradition would confidently differentiate as "race" and "culture." One of the disturbing implications of this blurring, for progressive analyses of racism, is that the "cultural" determinism embraced by modern anthropology and cultural studies has common roots with the "racial" determinism it is meant to contradict. Both see the individual as decisively shaped by his or her inheritance, whether biological or cultural. Today, the "natural" or appropriate response to the history of racial stereotypes of the Irish might seem to be to reject racial stereotyping outright. For Stephen Dedalus, however, and apparently also for Joyce, there was an other possible response: to affirm Irish "racial" difference and find in it a source of strength. In doing so, Stephen shares many of the crucial assumptions of Irish nationalists whose overt political and cultural agenda he opposes. In particular, he rejects political activism in favor of cultural renewal and associates this cultural renewal with expressing the essence of the Irish race. Similarly, the Gaelic League argued that the revival of the Irish language must precede political autonomy, which it considered "an accidental and an external thing."[65]

If Stephen sees himself as a Christ-figure, then the "uncreated conscience of [his] race" appears to be God the creator, while the "race" itself approximates the Church, the body of faithful in need of redemption. These conceptions of the Christ-figure as embodying the genius of the race may owe something to Joyce's reading (in 1905) of two influential works on the life of Jesus, by David Friedrich Strauss and Ernest Renan.[66] Strauss elaborated a Hegelian interpretation of the Incarnation which emphasized the dialectical nature of the Christ-figure, who shares the infinite capacities of God and the finitude of humans. Renan conceived of Jesus as embodying the characteristics of his race at the moment when it was being decisively transformed by its contact with Graeco-Roman civilization. Stephen's conception of the "race" mixes notions of historical fate, biological inheritance or blood, and spiritual unity. In his new theology, Stephen finds a place for a number of doctrines of the Roman Catholic church. The *creatio ex nihilo*, God's creation of the universe out of nothing, concerns him first in the class of elements at Clongowes school when he ponders his own place in the universe, having written in his geography book, on successive lines, his location:

> Stephen Dedalus
> Class of Elements
> Clongowes Wood College
> Sallins
> County Kildare
> Ireland
> Europe
> The World
> The Universe (p. 15)

Stephen wonders what belongs before the Universe, and arrives at a version of the ontological proof of God's existence: "It was very big to think about everything and everywhere. Only God could do that" (p. 16).[67] What troubles him next is that God has different names in different languages, a problem he eventually abandons after thinking, "though there were different names for God in all the different languages in the world and God understood what all the people who prayed said in their different languages still God remained always the same and God's real name was God" (p. 16). Stephen accepts that there must be some ultimate cause at the root of the way in which the world is ordered. The Church tells him that this is God, "the supremely good and loving Creator Who has called [the] soul into existence from nothingness." The problem for Stephen seems to be that each person can only imagine God in language, and that each language gives God a different name. Stephen's very specific location has of course shaped his conception of God. By starting, like Descartes, with the thinking subject (himself), Stephen replays the anxieties of modern western philosophy. As a child, Stephen cannot solve this conundrum. When he comes to embrace the "conscience of the race" as that which is "uncreated," he will see in the values he has learned from his nation, rather than in a universal God, the first cause that has called his soul into existence from nothingness.

Apart from the fact that he has inherited the notion from his father, one of Stephen's reasons for conceiving of the Irish nation as a "race" apparently stems from his conception of the race as a community to which a person belongs even *before* learning a language. Part of the fallen condition of the Irish race is, of course, that it has abandoned its own language in favor of the language of the conquerors. Stephen, whose idea of the race owes more than he would like to think to contemporary Irish nationalism, still rejects the nationalist program of reclaiming the Irish language: "My ancestors threw off their language and took another. They allowed a handful of foreigners to subject them. Do you fancy I am going to pay in my own life and person debts they made? What for?" (p. 203). Stephen does not, however, imagine that he can find in the English language a pure and unmediated relationship with his race. He feels alienated in his use of English. When speaking to the dean, an English convert to Catholicism, he says to himself:

The language in which we are speaking is his before it is mine. How different are the words *home, Christ, ale, master,* on his lips and on mine! I cannot speak or write these words without unrest of spirit. His language, so familiar and so foreign, will always be for me an acquired speech. I have not made or accepted its words. My voice holds them at bay. My soul frets in the shadow of his language. (p. 189)

"Language" is one of the nets in which the Irish soul is captured upon birth. Stephen hopes to return to something even more primary, although he recognizes that he can do so only through language. Thus, he accepts the Gaelic League's conception of the Irish as alienated from themselves by their use of English, but rejects the solution of a return to Irish. It is through working out the implications of this alienation, rather than through a nostalgic return to a lost origin, that Stephen will bring his soul out of the shadows.

Similarly, Stephen rejects the term "nationality" and much of the rhetoric of national renewal. Here again, he seems to be searching for a conception of Irish identity prior to its identification with the formal politics of citizenship in a modern liberal state. In this respect, again, he models his concept of membership in the race on notions of community he has inherited from the Church. As Cranly tells Stephen just before he rejects Christianity, "The Church is not the stone building nor even the clergy and their dogmas. It is the whole mass of those born into it" (p. 245). In the race, Stephen finds an even more primary source of communal identity. He embraces the concept of the "race" because one belongs to the race by right of birth, before even learning a language or being baptised. Whether this membership in the race depends primarily on one's blood or on one's being born in a particular location is a problem that Stephen considers without resolving. It seems likely, from the evidence of *Ulysses* and *Finnegans Wake*, that Joyce himself gradually broadened his definition of the race to which he belonged.

Most of the eleven uses of the word "race" in *A Portrait* confirm this association of the racial conscience with an identification prior to all other forms of membership in social groups.[68] Several point in particular to the link between race and maternity, suggesting one of the reasons for Stephen's refusal to serve his "fatherland," namely that fatherhood itself is ultimately a "legal fiction" and maternity is a more intimate source of identity.[69] Because he has rejected the intimate sphere, Stephen's own contribution to the race will be strictly spiritual, but he nevertheless links it closely with reproduction. It is in women, and especially peasant women, that he expects to find the racial conscience embodied. He listens with fascination to Davin's story of a peasant woman who had asked him to spend the night with her. Stephen pictures this peasant woman as "a type of her race and of his own, a batlike soul waking to the consciousness of itself in darkness and secrecy and loneliness" (p. 183). He also hopes to communicate this essence to the daughters of Irish patricians. As he contemplates leaving the Church, Stephen observes a party in the Maple Hotel, and wonders, "How could he hit their conscience or how cast his shadow over the imaginations of their daughters, before their squires begat upon them, that they might breed a race less ignoble than their own? And under the deepened dusk he felt the thoughts and desires of the race to which he belonged flitting like bats, across the dark country lanes" (p. 238). This passage ends with the observation: "him no woman's eyes had wooed." Stephen thus associates the racial conscience with women and sexual reproduction, or perhaps virgin birth, since it is merely his shadow that Stephen will cast over the imaginations of the young Irish women.

Stephen's hostility to formal politics, whether democratic and progressive or organic-nationalist, confirms this association of race with the inheritance of a group membership prior to all cultural associations. The racial conscience is "natural," not in the sense that it belongs outside history or culture, but in the sense that it precedes the individual's formal incorporation into the cultural groups associated with the nets of "language, nationality, and religion." Stephen recognizes the significance of formal politics, and particularly of Parnell, in having shaped the Irish race, but he seems to view politics as a lost opportunity and thus treats with skepticism any attempts at political renewal. While shaped by events in the public realm, Stephen's concept of the race can be of little use in the formulation of a pragmatic political agenda, since it is as hostile to movements of cultural renewal aimed at securing the rights of the "nationality" or the "fatherland" as to progressivist theories of history aiming at the rights and worth of the "human individual." Stephen even seems to sense this irrelevance of his forging of the racial conscience to formal politics somewhat guiltily in his various exchanges with the democrat MacCann. While Stephen's own theory of the race does not serve any explicitly political agenda, it nonetheless participates in a number of contemporary political trends. In particular, his conception of himself as a redeemer eerily prefigures the sacrificial language surrounding the uprising of Easter, 1916, the year of publication of *A Portrait*. In seeking to forge in the smithy of his soul the uncreated conscience of his race, Stephen draws upon the organic nationalist conception of the intimate relationship between the individual and his ethnic group which precedes all cultural ties and fundamentally conditions the individual's experience. It is more primary than culture, but it necessarily implies a combination of historical, cultural, biological, and spiritual conditions. In this ultimate existential unity between the individual and the race, Stephen, much like the Gaelic nationalists whose merely superficial nationalism he opposes, seeks to overcome the conflict between the individual's moral autonomy and his status as a product of a given set of historical and social forces. Stephen rejects religion because it proposes a false standard of human conduct, language because it is a purely conventional social structure that for the Irish in particular always involves oppression, and nationality because it reflects the merely formal, institutional conception of community implicit in modern liberal politics. He seeks instead a moral unity not with all of humanity nor with the principle of individuality, not with the nation nor the fatherland, but with the conscience of his Godforsaken, priestridden race.

MODERNIST NARRATIVE TECHNIQUE AND THE RACIAL CONSCIENCE

Joyce's narrative technique seems to offer some hope that Stephen will succeed in achieving this mystical union. The traditional novel of disillusionment leads the hero from a highly subjective, "unrealistic" attitude toward the external world to a more objective, disillusioned view. Only the existence of an objective, "realistic" mode of perceiving the world, represented by the narrator, makes it possible for the individual character to overcome his own limited, subjective view and to reach the maturity that consists in accepting the socially sanctioned, relatively adequate perspective on reality. In *A Portrait of the Artist*, where the intertwining of narrator's and character's perspective makes the existence of the mature, socially sanctioned perspective problematic, Stephen cannot hope to overcome his own subjectivity in the same way. Joyce was among the most ambitious of the modernists in his attempts to rethink the social logic of realist forms. Hugh Kenner, Wayne Booth, and others have noted the mingling of the character's and the narrator's voices in *A Portrait*, what Kenner has called Joyce's "doubleness of vision."[70] The distinction between the outer world and the mind of the protagonist is less sharp than in realist novels, and it is not always possible to separate perception from reality. The most remarkable formal innovation of *A Portrait* is, of course, the disappearance of the narrator's "objective" social knowledge. In Balzac, there exists an "objective" external reality, albeit one ruled by social conventions. Through his encounters with these conventions, the hero learns to interpret "reality" correctly (that is, in the same way as everybody else). For Joyce, the shaping effects of consciousness itself are so important that the hero, by virtue of his perceptions, effectively transforms the outside world.

Like Balzac, Joyce relies on a constant tension between the observer's perspective, embodied in the narrator, and the participant's, embodied in the character. Yet, in *A Portrait of the Artist as a Young Man*, practically every sentence mingles the objective third-person account of events with the subjective impressions of the growing artist and creates a type of irony akin to what Balzac generates with his frequent use of the expression *"Lucien trouva."* In *A Portrait*, not only does Joyce do away with quotation marks when relating the character's impressions, but he also severely limits his use of verbal markers, such as "Stephen thought." Most sentences in the book record Stephen's impressions of events or his musings occasioned by events, as in the sentence from the first page of the book, "When you wet the bed first it is warm then it gets cold." Where Stephen himself is the grammatical subject of the sentence, the verb often describes an act of perception, and the grammatical object appears to the reader as if through Stephen's eyes. For example, in the statement "Stephen looked at the plump turkey which had lain, trussed and skewered, on the kitchen table," "trussed and skewered" appear to be Stephen's words for the turkey and the sentence seems to recall Stephen's earlier perception of the turkey in the kitchen. In every event that the novel records, the narrator's description is imbued with Stephen's impressions, which are themselves the main events of the narrative. Most of the sentences describing Stephen's actions refer to his perceiving something. Even in a relatively simple declarative sentence that apparently records an objective event in which Stephen is a participant rather than an observer, the two perspectives are mingled, as in the description of his beating at Clongowes School, which includes many sentences like the following: "Stephen drew back his maimed and quivering right arm and held out his left hand." Although the narrator is describing, as if from without, an action of Stephen's, he does not exclude Stephen's own feelings from the description.

This narrative voice, then, represents an "objectivity" itself shaped by the same forces that shape the hero. There remains a distinction between character and narrator, but the possibility of a consensus as to the nature of external reality and of society seems to have disappeared. The narrator is neither simply the protagonist telling his own story, nor an omniscient outsider capable of describing the general social consensus as in Balzac. Rather, he is a projection of the individual and idiosyncratic perspective of the protagonist himself. (Only after the first world war, notably in *Ulysses* and the novels of Virginia Woolf, will a more "pluralist" conception of reality be represented through the use of multiple perspectives.) The narrator himself is tainted by the very "illusions" that Stephen has inherited from the national consciousness, and there is no objective, outside view, untainted by belonging to a particular culture, that can correct them. This formal characteristic of *A Portrait of the Artist*, its fusion of objective and subjective modes of description, is the hallmark of modernism in the novel. The highly subjective transcriptions of individual characters' consciousnesses in modernist novels color (or pollute) the apparently objective observations of the narrator, thus calling attention to the fact that any account of events, by virtue of being formulated in language (that is, by virtue of being an account) comes laden with interpretation, that no purely objective, purely descriptive account is possible. What makes *A Portrait of the Artist as a Young Man* remarkable, then, is not that the young man describes his experiences as they appear to him, but that the artist, the narrator, who speaks of Stephen in the third person, himself borrows the categories of the young man's mind not occasionally (as in Flaubert's free indirect discourse, for example) but in a sustained way throughout the entire narrative. This mode of representation puts a new emphasis on the constitutive tension of the novel form – the tension between first- and third-person accounts of events. Joyce intensifies the conflict between these two perspectives and thus extends the techniques of realism. This extension of realism however also leads to a transformation of realism into something different, and it does so by abandoning the possibility of overcoming subjectivity and achieving objectivity. It thus affirms what *Lost Illusions* only considered as a frightening possibility – the idea that objectivity arises out of subjectivity, that there are no laws but only conventions or mores.

At the end of the novel, the transcription of Stephen's diary, written in the first person, offers an apparent resolution of the tension: the young man with his subjective impressions becomes the narrator and a purely subjective first-person account replaces the tainted objectivity that has constituted the narrative up to that point. The intensified conflict between the third- and first-person perspectives in *A Portrait* leads to a collapsing of the two voices, and this collapsing corresponds to Stephen's attempt to overcome the bifurcated perspective on life in this world implied by the realist literary tradition and by liberal politics. The emergence of Stephen's apparently authentic voice in the diary relies of course on the romantic trope of the attainment of objectivity through immersion in subjectivity. Like Wordsworth in the *Prelude*, for example, Stephen comes to a realization of the retrospective unity of his whole life. The fact that his entire experience has contributed to the formation of his present identity seems to lend his current subjective impressions an air of objective necessity. The diary, then, represents for Stephen the final step in his coming to consciousness of his own destiny and his overcoming of the bifurcation between his social and ethical selves. Joyce's own attitude to Stephen's endeavor is, of course, less certain. On the one hand, external evidence suggests that Joyce too saw his art as a contribution to the future of his race. However, the subtle irony of *A Portrait*, as Booth has noted with some exasperation, makes it impossible to say clearly whether Joyce endorses or mocks Stephen's goals. It is clear that Stephen undertakes a task beyond the scope of his apparent abilities. His ideas, and particularly his poetry, remain marked by his immaturity. His behavior in *Ulysses*, too, suggests that his trip to the Continent has failed to make a mature artist of him. Yet, the overwhelming irony here seems to consist not so much in Stephen's own immaturity as in the immensity of the task he sets himself, a project that can never fully be achieved, even by the production of *Ulysses* and *Finnegans Wake*. Stephen's use of the word "conscience" to describe the source of his work in the Irish race emphasizes the difficulty of his task. For to forge a conscience involves not only the mystical unity with the race that I have described, but also a continual distancing from the race. Stephen's (or Joyce's) work must present a challenge to the nation that will allow it to develop. Throughout *Ulysses*, and notably in the "Scylla and Charybdis" episode, Stephen will concern himself with the mystery of the Trinity and the idea that the Son is at once identical with and different from His Father. In the role of Son, it is the novelist's challenge to embody once again the ideal essence of the national consciousness while at the same time introducing a redemptive difference. In order to speak for the race as it should be, the artist must challenge the race as it actually is.

Stephen's statement of his own aesthetic theory suggests that Joyce saw his experiments with narrative technique as aspects of an attempt to overcome the bifurcation between sociology and ethics. Stephen suggests that the "epical form" emerges "out of lyrical literature when the artist prolongs and broods upon himself as the centre of an epical event and this form progresses till the centre of emotional gravity is equidistant from the artist himself and from others. The narrative is no longer purely personal" (p. 215). He gives as an example the "old English ballad *Turpin Hero* which begins in the first person and ends in the third." Alluding to Flaubert, Stephen compares this transformation to the creation: "The mystery of esthetic like that of material creation is accomplished. The artist, like the God of the creation, remains within or behind or beyond or above his handiwork, invisible, refined out of existence, paring his fingernails."[71] *A Portrait*, of course, proceeds in the opposite direction, from the third person to the first person.[72] At the end of the novel, Stephen begins his diary and thus becomes the narrator. Joyce, however, is not retreating from the "epical" to the "lyrical," so much as re-uniting the lyrical "I" with the epical third person (or, in the terms I have been using, the ethical, subjective "I" with the sociological, objective third person).

In *A Portrait of the Artist as a Young Man*, the artist re-enters his creation to overcome the distinction between lyric and epic. If the accomplishment of the epic resembles in Stephen's theory the mystery of creation, the accomplishment of Joyce's modernism resembles the mystery of God's incarnation, which permits redemption. After Stephen has explained his aesthetic theory, he and Lynch take shelter under the arcade of the national library. Lynch complains: "What do you mean by prating about beauty and the imagination in this miserable Godforsaken island? No wonder the artist retired within or behind his handiwork after having perpetrated this country" (p. 233). The echo of Stephen's father's complaint about the "Godforsaken priestridden race" is unmistakable. Stephen will resolve on a new type of art in which the artist enters into his creation and in doing so he will redeem the Godforsaken island. The debate with Lynch outside the national library seems an essential step in Stephen's development of his theory of a new type of art that will allow him to forge the racial conscience, and such an art must, like *A Portrait*, achieve a synthesis between purely lyrical subjectivity and epical objectivity, must reinsert the creator in his creation, must reunite the artist with his country.

Stephen's other main statement of his aesthetic theory in the final chapter of *A Portrait* confirms the centrality of the problem of race to his literary experiments. In expounding aesthetics to Davin, he points out that different races have different ideals of beauty: "The Greek, the Turk, the Chinese, the Copt, the Hottentot . . . all admire a different type of female beauty" (p. 208). One possible explanation of this variety is that aesthetics originates in a purely physiological impulse, which differs according to the different biological make-up of the various races: "every physical quality admired by men in women is in direct connection with the manifold functions of women for the propagation of the species." Stephen rejects this explanation as leading to "eugenics rather than to esthetic." Stephen thus denies the reasoning he associates with Darwin which ultimately reduces the differences among races to purely physical terms. He does not, however, propose as an alternative that beauty itself inheres in aesthetic objects or in women or that beauty can be judged universally. Rather, he suggests that each beautiful object appeals to a certain common set of relations which is presumably present in human minds: "though the same object may not seem beautiful to all people, all people who admire a beautiful object find in it certain relations which satisfy and coincide with the stages themselves of all esthetic apprehension. These relations of the sensible, visible to you through one form and to me through another, must be therefore the necessary qualities of beauty" (p. 209). This solution allows Stephen to reconcile the fact that each race interprets the world differently with a notion of a universal human nature. For, if the beautiful differs for each race, then paradoxically the way to reach the universal in human nature may be to submerge oneself in the particularities of one's own race. Only by embodying a racially specific perspective as perfectly as possible can one arrive at an embodiment of the shared human condition of belonging to a particular race. This suggestion certainly bears a resemblance to some modern multiculturalist theories and in particular to the notion of a "politics of identity," but it bears an equally striking resemblance to the racialist theories that Joyce's work is often seen as opposing.

Just as Balzac's disillusionment plot reproduces certain crucial assumptions of nineteenth-century liberalism, Stephen's proposal to overcome the dynamic of disillusionment embodies certain tendencies of early twentieth-century theories of the nation-state. In particular, like many contemporary "organic" nationalists, Stephen conceives of the individual not as autonomous but as largely (perhaps entirely) determined in all his actions by the circumstances of his birth and particularly by membership in a given national community. In Joyce, this determining force works primarily through historical conditioning but also perhaps through biological inheritance (Joyce never clearly makes the distinction). In Balzac, the nation functioned as a limit of individual experience; the nation-state provided the institutions and the mores within which the individual developed, but it was the intimate sphere of the household that formed the individual's character, and ultimately it was in intimate relationships that the individual could find the fulfillment of his or her personality; the liberal conception of a necessary bifurcation between an intimate sphere dominated by ethics and true moral freedom and a social sphere operating according to purely material laws of necessity has disappeared for Stephen. The nation represents the cultural and biological inheritance that cannot be overcome or ignored and the nation speaks through the writer. The individual is a product of racial or historical forces which he does not control, but by embracing the fact of his having been produced by a particular race and culture, he can achieve the mystical union with his race that will allow him to convert his determination into a source of freedom.

The nationalist urge toward moral unity leads Stephen to imagine himself as redeemer of his race. Joyce's own attitude toward this ideal seems to have been more complex and ambivalent than Stephen's, and in *Ulysses*, Joyce presents a rather different model of the artist's relationship to the nation. While Stephen continues in *Ulysses* to imagine himself as the thwarted author of a national epic, Joyce writes the epic itself, but takes it out of the hands of his heroic narrator. If in *A Portrait*, the ethical and sociological perspectives on the Irish nation fuse in the person of the author, in *Ulysses* the author effaces himself so that the experience of the Irish nation can speak itself directly onto the page. The early Church saw the body of all believers as constantly reenacting the drama of Christ's resurrection. Similarly, when Joyce takes the role of narrator-hero away from Stephen in *Ulysses*, he puts the multiple voices of the Irish people on the stage in place of the single heroic, charismatic personality. That Leopold Bloom, a Jew, plays the central role in the later novel shows Joyce's renewed commitment to the civic, rather than the racial, definition of the nation. Bloom, like Stephen, dreams of being a second Parnell. In his fantasy of political power, he stands for "mixed races and mixed marriage," and a central problem of the entire narrative is how to reconcile Bloom's Jewish racial identity with his Irish nationhood, how to create a sense of national identity not marred by the anti-semitism of "the Citizen" and so many other Irish characters.[73]

Despite this attempt in his later work to de-racialize the conception of nationhood embraced by Stephen, Joyce does retain certain of Stephen's ambitions for the novel-form. These ambitions play a role in what I would like to call the "figural" vision of history in *Ulysses*. To describe thoroughly that great novel's relationship to the problem of Irish nationhood would require an extended discussion, so here I will simply offer a few remarks on its formal characteristics as they correspond to some of the problems of historical existence hinted at in Stephen's plan to "forge in the smithy of [his] soul the uncreated conscience of [his] race." When Stephen positions himself as a Christ-figure, he reverses many of the assumptions about the relationship of the individual to society that underlie literary realism. In particular, the heroic individual who can play this role for the Irish nation is no longer just any individual, no longer typical in the sense of sharing the nature of real, historical individuals who stand for nothing but themselves. Rather, Stephen takes upon himself (or Joyce endows him with) a special kind of symbolic importance. In addition to being an unusually bright but not superhuman young man living in Dublin, he is at the same time typical in the older sense of re-enacting a Biblical type and thus bringing to life an aspect of the universal, eschatological story of the redemption. In *A Portrait*, Joyce only hints at this quasi-allegorical character of Stephen's story, although the dense web of allusion in the novel gives the reader a sense of reading something other than a traditional novel of disillusionment or *Bildungsroman*. In *Ulysses*, however, while christological themes are less central, the difference from literary realism becomes increasingly apparent. One of the crucial features of this difference is the fact that the characters of *Ulysses*, without realizing it, continually re-enact mythical patterns. Most obviously, there are parallels with Odysseus, Telemachus, and Penelope, but there are also links to *Hamlet*, *Don Giovanni*, and numerous other texts, and there is the broad mythic and symbolic pattern that is *Ulysses* itself. These characters, while remaining concrete and historical like the characters in any realist novel, cannot be fully understood without reference to the mythical patterns which they are re-enacting. The effect of these mythical patterns is to elevate the characters into almost world-historical figures, but without draining them of their very concrete historical reality. The model for this type of epic is, of course, Dante's *Divine Comedy*, and in referring to Joyce's mode of writing as "figural," I draw on Erich Auerbach's important study, "Figura," which describes Dante's poem as the culmination of a way of thinking about the relationship between Biblical history and everyday life: "the individual earthly event is not regarded as a definitive self-sufficient reality, nor as a link in a chain of development in which single events or combinations of events perpetually give rise to new events, but viewed primarily in immediate vertical connection with a divine order which encompasses it, which on some future day will itself be concrete reality; so that the earthly event is a prophecy or *figura* of a part of a wholly divine reality that will be enacted in the future."[74] In *Ulysses*, with its emphasis on metempsychosis, the events of the plot function as such *figurae*, but their fulfillment lies not simply in the future. They are at once re-enactments of past mythical events and perhaps gestures towards a future historical reality, one that, in the shape of an independent Ireland, was just emerging as Joyce wrote the novel.[75] *A Portrait* offers some of the first tentative steps towards the introduction of the figural mode into the genre of the novel that was to be accomplished in *Ulysses*. Essential to this process was the conception of *A Portrait* as, at the same time, a story of a single individual in a particular point in space and time and a re-enactment of the Biblical story of redemption.

In *A Portrait of the Artist as a Young Man*, Joyce created a novelist-hero who saw himself as a Christ-figure in relation to his race. His solution to the dynamic of disillusionment, while perhaps more elegant and complete than many others, is also typical of a set of responses to the tradition of the realist novel developed by a number of important novelists in the years leading up to the First World War. Conrad, Proust, and d'Annunzio drew on the materials of their own lives to create narrator-heroes capable of embodying a sort of racial essence. In so doing, they contributed many of the central technical devices of modernism in the novel. Like Joyce, each of these novelists was raised Catholic. Less spectacularly than Joyce, each of them lost whatever religious faith he had grown up with, although d'Annunzio remained formally in the Church. Each was committed in various ways to secularism and, again apart from d'Annunzio, to the preservation of civil liberties and most of the other political institutions of a liberal society. They each responded in their work to crises in liberal institutions, and in the very idea of the nation, that threatened to undermine the European system of liberal nation-states from the last decades of the nineteenth century to the outbreak of war.

While these responses show a family resemblance to one another, they by no means constitute a unified front. Rather, the various literary techniques developed by the modernists correspond to a wide range of responses to the crisis of liberal nationalism. What they had in common was a questioning of the epistemological, metaphysical, and political assumptions underlying literary realism and the liberal nation-state. This study examines the novelists' responses to these intellectual and political crises, but offers only an overview of the historical causes of the crises themselves. I shall present the problems of the nation-state as they contributed to the rethinking of the novel, and hope to show how the rethinking of the novel form itself contributed, albeit marginally, to new conceptions of the nation-state that we in the late twentieth century have inherited. My focus, however, is on the ways in which the novelists grappled with these problems in their literary works and on the relation between this grappling and the novelists' formal experiments. In the broadest sense, each of them attempted to achieve a mystical union with the spirit of his nation. In the novel generally, as Lukács wrote, life is a going out onto an Earth in which we are exiled from God, a world ruled by merely conventional morality, with no divine sanction for authority or divine guarantee of justice. A redemption on the earth is impossible in the realist novel; the world is only the world and cannot become Paradise. In the modernist novel, the possibility of regaining Paradise on Earth becomes central again and the nation becomes the means for this redemption. The national bond represents the possibility of transcending the apparent meaninglessness of life on Earth, of "transmuting the daily bread of experience into the radiant body of everliving life." Through the novelist-hero's mystical union with the racial conscience, these modernist writers hoped, the experience of life in a world abandoned by God would be redeemed and the word again made flesh.

CHAPTER TWO

The crisis of liberal nationalism

The Paris Peace Treaties of 1919 and the founding of the League of Nations appeared to contemporary liberals to ratify the victory of the liberal principle of national self-determination championed by the Allies over the imperialism of the Central Powers. Under the Treaties, the Allies attempted to "redraw the political map [of Europe] on national lines" and thus to establish an international system of liberal nation-states.[1] The nations were to enter into a form of social contract with one another, under which they would be, in Woodrow Wilson's words, "governed in their conduct towards each other by the same principles of honour and of respect for the common laws of civilized society that govern the individual citizens of all modern States."[2] Thus, not only would each nation develop liberal institutions of its own, but the relations among nations would, for the first time, be based on the principles of rule by law, impartial justice, and popular sovereignty, rather than on "the great game, now for ever discredited, of the Balance of Power."[3] Almost immediately, however, the United States Senate refused to ratify the treaty that founded the League of Nations; the difficulty of establishing national states in Eastern and Central Europe became apparent; and hopes of an era of peaceful co-existence modeled on a liberal interpretation of the principle of nationality began to fade. Given its first great opportunity to reshape the world according to its own theory of human relations, liberal nationalism failed.

The historical causes of this failure are complex. The immediate reason for the weakness of the League of Nations was the refusal of Republicans in the United States Senate on November 19, 1919 to ratify the Treaty of Versailles, on the grounds that it limited American sovereignty. The United States never joined the League of Nations. The punitive reparations that the English and French governments demanded of Germany also jeopardized the long-term survival of liberal institutions there. More generally, the attempt to remake Europe on the model of England and France failed because the collapsing multi-national empires of Eastern and Central Europe, with their mixed populations, did not offer fertile soil for the development of liberal nation-states. As Eric Hobsbawm has suggested, "The logical implication of trying to create a continent neatly divided into coherent territorial states each inhabited by a separate ethnically and linguistically homogeneous population, was the mass expulsion or extermination of minorities" (p. 133). In a broader historical context, however, liberal nationalism had already, by 1919, experienced a major crisis, and the First World War was at least in part a result of the limitations of the theory and functions of the nation-state that had developed over the course of the nineteenth century. The immediate politial causes of this crisis have been examined elsewhere. In this study, I focus on the role of the political idea of the nation-state in the crisis of the liberal system. In England and France themselves, the liberal nation-states *par excellence*, liberalism was under enormous stress, and this stress can be understood as a result of inherent tensions within the liberal model of the nation-state. The failure of the Paris Peace Conferences may have resulted, as Hannah Arendt argued in *The Origins of Totalitarianism*, from the "tragedy of the nation-state," which consisted in the conflict between the concepts of "nationality" and "state":

In the name of the will of the people the state was forced to recognize only "nationals" as citizens, to grant full civil and political rights only to those who belonged to the national community by right of origin and fact of birth. This meant that the state was transformed from an instrument of law into an instrument of the nation. (p. 230)

This chapter investigates the tensions within liberal thought about the nation-state as they manifested themselves after the apparent liberal-democratic triumphs of the Reform Acts of 1867 and 1884 in England and the founding of the Third Republic in France. Later chapters will suggest that the modernists' literary experiments involved an engagement with a set of concerns they shared with the theorists of the liberal nation-state. In particular, I will focus here on two crucial discourses about the nation-state, the discourses of character and of will, that would, respectively, shape the narrative techniques of Joseph Conrad and Marcel Proust.

From a late twentieth-century perspective, the admission of the national principle at the Paris Peace Conference may appear as a failure on the part of liberalism, but from the Wilsonian point of view, it was an extension of the principle of self-determination, and especially of social contract theory. Most liberals held national self-determination to be crucial to the functioning of representative government. Thus, in the second half of the nineteenth century, British liberals championed the causes of oppressed nationalities, including the Italians, Greeks, Poles, Bulgarians, and Hungarians, and eventually even the Irish. By 1911, during the debate on the Irish Home Rule bill, L. T. Hobhouse, a "New Liberal," argued that the British must recognize the national rights of the Irish because "National and personal freedom are growths of the same root, and their historic connection rests on no accident, but on ultimate identity of idea."[4] Hobhouse saw peaceful internationalism as the future of liberalism, and argued that "the world-state of the not impossible future must be based on a free national self-direction as full and satisfying as that enjoyed by Canada or Australia within the British Empire at this moment" (p. 115). As J. A. Hobson noted in 1902, the vision of internationalism shared by many British New Liberals was anathema to the imperialists.[5] It suggested a world-wide federation of independent, liberal nation-states, which would necessarily conflict with the maintenance of British, and perhaps even of European, supremacy. The liberalism envisioned by these progressive pre-war thinkers, though familiar again in the last decade of the twentieth century, seemed outdated in the aftermath of the First World War. The "strange death of Liberal England," the war itself, the Russian Revolution, and the rise of fascism suggested to many contemporary thinkers that the future was one of "collectivism" or "corporatism" and that liberal democracy would wither away.[6] Two sets of forces had already, from the 1880s onward, begun to undermine the liberal consensus in England and France: the socialist movement on the left and the various forms of jingoism, imperialism, and authoritarian nationalism on the right. In 1919, shortly after the Bolshevik Revolution, it seemed that the left posed the more immediate threat, and the parties of the center allied with the parties of the right in attempts to defeat socialism. Ultimately, however, the rise of fascism showed that imperialism and racism might amount to a greater danger to liberal politics in the long term.

The second and third Reform Acts of 1867 and 1884 extended the franchise in the United Kingdom to the point at which it could be considered a "liberal democracy," although women and some adult men remained excluded.[7] After 1875, the Third Republic in France began to seem secure against attempts at a restoration of the monarchy or the Empire.[8] It was during the last decades of the nineteenth century, then, that the liberal-democratic conception of the nation-state first seemed to triumph in these two countries. In formal politics, however, the establishment of liberal democracies led not to a triumph of the "liberal," centrist parties, but to an increasing polarization of politics. The rise of labor movements was one significant threat to political liberals that should not be ignored. By 1906, the British Liberal Party had lost some electoral ground to the Labour Party and the French Left-wing Bloc had disintegrated, leaving a moderate republican government under Prime Minister Georges Clemenceau without socialist support. Another category of challenges, however, is central to understanding the changing conception of the nation-state among liberals and their critics in this period. These challenges belong not so much to the realm of the class struggle and economic issues as to that of the nature of political institutions and the appropriate relationship between the state and the ethnic make-up of society.

In Great Britain, these conflicts revolved around the question of empire, especially in Africa and Ireland. The great leader of mid-Victorian liberalism, William Ewart Gladstone, had to resign as Prime Minister in 1885, the year after the third Reform Act, largely because of popular outcry over his failure to support imperialist policies more vigorously, and specifically over the death of General Gordon at Khartoum in January, 1885. Gladstone returned to power briefly in 1886 and 1892–3 and introduced bills to allow Irish Home Rule, but a large portion of the Liberal Party, the Unionists, led by Joseph Chamberlain, deserted him and allied themselves with the Conservatives. In the 1886 election, the Conservatives and Unionists defeated the Liberals by a wide margin, and their alliance dominated British politics until 1905. To Hobhouse, writing a generation later, the "party fissure" after 1885 seemed to have taken place "on false lines," displacing attention from the class antagonisms of the "social question" to the problems of Ireland and Empire, and leaving some members of the upper and middle classes in the Liberal Party (p. 106). It seems more reasonable, however, to admit that the Unionists defined themselves in terms of their attitude to Ireland, not to economic issues. It is therefore possible to see in this first splitting of the Liberal Party the rise of a modern conservative nationalism (still represented, for example, in the "Euro-skeptic" wing of the Tory party) and its separation from an internationalist liberalism such as that later embraced by New Liberals like Hobson and Hobhouse. The New Liberals would support a Wilsonian vision of a world of equal nation-states, while the Conservatives and Unionists carried on the older Whig tradition of the defense of specifically English liberty. The crisis of the ideology of liberal nationalism did not lead directly to a crisis of the political system itself. The multinational character of Great Britain itself did not prevent it from functioning as a liberal nation-state after Irish independence. Recent constitutional changes that have created regional assemblies in Scotland and Wales seem to represent a renewed form of liberal nationalism, which is compatible with the internationalism of the European Union. In the EU, as in the Wilsonian vision, liberal national democracies share sovereignty through an international body, though in this case one that is restricted to a sort of super-national polity made up of the inhabitants of the old territory of Western Christianity. A century ago, however, the problem of imperialism seemed destined to undermine the liberal national idea, and the perceived crisis motivated a rethinking of the nation-state both in formal political philosophy and in literary works, such as those of Joseph Conrad.

In France, the crisis of the liberal nation-state as a functioning political system was much more in evidence during the Dreyfus Affair and its aftermath. Historians of the Third Republic have represented the period from 1871 to 1914 as characterized by the attempts of succeeding regimes to achieve mass support for republican institutions and to overcome an "endless crisis" of legitimacy.[9] One important source of instability was the clamor for "la revanche," revenge for the lost provinces of Alsace and Lorraine, which had been ceded to Germany by the Treaty of Frankfurt after the Franco-Prussian war. Although abortive *coups d'état* such as the one led by General Georges Boulanger in 1889 did not succeed in defeating the Republic, and traditional conservative elements became increasingly reconciled to it, the Dreyfus Affair of the 1890s revealed the persistent instability of the liberal-democratic regime. In the agitation surrounding Dreyfus's retrial, in which the young Marcel Proust was deeply involved, large portions of society, and notably the army, became mobilized either for or against the Jewish officer who had been convicted of treason on the basis of evidence manufactured by another officer, Major Esterhazy. The mass appeal of the various "Ligues" – of Patriotes, of the Patrie Française and of Action Française on the right, and of the Droits de l'Homme on the left – made the question of the nation-state of crucial political importance. In 1898, after the conviction of Zola and during Dreyfus's retrial, the British army under Kitchener forced the French army under Marchand to withdraw from Fashoda (not far from Khartoum, which Kitchener had recently retaken). This defeat, blamed largely on the "enemy within" (the intellectual and pro-Jewish left), heightened nationalist outrage.[10] The defense of the army and the attack on Dreyfus led to the rise of a new nationalist right wing. The anti-semitism of the period created, or revealed, deep divisions within society. The defenders of the republican ideals of 1789 ultimately triumphed, largely because of the fear of authoritarianism and clericalism aroused by the spectacle of this new right wing. As a result, the radical republicans and socialists were able to introduce a series of measures, culminating in the law on the separation of church and state in 1905, which confirmed the laicization of the state and thus established a central, and controversial, feature of the twenti-eth-century French republics. As the recent case of young Muslim women being forbidden from wearing their head-veils to school suggests, however, the laicization of the state did not permanently resolve the problem of the relation of the secular state to ethnic minorities within the nation. Furthermore, while the nationalists' electoral fortunes ebbed, a "new nationalism" became standard political fare in the moderate parties and helped to hasten the outbreak of the First World War.[11]

The political context of the crisis of liberal nationalism, then, was the struggle over the definition of the nation and its relationship both to the colonized peoples and to minorities within the nation that led to a reshaping of formal politics in England and France. Although the polit-ical events that I have briefly sketched here were the proximate causes of the crisis of liberal nationalism, its roots lay in the political dynamic created by the Enlightenment attempt to reorganize human institutions on the basis of reason. As I shall suggest in this chapter, the varieties of liberalism that had their roots in the Enlightenment were undermined over the course of the nineteenth century by evolutionary and historicist modes of social thought that emphasized the often irrational role that the national community played in the establishment of a liberal polity. By the end of the nineteenth century, the very attempt to understand on a scientific basis the causes of human behavior seemed to lay bare the inability of human communities to organize themselves on a rational basis without appeal to mystical and traditional notions like the national character or the national will. Liberalism had presented liberty and equality as essential characteristics of human beings, but the social sci-ences tended to suggest that, on the contrary, liberty and equality are his-torical products of very particular communities. The descriptive claims of the social sciences thus helped to undermine the normative demands of political liberalism.[12]

The immediate intellectual context of this crisis, of which the mod-ernist novelists were aware in varying degrees, was the "revolt against positivism" of the 1890s. While it can be specifically applied to the sociologies of Auguste Comte and Herbert Spencer, which John Stuart Mill partly endorsed, I use the word positivism here, following H. Stuart Hughes, to designate "the whole tendency to discuss human behavior in terms of analogies drawn from natural science."[13] More precisely, positivism involved an attempt to create a social science on the model of natural sciences that would treat the tension between sociological and ethical conceptions of the self, as unproblematic. Positivists might ignore the questions of traditional ethics, but more frequently they sought to find in a deterministic sociology a scientific basis for solutions to ethical problems, an "ethology" in John Stuart Mill's formulation, or a "science of ethics," as Leslie Stephen proposed. A resurgence of interest in Kant and the German Idealists in the 1890s indicated a growing awareness of the inadequacies of such a project. Writers influenced by Nietzsche felt increasingly the potentially disruptive implications of the tension between the ethical person considered, in Kant's words, "under the Idea of Freedom" and the sociological person considered as a product of given social circumstances. Earlier liberal theories that attempted a compromise between the two, or that tried to find in the necessary tension between them a realm of human freedom, came increasingly to seem inadequate. For they were open to attack both from unswerving determinists, such as Spencer and Marx, who treated the ethical self as no more than an illusion, and from spiritualists or intuitionists, such as Henri Bergson, who perceived a realm of ultimate freedom that was above all determinations. Intellectually, it seemed, the center would not hold. It required a new set of social theories and philosophies, notably those of Weber, Freud, and Husserl, to provide convincing answers to the competing claims of absolute free will and absolute determinism. In the meantime, however, the idea of the nation, which had played an important but unexamined role in the liberal positivist tradition, seemed to offer a solution to the failings of that tradition. Leslie Stephen himself, the great positivist philologist Ernest Renan in France, and less liberal-minded thinkers such as the eugenicist Karl Pearson and the nationalist politician and novelist Maurice Barrès, found in theories of the national character or the national will what they took to be convincing solutions to the crisis of positivism and liberalism. Renan and Barrès in particular seem to have influenced both Joyce and Proust directly, and Barrès was both a friend of and a political model for d'Annunzio.[14] Conrad's reading was restricted to somewhat earlier currents, notably the social Darwinism of Alfred Russel Wallace, but his attempts to respond to it

resemble those of later evolutionist thinkers. To understand the modernist novelists' concerns with the nation-state, it is worthwhile to examine
these attempts by thinkers who influenced their generation to resolve the
ambiguities of liberalism by an appeal to the nation.

Hobsbawm has suggested in his brief survey of liberal theories of the
nation that mid-nineteenth-century liberals endorsed the principle of
nationality as a necessary but sometimes almost accidental element of
the theory of representative government, "a phase in human evolution
from the small group to the larger, from family to tribe to region, to
nation and, in the last instance, to the unified world of the future" (p. 38).
In this context, Hobsbawm suggests that the principle of nationality was
linked to liberalism "by long association rather than by logical necessity:
as liberty and equality are to fraternity" (p. 40). This link, Hobsbawm
implies, was almost arbitrary, and liberalism could have done just as well
with small republics such as Rousseau and Kant had imagined, with a
world government, or with multinational states. Hobsbawm here under-
estimates the centrality of the idea of the nation to many liberal thinkers of the nineteenth century, and particularly to those who saw little
hope of the establishment of a universal government. Even though
liberal thinkers may not themselves have paid particular attention to the
specifically national content of their theories, the question of the nation
often pervaded their thought. As Stefan Collini has noted, "English historians, in particular, have tended to treat nationalism as something that
happened to other people."[15] Yet the idea and ideal of the liberal nation-
state motivated much political activity in Britain as in France.

Nineteenth-century liberals did not wholeheartedly embrace what C.
B. MacPherson called "possessive individualism," a vision of the human
being as *homo economicus*, ruled solely by the motive of financial gain and
connected to other human beings only by the cash nexus.[16] Almost all
actual nineteenth-century liberal thinkers explicitly stated their concern
not only with the self-regarding but also with the other-regarding, or
altruistic, motives of human behavior. What liberal nationalists often
shared was a faith in the nation-state as the unit of human society appropriate to representative democracy. The nation-state could forge solidarity in an era marked by competition among individuals and thus
encourage the process of civilization. Only within a well-developed
nation-state, many liberals argued, could the liberty and equality of all
individuals be secured while justice and the rule of law were maintained.
The nation seemed particularly important as the liberal oligarchies of
the mid nineteenth century gave way to democratic mass politics, for the

nation-state served both as the expression of the popular will and an important force in shaping the characters of individuals and making them capable of self-government. States smaller than a nation risked being held back by provincialism, while multinational states, such as the Russian, Ottoman, and Austro-Hungarian empires, encouraged ethnic rivalries and the suppression of minority groups.[17] Many liberals did look forward to an era of internationalism that might replace the nation-state with a more universal form of government, but except to the most idealistic (and those leaning towards socialism), this future of international peace seemed more likely to be secured by a covenant among sovereign nations than by doing away with nationality altogether. The League of Nations was in a very real sense the culmination of liberal nationalist principle, for it kept the idea of the sovereign nation from nineteenth-century liberalism but also promised to usher in the long dreamed-of era of international co-operation, based on a social contract among the nations. The debate over the League of Nations also revealed some of the limits of Western liberals' conception of fraternity. In particular, the idea of "race," defined in a variety of ways, often signified the limit of liberalism's attempts to develop a universalistic theory based on the liberty and equality of all people. Exemplary of this limitation of liberal thought was the refusal of the delegates of the British Empire at the Paris Peace Conference to accept the Japanese proposal for a clause recognizing racial equality in the Covenant founding the League of Nations. Wilson supported this refusal out of considerations of *Realpolitik*.[18] Although this decision was a minor incident from a political point of view, it pointed to the ambiguity of the category of "race" in liberal thought, which has been a central reason for attacks on liberal universalism as an ethnocentric political theory. In the wake of new biological and historical theories of racial difference, liberals in late nineteenth-century England and France attempted to develop theories of the nation-state that would avoid the radically universalistic implications of both Kantian and utilitarian liberalism by grounding the principles of liberty and equality in the shared community of the nation-state. In so doing, they revealed the limits of their liberalism, for they could not successfully account for what seemed to them the irreducible differences of "race."

THE DECLINE OF THE NATION-STATE

In liberal theory, the national bond was precisely a form of fraternity that permitted people to live on terms of legal equality with one another without destroying the social order. In her essay on Lessing, Hannah Arendt calls attention to the distinction between the classical concept of friendship, *philia*, and the Enlightenment's notion of fraternity. Arendt herself is highly skeptical of fraternity and the related Rousseauian value of compassion, which, she argues, implies that what links people together is a shared human nature. Like Lessing's Nathan the Wise, she values friendship, "which is as selective as compassion is egalitarian." Friendship, she says, preserves the sense that the world itself is not humane, but only our ability "to discuss it with our fellows" makes it so: "we humanize what is going on in the world and in ourselves only by speaking of it, and in the course of speaking about it we learn to be human."[19] As Seyla Benhabib has pointed out in her interpretation of Arendt's essay, Aristotle took friendship to be a prerequisite of justice in the relations among free and equal citizens of the *polis*.[20] Only a degree of friendship, a form of mutual recognition akin to what the Victorians called "sympathy," could guarantee the goodwill towards one another of the citizens that would permit them to live in harmony with one another, as Aristotle claimed in the *Politics*: "Friendship seems too to hold states together, and lawgivers to care more for it than for justice; for concord seems to be something like friendship, and this they aim at most of all; and when men are friends they have no need of justice, while when they are just they need friendship as well, and the truest form of justice is thought to be a friendly quality."[21] Arendt sometimes seems to hope for a return to the Aristotelian notion of friendship as a basis for modern political communities, but this hope seems futile in a modern democratic age, because any such return would require the exclusion of those whom the community does not recognize. The modern, Christian-derived notion of fraternity seems to imply that only what is common to us by birth (our equality before God, or our "natural" rights) can be the basis for our membership in a community and the recognition of our political equality and liberties. Political liberalism thus tends to base justice on "fraternity," the ability to live together people share not simply by virtue of their mutual recognition but because they are born into the same group. The Enlightenment promised that all men would become brothers, but in liberal nationalist discourses in the wake of the French Revolution, when the faith in universal brotherhood was at a low ebb, only those born in a certain territory or with a certain blood-line were considered brothers and therefore capable of the fraternal relations that allowed liberty and equality to co-exist with justice. Modern liberalism thus attempts to make the sense of shared belonging into the basis of a political order, to make fraternity the basis of friendship. The nation-state is the political form that this fraternity takes, namely one that demands of all citizens born into the nation that they recognize their fellows as free and equal members of the national community.[22]

Arendt traces two movements that contributed to the rise of totalitarianism: anti-semitism, which was manifested in its characteristic modern form in the Dreyfus affair; and imperialism, which especially in England contributed to the development of racist ideology. Both anti-semitism and imperialism, Arendt argues, are closely related to, almost historical by-products of, the rise of the bourgeois nation-state. Yet these movements also contain the historical seeds of the decline of the nation-state. Arendt's analyses of the fates of the concepts "equality" and "liberty" are exemplary in this respect. She explains the rise of anti-semitism as a result of the "perversion of equality from a political into a social concept," the demand that political "equality of condition" lead to a reduction of the differences among people, to a sort of social leveling: "The more equal conditions are, the less explanation there is for the differences that actually exist between people" (*Origins*, p. 54). What the Enlightenment had taken to be a natural attribute of people, equality, turns out to be a political, and therefore in a sense a merely conventional, concept that cannot justify itself by an appeal to nature. In imperialism, Arendt saw a similar process at work. In particular, she criticized Burke's conception of liberty as an "entailed inheritance": "The concept of inheritance, applied to the very nature of liberty, has been the ideological basis from which English nationalism received its curious touch of race-feeling ever since the French Revolution" (p. 176). Arendt at first seems to be criticizing the transformation of what the Enlightenment had regarded as a natural attribute of all people, liberty, into a type of property to be governed by the merely conventional laws of inheritance. However, Arendt later finds in the condition of stateless people in the twentieth century "an ironical, bitter, and belated confirmation of . . . [Burke's] assertion that human rights were an 'abstraction,' that it was much wiser to rely on an 'entailed inheritance' of rights which one transmits to one's children like life itself" (p. 299). As the rest of Arendt's analysis of imperialism makes clear, it is the transformation of this concept of inheritance from a legal to a biological concept that gives it its potentially totalitarian implications.

Although Arendt does not phrase it precisely in the same way, what she criticizes in Burke, but then finds ironically true, is similar to what she criticizes in anti-semitism: the mistaken tendency, inherited from the

Enlightenment, to understand political concepts (liberty and equality) as resulting from natural attributes of human beings. Although her analysis of liberty is much less precise than her discussion of equality, both support her central claim that once the "absolute and transcendent measurements of religion or natural law have lost their authority," so must the distinction between justice (the right) and utility ("what is good for – for the individual, or the family, or the people, or the largest number"). Utility, Arendt argues, becomes the measure of all goods precisely because of the lack of a transcendental conception of justice. The "perversion" of the concepts of equality and liberty results from the same process: what had appeared to be guaranteed by nature, the liberty and equality of all people, turns out to be only a conventional or political concept. After the loss of the "transcendent" measurements of religion or natural law, attempts to ground this concept in "natural" categories entail perverting it, and making politics a slave of false transcendent constructs. Two influential transcendent constructs with which the modern age has attempted to replace the natural law have been the laws of natural science and the philosophy of history.

The crisis of liberal nationalism resulted largely from the attempt to overcome perceived deficiencies of the liberal political system: notably, the "merely formal" status of the liberal ideals of liberty and equality and the lack of a metaphysical guarantee of justice in liberal political systems. The discourses of liberal nationalism often looked to the idea of the nation to provide such metaphysical guarantees, which traditional religious belief and the theories of natural rights and utilitarianism were no longer able to supply. It was particularly in the positivist attempt to adapt traditional modes of political and moral speculation to "scientific" methods, and especially to develop a scientific account of the plurality of human cultures and races, that nineteenth-century liberals invested the nation with metaphysical powers. What all of these modes of explanation – religion, natural rights theory, utilitarianism, and social-scientific positivism – tended to demand of the nation was what Bonnie Honig has described as the "displacement of politics."[23] This displacement consisted in the attempt to guarantee a just social order free of political conflict through appeals to some theory allegedly higher than politics itself, and thus to create a world in which politics and the clash of competing interests would be supplanted. Later, right-wing "nationalist" thinkers were able to draw on the metaphysical ideas of the nation already available to them in liberal thought. It was in particular the attempt to develop these traditional discourses of the liberal nation-state in the context of the problem of race after Darwinism, comparative philology, and the loss of faith in the Biblical account of the unity of human nature that caused the wreck of traditional liberal discourses about the nation. In the context of the revolt against positivism, the modernists felt a heightened sense of conflict between the idea of the nation as will (as a binding convention among autonomous subjects) and the idea of the nation as character (as a quasi-natural essence shaping the individual). For Conrad, Proust, Joyce, and d'Annunzio, the question of the nation was a central focus of the problem of being both subject and object of historical forces. Their thoughts about the nation-state bear a remarkable resemblance to Georg Lukács's contemporary attempts, in *History and Class Consciousness* (1922), to find in the notion of the proletariat as "identical subject-object" of history a solution to the "antinomies of bourgeois thought" bequeathed by Kant.[24] Ultimately, the development of new conceptions of "culture," to which the modernists themselves contributed, allowed the re-integration of liberal theory, but at the cost of having exposed the fundamental weakness of the concept of nation which had been so central to it.

THE LIBERAL COMPROMISE BETWEEN WILL AND CHARACTER

When J. A. Hobson, in 1902, upheld the principle of nationality in opposition to imperialism, he cited the most well-known English liberal definition of nationality, that of John Stuart Mill in his *Considerations on Representative Government* of 1861:

A portion of mankind may be said to constitute a Nationality, if they are united among themselves by common sympathies, which do not exist between them and any others – which make them cooperate with each other more willingly than with other people, desire to be under the same government, and desire that it should be government by themselves, or a portion of themselves, exclusively. This feeling of nationality may have been generated by various causes. Sometimes it is the effect of identity of race and descent. Community of language and community of religion contribute greatly to it. Geographical limits are one of its causes. But the strongest of all is identity of political antecedents; the possession of a national history, and consequent community of recollections; collective pride and humiliation, pleasure and regret, connected with the same incidents in the past.[25]

Mill endorsed the case for uniting a given nationality under a single state as an extension of the theory of self-government and because he thought that multi-national states tended to encourage ethnic rivalries. He perceived national states as the natural form of representative government for nineteenth-century Europe, but held open the hope for some more universal form of government in the future. Mill's definition of nationality combines two crucial criteria that were to remain intertwined in most future discussions of the topic: the sympathies felt for one another by the members of a given group and the historical and other external causes tending to encourage those sympathies – race, descent, language, religion, geography, and especially political antecedents.

The balance of the "causes" of the "feeling of nationality" and the "sympathies" that result from those causes in Mill's definition of the nation continues to motivate liberal theorists of the nation-state today. In *Nations and Nationalism*, Ernest Gellner offered two provisional definitions of the nation, the cultural and the voluntarist:

1. Two men are of the same nation if and only if they share the same culture, where culture in turn means a system of ideas and signs and associations and ways of behaving and communicating.
2. Two men are of the same nation if and only if they recognize each other as belonging to the same nation . . . [N]ations are the artefacts of men's convictions and loyalties and solidarities.[26]

Gellner then goes on to develop a convincing account of the ways in which the nation-state facilitates the work of a modern, industrial society, by enabling the diffusion of a shared "high," literate culture. A high degree of literacy and numeracy is essential to the modern division of labor. Given that access to education in one's own language determines social status and rewards, it is understandable, perhaps inevitable, that groups who inhabit states where the power-holders do not speak their language would agitate for states of their own, where their own high culture is supported by state institutions, from the primary school to the university and the legal system. After developing this account of the relationship of the modern nation-state to industrial society, Gellner emphasizes the need to understand that under the social conditions which make national cultures appear "the natural repositories of political legitimacy,"

nations can indeed be defined in terms both of will and of culture, and indeed in terms of the convergence of them both with political units. In these conditions, men will to be politically united with all those, and only those, who share their culture . . . The fusion of will, culture, and polity becomes the norm, and one not easily or frequently defied . . . These conditions do not define the human condition as such, but merely its industrial variant. (55)

Like Mill, then, but with slightly less emphasis on freedom of choice, Gellner sees the nation-state as the normal political form of industrial (Mill would have said civilized) society. This notion of a community which is at once shaped by circumstances and freely willed, a product of the evolution of "national character" and an expression of a "daily plebiscite," was the common-sense liberal attitude to the nation-state in the middle of the nineteenth century, and has become so again today. As a sociological description of the state of affairs in the liberal-democratic nation-states of the developed world, Gellner's and Mill's descriptions may seem quite accurate, and there are few – apart from radical nationalists – who would be likely to object to their basic substance.

For Mill, it is a short step from explaining the nature of the principle of nationality to justifying the nation-state as an appropriate form of political organization. Mill quickly goes on to make normative claims, again stressing the dual character of the national community. "[A]ny division of the human race" ought to be "free to . . . determine, with which of the various collective bodies of human beings they choose to associate themselves," so people in a given territory should be free to choose a state that suits them, and people generally seem to prefer nation-states. Quite apart from this argument on the basis of free choice, however, there is "a still more vital consideration," namely that "Free institutions are next to impossible in a country made up of different nationalities" (p. 309). Mill goes on to argue that because different nationalities lack the "united public opinion, necessary to the working of representative government," which is based on a shared political culture, they are unlikely to have sympathy for one another. Resentments among national groups, particularly as they affect the army, will thus interfere with the development of free institutions, as the example of the Habsburg empire illustrates.

Mill's attempt to defend the national form of representative democracy by an appeal both to choice or "sympathy" and to conditions, circumstances, or "causes" is significant because the question of the nation-state became a crucial problem for the limits of liberal and democratic politics. The existence of given national cultures or, as the Victorians called them, "national characters" appeared to be a forceful argument against the spread of representative institutions outside the Anglo-Saxon world (especially after the rise of Napoleon III in 1848–1851, which undermined the French claim to an equal share in the liberal tradition). By accepting the argument that nationality was largely a product of circumstance, Mill risked ceding ammunition to the opponents of liberalism, for it was not far from the acceptance of different governments for different national characters to Burkean arguments for an extremely gradual approach to constitutional reform. Mill summarizes the central position of the Burkean tradition:

[A people's] will has had no part in the matter [of its fundamental political institutions] but that of meeting the necessities of the moment by the contrivances of the moment, which contrivances, if in sufficient conformity to the national feelings and character, commonly last, and by successive aggregation constitute a polity, suited to the people who possess it, but which it would be vain to attempt to superinduce upon any people whose nature and circumstances had not spontaneously evolved it. (p. 3)

In this caricature of Burkean Whiggery, Mill falls back upon a key opposition that was to shape debates about the nature of nationality: the opposition between will and character. These two forces are to the idea of the nation what the ethical and sociological conceptions of the self are to the individual. References to the national will or the will of the people emphasize the nation's ability to constitute itself through an act of political freedom akin to the rational individual's acting, in Kant's words "under the Idea of freedom."[27] References to national character, on the other hand, tend to emphasize the shaping of the people's will by forces beyond conscious control, the forces Mill enumerates as "causes" of the sympathy members of a given nation feel for one another, and what a Kantian would call the sources of their "heteronomy."

Mill's dual method of defining nationality, the emphasis on sympathies and on the circumstances that make those sympathies possible, reinforces the claims of the first chapter of the *Considerations on Representative Government* concerning the extent to which "Forms of Government are a Matter of Choice." Writing in a mode reminiscent of Tocqueville, Mill attempts here to strike a balance between those who claim that "forms of government . . . being made by man . . . man has the choice either to make them or not, and how or on what pattern they shall be made" and those who claim that "The government of a country . . . is, in all substantial respects, fixed and determined beforehand by the state of the country in regard to the distribution of the elements of social power . . . [and that a] nation, therefore, cannot choose its form of government" (p. 13). Mill seems to have in mind his father and Jeremy Bentham as advocates of "choice" and the Whiggish and Conservative British opponents of parliamentary reform as advocates of determinism. Mill's solution, similar to Tocqueville's, is to claim that while a government must be appropriate to the state of civilization of a given country, it should be possible "to exercise, among all forms of government practicable in the existing condition of society, a rational choice" (p. 17). Ultimately, then, Mill's own sympathies are with the proponents of choice, although he recognizes the need to understand the historical limitations of the range of choices available at any given time, an argument brought home to him by Macaulay's criticisms of his father's political writings. Mill attempts to strike a balance between these two forces, and his balance is typical of mid-nineteenth-century liberalism in that it emphasizes the need to recognize this bifurcation between character and will as an organizing tension of life in a community and as linked to the nature of existence in history, which constantly transforms people's needs. One other typically liberal aspect of his discussion of the problem is his claim that the strongest cause of national sympathies is "identity of political antecedents." By focusing on shared political history as the source of national feeling, Mill again emphasizes the importance of humans' capacity for free self-development through political institutions. By making politics, rather than language, religion, or race, central to the development of the nation, Mill can maintain his trust in the capacity of free choice, exercised through political institutions, to encourage individual virtue and social progress. As Stefan Collini has pointed out, Mill's faith in the virtues of citizenship links him to the classical tradition of political thought and separates him from many English liberals who lack his faith in politics themselves as the site of truly free human endeavor.[28]

Not only Mill's, but also more recent liberal theories of nationality, such as Gellner's or Yael Tamir's, raise certain questions about ethical and political principles that Gellner does not seem concerned to answer but that Mill recognized as unresolved problems about human nature.[29] In particular, if the national state is in a certain sense the natural or normal form of the state in industrial or civilized society, then what does this imply about what might be called the "philosophical anthropology" of modern, liberal political systems?[30] Liberal nationalism often suggests that the pre-political, perhaps even pre-ethical, *sentiments* of "friendship" and "fraternity" are in important senses prior to notions such as equality and freedom. In other words, the existence of a liberal democratic political order depends not on a generally shared characteristic of human nature (such as rationality) but on a particular set of sentiments which arises in the human being only in certain contingent circumstances, only when particular sorts of "sympathies" operate. If this is true, then the most central fact about moral subjects is not that they are created "free and equal," but that, like Stephen Dedalus in Joyce's

A Portrait, they enter the world with ethical commitments and attachments that can only be prior to their commitments to humanity as a whole or to God.

Modern liberal principles ultimately result from a situation of radical epistemological and moral uncertainty as to the ends of human action. The usual claims of liberal politics, often enshrined in the constitutions of modern nation-states, are that each person should be recognized as free and equal in respect of her rights, regardless of her attachment to a particular culture or of other attributes such as race, religious conviction, sex, and more recently sexual orientation. Political philosophers, notably John Rawls and Jürgen Habermas, have often been engaged in a project of justifying these constitutional arrangements on the basis of claims concerning the universal characteristics of human beings as such, claims derived ultimately from Kantian ethics.[31] Typical of such attempts, ever since Kant, has been the desire not to rely on too "thick" a description of human nature. In particular, neo-Kantian forms of universalistic liberalism rely on a notion of the self as "prior to its ends," that is, a self that affirms no particular values and can be conceived of as outside of any existing social relations, as a person in the abstract. One frequent objection to Kantian attempts at a universalistic liberalism, made for example by Michael Sandel and by Bernard Williams, is that they offer an inadequate philosophical anthropology, which is to say that they do not describe human nature accurately or in sufficient detail to form the basis of a meaningful political or ethical theory. Attempts to develop a more convincing philosophical anthropology often begin by rehabilitating teleological ethics, which assert that the particular ends (such as happiness) pursued by the self, and the self's location within a network of social relations, are not irrelevant to ethical thought. As Yael Tamir has suggested, liberal nationalism "rejects the view [typical of Kant] that to reason ethically, to consider things from a moral point of view, means to rely exclusively on an *impartial* standpoint" (p. 106). The theorists of the liberal nation-state I examine here differ for the most part from Kant in that they do not attempt to justify their conceptions of political justice by reference to a model of the rational self as capable of abstracting itself entirely from its prejudices and inherited values to arrive at universally applicable principles of action. To this extent, they may appear to offer alternatives to Kantian liberalism, to provide a more complete account of the motivations characteristic of human nature, and thus to provide a potential model of social relations that does not rely on the now much maligned "Archimedean point" outside of political and ethical preconceptions as a guide to moral and political questions. In fact, both Burke and Rousseau, who inspired later liberal nationalist theories, were themselves turning back to the Aristotelian tradition for a more compelling philosophical anthropology to oppose to the early social contract theories. Ultimately, however, these attempts to ground forms of liberal theory in conceptions of the central importance of social identifications to human nature led to crucial modifications of liberalism. The most fundamental problems associated with liberal nationalism arose out of the attempt to find in the organization of humanity into national states a solution to the epistemological and moral uncertainty resulting from the decline of traditional "transcendent" guarantees of the liberty and equality of all men. The discourses of national character and national will seemed to offer guarantees of a just relationship among people that would ground the claims of liberty and equality in the supposed fact of national fraternity, but in so doing they had to abandon many of the earlier transcendental claims of liberalism. The generation of the modernists was to be faced with the resulting crisis, the notion that liberal politics depended on the nation-state system and that the nation-state system could no longer guarantee the fundamental principles of liberty and equality.

NATIONAL WILL VS. NATIONAL CHARACTER

The ideas of a "national will" and a "national character" took on the form in which they appeared to Mill during the French Revolution. Both "will" and "character" served as terms for defining the common interest of the nation and alternatives to the natural law and utilitarian theories of interests that underlay seventeenth- and eighteenth-century proto-liberalism.[32] The revolutionaries, borrowing and transforming Rousseau's idea of the "general will," identified it with the concept of the nation. By renaming itself the "national assembly" and claiming to represent the entire nation, the Third Estate established a crucial claim of modern forms of nationalism: that the nation of equal citizens, rather than the state or the monarch, is sovereign.[33] In the *Declaration of the Rights of Man and of the Citizen*, the national assembly proclaimed that "The nation is essentially the source of all sovereignty; nor can any individual, or any body of men, be entitled to any authority which is not expressly derived from it." This notion of national, popular sovereignty builds on the voluntarist tradition in liberal political thought, according to which the state derives its authority from the consent of the ruled. Edmund

Burke opposed the concept of national, popular sovereignty with a defense of the principles of the British constitution, drawing on the notion that political communities derive their authority from nature rather than convention or consent. He argued that the constitution was suited to the national character as a result of its gradual historical development; it was "made by what is ten thousand times better than choice; it is made by the peculiar circumstances, occasions, tempers, dispositions, and moral, civil, and social habitudes of the people, which disclose themselves only in a long space of time. It is a vestment, which accommodates itself to the body."[34] These two notions of government then, that it should express the will of the nation and that it should accommodate itself to the character of the nation, regardless of its will, face each other as the opposite poles of nineteenth-century theories of the nation-state.

The revolutionaries' assertion of the sovereignty of the nation and Burke's emphasis on the "habitudes" of the people correspond to competing theories of the common good which both the revolutionaries and Burke associated specifically with the word "nation." Throughout the eighteenth century, aristocrats had frequently appealed to the traditional rights of "the nation" in opposing the centralizing efforts of various monarchies, and Burke in particular echoes many traditional defenses of the British constitution.[35] What marks off both the Burkean and revolutionary uses of the word is that they imply variations on "social contract" theories of society. Burke and Rousseau are both often presented as critics of Enlightenment liberalism and sometimes even as precursors of "organic" nationalism.[36] However, both thinkers shared a number of fundamental beliefs of Enlightenment liberalism, and, in very different ways, they would contribute to the later rhetoric of liberal defenses of the nation. What characterized nineteenth-century liberal nationalism and distinguished it from earlier forms of liberalism was its recognition of a central tension between the notions of popular sovereignty and of individual rights, both of which were important to the liberal tradition deriving from Locke. Lord Acton, a Burkean Whig of the late nineteenth century and a favorite of modern conservatives, was to compare the French and English conceptions of nationality:

that absolute right of national unity which is a product of democracy, and that claim of national liberty which belongs to the theory of freedom. These two views of nationality, corresponding [respectively] to the French and to the English systems, are connected in name only, and are in reality the extreme opposites of political thought.[37]

"Democracy" and "the theory of freedom" remain the competing strains within liberal thought, today often labeled "egalitarian" and "libertarian" liberalism.[38] In the early nineteenth-century Whiggish liberalism from which Acton derived his categories, the two types appeared to be "the extreme opposites of political thought." Today, however, they appear as two strains held in tension within the liberal-democratic tradition. Tocqueville and Mill were the most important nineteenth-century thinkers to attempt the reconciliation of liberalism with democracy, freedom with equality, that is still a central concern of liberal political thinkers. As they were to develop in the later nineteenth century, the English "theory of freedom" would rely on a combination of utilitarian ethics with the discourse of national character derived from Burke, while French "democracy" would emphasize a voluntarist ethics derived from Rousseau and the notion of the national will developed in the French Revolution. Both theories made the national state into the transcendental guarantor of liberty and equality, although they did so from different perspectives, and they both also saw in the concept of race a radical limit to the possibilities of liberal universalism.

Rousseau and Burke both reject key aspects of the "social contract" theory, while adapting other elements of it to their own uses. In the first liberal or proto-liberal political theories, seventeenth-century thinkers put the rational, autonomous, self-interested individual at the basis of political society and made the consent of these individuals the source of political sovereignty. Locke asserts that men in the state of nature are "free, equal, and independent."[39] They enter into society and, in so doing, establish a sovereign authority. The government was to act for the good of the community and individuals were to retain their rights to life, liberty, and property. By joining the community, the individual submits to the will of the majority, and those born into the society after its original founding submit to it by tacit consent. Locke assumes that the law of nature is "plain and intelligible to rational creatures," and therefore that in civil society it can be determined by the legislature and followed by impartial judges. Like the later utilitarians, Locke assumed that the common good of society would ultimately not conflict with the interests of the individuals who make up society. According to Locke's *Second Treatise*, the government must guarantee the rights of life, liberty, and private property and must rule according to established laws, "directed to no other *end* but the *Peace, Safety*, and publick good of the People" (p. 130). As long as this radical distinction between private and public concerns is maintained and the rights of individuals are protected, Locke assumes that the interest of the community will not conflict with the interests of the individuals who compose it. Given a sharp distinction between the private and public spheres and appropriate restraints on the infringement of each individual's rights, Locke assumes that the common good will never conflict with the rights of each individual. For this reason, he pays scant attention to the problem of the moral foundations of justice; he concerns himself only with justice as a legal system for deciding disputes among individuals. Put another way, he does not distinguish clearly between what is right and what is good for the individuals who make up society.[40]

Both Rousseau and Burke objected to Locke's version of the social contract theory on the related grounds that the aggregate good of all the individuals in a society is not necessarily equivalent to the good of the society as a whole and that individuals, as they actually exist in society, are not free, equal, or independent. From a central shared objection to the counter-factual nature of previously existing social contract theory, Rousseau and Burke developed sharply contrasted theories of the relationship between the common good and the interests of individuals. As Rousseau put it, he was "taking men as they are and laws as they might be . . . to bring together what right permits with what interest prescribes, so that justice and utility do not find themselves at odds with one another."[41] Burke preferred to take both men and laws as they were. What Burke and Rousseau share philosophically is a return to Aristotle, which entails a rejection of the modern liberal notion, articulated by Locke, that government should be neutral as to the ends pursued by private citizens.[42]

During the nineteenth century, the "national will" became the preferred form of democratic legitimacy and the "national character" the preferred justification for postponing equality in the name of liberty. What undermines both Rousseau's and Burke's accounts of the common good is the conflict between an Aristotelian teleological ethics and modern liberalism's assumption that knowledge of the purposes or ends of human life is fundamentally problematic. This central problem of the moral and epistemological uncertainties of the modern, scientific world-view became evident as the social sciences developed in the nineteenth century, with their claim to explain human behavior in terms of the modern scientific notion of efficient cause rather than the Aristotelian final cause (*telos*). It was with the crisis of positivism at the end of the nineteenth century that this tension within the liberal democracies seemed to become unbearable. By then, "will" and "character" had become metaphysical, almost theological, concepts within the discourses of liberal nationalism, and had lost their usefulness for ethical and political philosophy. Because they did not distinguish clearly between "fact" and "value," "is" and "ought," the liberal nationalist discourses seemed inadequate to the attempt to develop a purely factual science of society. By attempting to transform the tradition of practical philosophy into a modern science, the philosophers of national character and will lost sight of the possibility that philosophy could provide any sort of clarification of matters of value. The "ought" and the *telos* were dismissed as unscientific, and the practical philosophers found themselves at the service of a radical determinism. The roots of these confusions lay in the writings of Rousseau and Burke.

THE RIGHTS OF MAN AND OF THE CITIZEN

The Declaration of the Rights of Man and of the Citizen asserted the principle of national, popular sovereignty and the claim that all men are "free, and equal in respect of their rights." The very title of the Declaration, however, brought into high relief a tension that has marked discussions of the nation-state ever since, the tension between the apparently universal rights of man, which should belong in principle to all men (or, from a more modern perspective, to all people) and the rights of the citizen, member of a sovereign nation, which by definition is limited to a given territory. All people should enjoy the same rights, but only some people are citizens of any given nation. The liberal-democratic nation-state has grappled with the potential conflict between the rights of the citizen and the rights of the human being ever since. The tensions between popular sovereignty and human rights were a central theme of Rousseau's political writings, but in the Revolution, those writings were used to exalt popular sovereignty, associated specifically with the idea of the nation, over human rights, in a mode that prefigured the totalitarian possibilities of revolutionary movements ever since. The danger of the voluntarist definition of the nation, adapted by the revolutionaries from Rousseau's theories, was that it made membership in the national community the primary guarantee of human rights and indeed treated the political aspect of human nature, citizenship, as the only distinctively human quality. In the theory of absolute national sovereignty, citizenship became the only effective grounding of human rights. Rousseau's idealization of the Greek *polis* risked abandoning the principle of human equality embodied in natural-rights theory, for it created two classes of people, citizens and non-citizens. This process made possible the later confusion of the political concepts of "equal rights" (or "equality of condition") with natural equality and racial homogeneity which was fundamental to the nationalist movement in France from the 1890s onward and was a crucial problem for Proust. The discourse of "national will," then, identified abstract justice with the common good, the state as the instrument of law with the state as instrument of the nation, but only at the cost of making citizenship in a nation-state the essence of human nature.[43]

Rousseau takes the people to be sovereign and their sovereignty to be inalienable. He therefore recognizes the dual status of the individual's involvement in the community. The individual both pursues private interests and plays a role (as part of the sovereign people) in establishing the laws that are meant to regulate the entire community for the sake of the public good. Rousseau's main amendment to earlier formulations of the social contract theory was to argue that the guarantee of the rights of individuals, which Locke took to be central to civil society, is insufficient to ensure the pursuit of the common good, since any given person exists both as a private individual with interests of his own and as a member of society with a responsibility for ensuring the public good. Rousseau's solution to the conflict between the citizen's private interests and his obligation to pursue the common good as part of the sovereign people was to distinguish between the "general will" ("volonté générale") and the "will of all" ("volonté de tous"). He associates the general will with the common good, or the interest of the entire community. The will of all, on the other hand, represents the interest of the community as the individuals in the community perceive it. Rousseau argues that only if all individuals, as subjects, submit themselves to the common good and make laws with the common good, rather than their own personal interests, in mind can the general will be achieved:

But when the social bond begins to relax and the state to grow weak, when private interests begin to make themselves felt and small societies begin to influence the large one, the common interest changes and finds opponents. Unanimity no longer reigns in the votes; the general will is no longer the will of all. Contradictions and debates arise, and the best advice does not pass without disputes.[44]

Rousseau thus establishes a sharp distinction between the interest of the entire community, which he equates with what is right, and the private interests of individuals, which are bound to undermine the general will. He distrusts any intermediate associations within society, as tending to distract individuals from consideration of the common good. At one level, and particularly as developed later by Kant, this identification of the general will with what is right involves a further development of liberal theory, for Rousseau suggests that each individual must distinguish between her or his private interests and the public good.[45] However, by attempting to overcome the distinction between "utility" and "justice," Rousseau also opens up the possibility of a totalitarian interpretation of his work.[46] The assumption that the common good of the community, "the general will," is also what is "right" or "just" threatens to efface the distinction between the private and public spheres that is crucial to liberal theory. Rousseau argues, for example, that "since the sovereign is formed entirely from the private individuals who make it up, it neither has nor could have an interest contrary to theirs" (I.vii). The interest of the community as a whole, then, is assumed to be identical with the interests of all the individuals in it. The notion of the "general will," then, introduced to correct the assumption that the interest of the community is no more than the aggregate of the interests of all the individuals in it, can at least in some interpretations lead to a conception of the interest of the community as the single overriding concern of government and the rights of private individuals as entirely subordinate.

That interpretation of Rousseau became influential in the French Revolution. The Declaration of the Rights of Man and of the Citizen declares not only that the nation is sovereign but also that "The law is an expression of the will of the community."[47] It does not address the problem of the potential conflicts between the will of the community and the true interests of the community or between the will of the community and the "natural and imprescriptible rights of man."[48] As François Furet has argued, the notion of a unified popular or national will that is invariably just motivated many of the excesses of the Revolution.[49] One of the most influential theorists of the unified will of the nation, which could not be opposed, represented, or divided, was the Abbé Sieyès, who identified Rousseau's general will with the concept of the "nation." For both Locke and Rousseau, the question of whether a given society was a nation or not was relatively unimportant. Sieyès, however, used the concept of the nation as the grounds of his attack on the nobility, arguing in a rather circular fashion that the nation consisted of all those whose work was necessary to sustain the nation. He claimed that the third estate contained in itself "everything that is necessary to form a complete nation" and that if the privileged order (the nobility) were removed, "the nation would be not something less but something more."[50] The crucial concept here, for the future of the Revolution, was that there must not be orders or castes within the nation. The concept of the national will reverberated throughout nineteenth-century France as the claim that there could be only one interpretation of the common good, that the common good was equivalent both to justice and to the interests of all the individuals in society, and that anyone who opposed it was also opposing the nation itself. When, in the rhetoric surrounding the Dreyfus affair, this fantasy of a unified national will combined with the demand that, in order to enjoy political equality of condition as a citizen, one must be similar, or naturally equal, to all other French citizens, it helped to create modern, anti-liberal nationalism.

Rousseau's writings became the model not only for revolutionary movements but also for Kant's "deontological" ethics, an ethics which places the demands of justice and duty before all else. One characteristic weakness of such ethics, explored already by Hegel and more recently by Sandel and Williams, is the demand that the virtues Rousseau associated with citizenship override all other commitments, including not only, for example, strictly immoral desires, but also merely personal needs that may be neither moral nor immoral but that make up most of any human being's life.[51] Kant treats the distinction between duty and inclination as absolute: one either acts autonomously, out of reverence for the "moral law within," or one acts according to one's merely contingent inclinations, which is to say non-morally. In Rousseau, this distinction is located at the level of politics. One either acts in accordance with the general will or against it; Rousseau expresses deep suspicion of purely private interests as tending to undermine the general will. The theory of the "general will" assumes, like Aristotle's ethics, that politics aims at the chief good for human beings, and it therefore subordinates all considerations to the problems of political life. As a result, as Ernest Renan would later realize, the general will demands a sort of forgetting of all of one's attachments other than that to the community as a whole. As an ideal, this is not only too demanding but also undermines the working of the general will itself, for it assumes that the only meaningful sort of freedom is that of the people acting unanimously in concert.

Rousseau relies on an equivocal use of the concept "freedom," to indicate both political freedom (freedom from socially imposed constraints) and metaphysical freedom (freedom from natural constraints). These two senses, which Kant defined as "negative" and "positive" freedom, often also correspond in political discourse, as Isaiah Berlin has shown, to (political) "freedom" and (political) "equality."[52] Equality, in other words, is treated as a positive form of freedom, and thus in the name of positive freedom, all sorts of infringements of "negative" freedom appear justifiable. This is at least one plausible interpretation of Rousseau's notion that "whoever refuses to obey the general will will be forced to do so by the entire body. This means merely that he will be forced to be free."[53] The revolutionary concept of a unified national will that secures equality and "positive freedom" for its citizens involves a transformation of the concept of freedom. In Rousseau, by virtue of the metaphysical powers invested in it, the will becomes a mere spiritual principle, presumed to be free and capable of acting in any way it chooses. Thus, the theory of democracy ultimately takes a "positive," metaphysical notion of freedom on faith in order to secure political equality. While it distinguishes sharply between political and metaphysical ("natural") conceptions of equality, it elides the distinction between political and metaphysical conceptions of freedom. The problem, as Berlin puts it, is simply that if one is going to trade liberty for equality one should say so, rather than claim to be trading one form of liberty for another. The implications of this identification of liberty and equality, however, work to the detriment not only of political liberty but also ultimately of equality itself. For Rousseau's conception of the general will leaves the discourse of national will open to objections on the basis of deterministic theories of human nature which, by undermining its concept of metaphysical freedom, could also call into question its ideal of political equality. In the Dreyfus Affair of the 1890s, this undermining of the concept of free will, or "positive liberty," would, in fact, underwrite what Arendt called the "perversion of equality from a political to a social concept."

Rousseau's emphasis on the shared will as the defining aspect of the nation was to be reformulated during the third republic by one of the leading intellectuals of French positivism, Ernest Renan. Contemporary liberal and anti-racist theorists of the nation have admired the democratic implications of Renan's famous definition of the nation as a "daily plebiscite" in his lecture "What is a Nation?" of March 11, 1882.[54] This lecture was one of Renan's attempts to develop a liberal theory of the nation-state for the French Third Republic that could heal the wounds of the various nineteenth-century revolutions. Unlike many of his English contemporaries, Renan saw the danger of theories that equated the race with the nation: "a very great error, which, if it were to become dominant, would destroy European civilization" (p. 13). One of Renan's implicit tagets in "What is a Nation?" is the racialist theory of Joseph-

Arthur de Gobineau, who had argued that the merits of any given nation depended on the mixture of racial types in that nation's blood (such as Germanic, Gallo-Roman, and Celtic in France).[55] Renan distinguishes two conceptions of race, the biological or zoological and the philological or historical. Whereas anthropologists may concern themselves with physiological and blood relations, "race, as we historians, understand it, is . . . something which is made and unmade" (p. 15). Renan thus differentiates two conceptions of race, corresponding to the twentieth-century ideas of "race" as biological inheritance and "culture" as those shared characteristics that do not depend on biological inheritance. Historians of the "constructivist" school admire Renan's recognition of the role invention has played in the creation of nations: "Forgetting, I would even go so far as to say historical error, is a crucial factor in the creation of a nation . . . [T]he essence of a nation is that all the individuals in it have many things in common, and also that they have forgotten many things" (p. 11). A good deal of Proust's commentary on the French nation-state develops a social psychology akin to Renan's thoughts here.

Renan denies the claims not only of race, but also of common interests and language to be at the root of nationality.[56] He speaks the true language of universalistic liberalism when he announces that "Aside from anthropological characteristics, there are such things as reason, justice, the true, and the beautiful, which are the same for all [human beings]" and that "there is something in man which is superior to language, namely, the will" (pp. 15, 16). He seems almost a more eloquent version of John Stuart Mill when he suggests that "More valuable by far than common customs posts and frontiers conforming to strategic ideas is the fact of sharing, in the past, a glorious heritage and regrets, and of having, in the future, [a shared] programme to put into effect, or the fact of having suffered, enjoyed, and hoped together." Especially when compared to the social Darwinism of contemporary English theorists of "national character," Renan's statement that "a nation is a soul, a spiritual principle" seems to offer a true model for liberal-democratic nationalism (p. 19). Without explicitly claiming that any sort of providence has established nations, Renan argues that it is quite reasonable to worship one's ancestors, for the cult of the nation is a sort of extension of self-love: "The nation, like the individual, is the culmination of a long past of endeavours, sacrifice, and devotion" (p. 19). Renan proposes, in effect, that a liberal nationalism become a sort of civic religion for the Third Republic. So it seems rather surprising to learn that among Renan's admirers were not only James Joyce and Marcel Proust, but also some of the most radical opponents of the Republic and its liberal parliamentarism, the anarcho-syndicalist Georges Sorel and the right-wing, anti-semitic nationalist Maurice Barrès. What could there be in Renan's liberal, universalistic nationalism to appeal to the anti-parliamentary, anti-semitic, and militarist nationalists of the period of the Dreyfus affair? I will argue here that Renan reproduces the weaknesses of Rousseau's voluntarism, but that these weaknesses are exacerbated by Renan's eagerness to rebut the racialist theories of the origins of nations. This latter concern led Renan to develop a conception of membership in the nation as demanding a suppression (a "forgetting") of racial and other differences among citizens that proved inadequate to withstand the development of a determinist, race-based nationalism.

Renan's strong voluntarist analysis of the nation-state suggests that it is only in the sharing of a will through the daily plebiscite that people become capable of living together in a liberal democracy. Mill already implied something of the sort in his argument as to the impediments to representative democracy in multi-national states, but whereas Mill makes his claim in favor of nations on more or less empirical grounds, Renan seems to be making a larger claim about human nature and suggesting that it is only in the nation that the will finds its true fulfillment. For example, Renan claims that

> Man is a slave neither of his race nor his language, nor of his religion, nor of the course of rivers nor of the direction taken by mountain chains. A large aggregate of men, healthy in mind and warm of heart, creates the kind of moral consciousness which we call a nation. So long as this moral consciousness gives proof of its strength by the sacrifices which demand the abdication of the individual to the advantage of the community, it is legitimate and has a right to exist. (p. 20)

Unlike Rousseau, Renan does not speak of forcing people to be free. The sacrifices the nation demands must be offered without compulsion. However, like Rousseau, he finds a higher sort of freedom in the sentiments that can cause a person to sacrifice private interests to the good of the community. While this is obviously a noble goal, perhaps the highest goal of liberal nationalism, it nonetheless rests on an identification of justice with the advantage of a given community. As a result, like Rousseau's *Social Contract*, Renan's "What is a Nation?" ultimately makes the national will the measure of justice and submission to the national will the measure of moral worth. Those who are not prepared to make the sacrifice are clearly, in Renan's formulation, not part of the nation, and those who hold other values to be higher than that of the nation must therefore be suspect as imperfect citizens. Renan thus reproduces the strong voluntarist ideology that makes the shared will of the nation the measure of justice and all subordinate identifications a temptation to betray the nation. Mill, in the *Considerations*, treated as unproblematic the fact that certain "causes" (including race and descent) may have helped to shape the "sympathies" felt by members of the same nation. Renan, on the other hand, eager to refute a certain form of political determinism associated for him with the racist theories of Gobineau, must emphasize unduly and unconvincingly the absolute freedom of the human will in choosing a nation. All of the causes that Mill enumerates as conducing to the feeling of nationality, Renan rejects. The nation must be more than a result of certain forces, historical, geographical, or biological. It must express a higher conception of human freedom, and this is so because Renan has accepted the principle, derived from Aristotle by way of Rousseau, that it is in the political life that human beings achieve their chief good.

Renan, like Rousseau and also like Kant, treats the universal (reason, truth, justice, beauty) as inevitably at odds with the particular (loyalty to a given race or religion simply because it is given). Renan rehabilitates, however, the basic error of Rousseau that Kant had corrected. For Kant made the object of duty the universal moral law which the reason can prescribe for itself. Renan, like Rousseau, imagines that this moral law can be identified with a given community, the nation. He thus reverses everything important in Kant's conception of a "kingdom of ends," the imagined and ideal "systematic union of rational beings through common objective laws."[57] For Renan, the kingdom of ends extends only to the borders of the French Republic. Although he aspires, like Kant, to a world in which each person obeys the universal laws of duty, he is quite content in "What is a Nation?" to encourage a Rousseauian cult of the national will which by its very nature conflicts with the reverence for the universal law that Kant took to be the foundation of ethics. So he maintains the irreducible opposition between the universalistic morality and all particular ends or values that makes Kant's ethics so impractical, but he throws away the crucial impulse of Kantianism towards universal justice, contenting himself with a simply national justice.

"What is a Nation?" retains the conception of the nation as a unitary, homogeneous group that the revolution adapted from Rousseau. Whereas the revolutionary ideology had emphasized the equality of all

citizens as a natural right of all men, however, Renan accepts the racialist premise that political equality somehow depends on racial homogeneity. He has transferred the voluntarist logic that demands the
destruction of all intermediary associations between the nation and the
individual to the realm of racial thought and imagined a nation made
up of an indistinct mixture of races, just as Sieyès imagined a nation
without castes or orders. Renan does not develop any racist fantasy of
achieving equality through genocide or eugenics. Rather, he clearly
wishes all races to stand on an equal footing in the French Republic. Yet,
he speaks as if the unified national will depended for its survival not
simply on a separation of race and politics, but also on the suppression
of public discussion of race, a forgetting of origins comparable to the
forgetting of the wars of religion. In his private correspondence with
Gobineau, Renan argued that the loss of racial distinctiveness among
(white) nations would ultimately have a positive, equalizing effect:
"Putting aside the entirely inferior races, whose admixture to the great
races would do nothing but poison the human species, I conceive for the
future a homogeneous humanity, in which all the original streams will
blend into a great river, and where all remembrance of the diverse prov-
enances will be lost."[58] In "What is a Nation?" this racial blending and
forgetting becomes a spiritual process, but the concept of the national
will that results is in an important sense less flexible than anything in
Mill. For, in the demand to exclude from the consideration of what
makes a nation anything that divides or differentiates a nation's citizens,
the voluntarist tradition invents for itself an impossible criterion: that a
nation can consist only of people willing to sacrifice any social identifications other than that of citizen. Furthermore, any such consent must
amount to an act of pure free will. Renan's conception of the nation
could account no more than Rousseau's for the fact that one is born into
a given nation and does not choose it. Even less satisfactorily than
Rousseau could Renan account for how one might be born with a
number of competing loyalties no one of which could be sacrificed completely. With Rousseau and Sieyès, this conception of the nation led to
the reign of Terror. With Renan and his generation, it led to the emergence of nationalist ideology in the Dreyfus affair.

   Rousseau appealed to the notion of positive freedom through incorporation in the general will in an attempt to guarantee the moral equality of all citizens, recognizing the fact that citizens could not be naturally
equal. Renan, similarly, appeals to the positive freedom of the will to
form a nation to maintain the equality of all citizens against the claims

of Gobineau that people from various races are not naturally equal. This reliance on the concept of free will makes Renan vulnerable to the argument that people are not in fact metaphysically free. It was no very difficult step for the right-wing nationalist propagandist, Maurice Barrès, to respond that people's actions are in fact determined, and therefore that the cult of the nation must in fact rest on a rejection of the universal values such as reason, justice, and truth that Renan associated with free will. Like Gobineau and Renan before him, Barrès acknowledges that there is no French race, strictly speaking. The French nation is, as in Renan, the product of historical forces and the individual is linked to it not solely by blood but by "the work of individuals and the sacrifices that have preceded him."[59] Barrès considers, however, that certain races can never be fully part of the nation, for more or less physiological reasons. The Jew's racial difference makes him incapable of becoming part of the nation, whereas other races, like the Lorrain, are capable of this integration. Here of course, there is a certain intellectual inconsistency, since he frequently treats the nation specifically as a physiological rather than a historical concept, but this does not seem to have troubled Barrès, who was motivated by the desire to make political and racial anti-semitism a sort of mortar capable of uniting the French nation. What is interesting is that Barrès's anti-semitic rhetoric reconfigures the voluntarist notion of the race as a mortal antagonist of the nation. Barrès explains that he finds "Judaism (a race opposed to mine)" repugnant:

The Jews have no fatherland [*patrie*] in the sense in which we understand that word. For us, the fatherland is the soil and the ancestors, the earth of our dead. For them, it is the place where they find their greatest [material] interest. Their "intellectuals" thus arrive at their famous definition: "The fatherland is an idea." But what idea? That which is the most useful to them, and, for example, the idea that all men are brothers, that nationality is a prejudice to be destroyed, that military honor stinks of blood, that we must disarm (and leave no other force than money), etc. . . . It is highly moral to obey the law . . . But I cannot accept any law but the one with which my spirit identifies. The more honor I have in myself, the more I revolt if the law is not the law of my race. The relativist seeks to distinguish the conceptions appropriate to each human type.[60]

Universality and the rights of man have become nothing more than Jewish conspiracies that elevate one race at the expense of all fatherlands. All values are relative to the nation, and one race invents the idea of the absolute as a sort of trick to divert attention from this truth. The near-total incoherence of Barrès's political opinions did not prevent him from appealing to a large part of the French public or from being admired and befriended not only by right-wing intellectuals but even by the occasional Dreyfusard of Jewish descent, like Proust. The voluntarist conception of the nation as a jealous God paved the way for Barrès's political antisemitism. Renan relies on a metaphysical concept, freedom of the will, to justify political liberty. Because he implicitly accepts that people may not be naturally equal in their abilities, Renan requires the idea of free will to justify the idea of political freedom. The anti-semite Barrès responds by rejecting both the freedom of the will and the ideal of political equality. As I shall argue below, it was at this stage of French history that Proust, who resembled Rousseau in so much else as well, would reconfigure the voluntarist tradition by describing personal identity in terms of the multiple manifestations of "involuntary memory" in the individual citizen and thus suggest both the limits of the "will" as a source of national unity and the possibility of rethinking the role of subsidiary identifications within the nation-state.[61]

THE RIGHTS OF MEN AND THE RIGHTS OF ENGLISHMEN

Like Rousseau, but with almost diametrically opposed intentions, Burke draws on Aristotelian tradition to criticize and expand the social contract theory. Rousseau was in fact the most important social contract theorist that Burke attacked. Burke's alternative to Rousseau's voluntarism, however, was not to defend either the "Divine Right of Kings" or the common eighteenth-century English notion of an "ancient constitution" that could not be altered under any circumstances.[62] Rather, Burke accepted a basic element of the social contract theory, the notion that society is founded upon convention. He reinterpreted the notion of society as a convention so completely, however, that it lost most of its radical implications, and in fact returned it to something much closer to what it seems to have meant to Aristotle. "Society is indeed a contract," Burke observes in perhaps the most famous passage of *Reflections on the Revolution in France*, but unlike "subordinate contracts for objects of mere occasional interest," society or the state cannot be dissolved at will: "it becomes a partnership not only between those who are living, but between those who are living, those who are dead, and those who are to be born" (pp. 146–147). Burke denies that the state embodies the will of the nation and attacks the revolutionary notion that sovereignty "not only originates from . . . [but also] constantly and inalienably resides in" the people.[63] Burke's method of reconciling the potentially competing theories of the state as instrument of the nation and the state as instrument of the law is to argue that the state reflects not the will of the sovereign nation at a given time but the character of the nation as it discloses itself over generations. Burke thus appeals to a teleological assumption, that the natural processes of society will over time lead to a harmony between the nation and its form of government, and that this harmonious natural process will serve both the interest of the nation (the common good) and justice (the right). As with the revolutionaries he criticizes, the nation itself becomes a central concept in Burke's attempts to reconcile justice and the common good, but for Burke it is the character of the nation, its natural tendencies of development over time, rather than its will, that guarantees this harmony, for "the will of the many, and their interest, must very often differ" (*Reflections*, p. 103). Whereas Rousseau embraces the universalistic, democratic implications of the social contract theory and gives rise to a universalistic theory of the liberal nation-state, Burke defends particularism and the development of the local character of the British constitution. What guarantees that liberal government will achieve the common good is a teleological, indeed Providential, conception of history. Although less formal, Burke's theory of history resembles Hegel's in trusting to the power of historical development to bring out the latent wisdom implicit in English customs.

One central motivation of Burke's attack on the French Revolution was his sense that the democratic claims to equality threatened to undermine traditional liberties: "In the famous law of the 3d of Charles I. called the *Petition of Right*, the parliament says to the king, 'Your subjects have *inherited* this freedom,' claiming their franchises not on abstract principles 'as the rights of men,' but as the rights of Englishmen, and as a patrimony derived from their forefathers" (p. 82). In this famous passage, Burke claims that actual legal rights are recognized by custom within a given state rather than by reference to a universal principle. The constitution embodies these customary rights, passed on from generation to generation, "an entailed inheritance derived to us from our forefathers, and to be transmitted to our posterity."[64] The association between Englishmen themselves and liberty became so common in English thinking as to cause Hannah Arendt to observe of Burke's concept of liberty as an "entailed inheritance": "The concept of inheritance, applied to the very nature of liberty, has been the ideological basis from which English nationalism received its curious touch of race-feeling ever since the French revolution."[65] Arendt argues that when this concept became attached to certain forms of Darwinism, it developed into the ideology of racism, offering a new "key to history." On its own, in fact, Burke's notion of national character, although it contained an element of pride, did not imply that the English were inevitably superior to or more suited for liberty than all other peoples. Burke himself merely suggested an early form of what Herbert Butterfield would later criticize as the "Whig Interpretation of History," the assumption that the movement of English history naturally led to the embodiment of the ideal of English liberty.[66] It was when the notion of national character became attached to a hierarchical theory of various types of institutions as belonging to different stages of civilization that it came to imply a sort of essence of Englishness that allowed liberalism to flourish in England and nowhere else.

Arendt treats the failure of the nation-state system to guarantee the rights of stateless people as an "ironical, bitter and belated confirmation" of Burke's arguments against the Declaration of the Rights of Man and of the Citizen. She does not, however, consider at length Burke's alternatives to the "Rights of Man." Burke's defense of the rights of Englishmen and condemnation of the rights of man has earned him a reputation as essentially a conservative, but he supported gradual reform of the constitution on the basis of a theory of the progressive and harmonious interaction of the national character (civil society) and political institutions (the state). Burke himself was a Whig, not a Tory. In fact, he believed in more or less the same civil rights that Locke had supported a century before: the rights to life, liberty, property, and a fairly large degree of political representation for the propertied classes.[67] Burke had defended these rights against what he believed to be the incursions of the monarchy in the 1770s and had supported the American Revolution because he saw it as fundamentally consonant with the principles of the Glorious Revolution of 1688.[68] Burke brought together three interrelated elements in English and Scottish political thought that were to remain closely linked with one another and with Burke's name throughout the nineteenth century: the importance of allowing the natural development of civil society (the "nation" side of the modern expression "nation-state"); the defense of time-honored customs, regardless of their apparent irrationality, as useful for facilitating society's natural development; and a theory of society as composed of competing group interests, not simply of autonomous individuals. In the nineteenth century, several of Burke's central concerns would unite the Whiggish strain within English liberalism in a defense of the specifically national character of English institutions. As John Burrow's studies of the Whig legacy have shown, what remained the most influential element of Burke's thought was the rejection of *a priori* arguments drawn from rationalistic theories of human nature.[69] For Burke, liberty had to be defined in more concrete, historical terms.

Burke's conception of the reconciliation of conflicting interests in the parliamentary process seems to offer an alternative to Rousseau's conception of all interests as subordinate to the general will. It is at odds with both the individualist assumption that the common good is the sum of all individual goods and Rousseau's claim that the common good is the general will, identifiable with justice. Instead, Burke conceives of the common good as the harmonious balancing of the competing interests within society. While "parliament is a *deliberative* assembly of *one* nation, with *one* interest, that of the whole," Burke defines this national interest as consisting in the reconciliation of the diverse interests of various segments of society: "All these widespread interests must be considered; must be compared; must be reconciled, if possible."[70] Burke conceives of these interests as corporate rather than merely individual. In contrast to Rousseau, Burke therefore defends parties and subordinate associations within the state as capable of contributing to the harmonious working out of the competing demands of a complex society: "To be attached to the subdivision, to love the little platoon we belong to in society, is the first principle (the germ as it were) of public affections" (*Reflections*, p. 97). By trusting in the ability of the political process to guarantee the harmonious development and, where possible, reconciliation of the nation's "various, multiform, and intricate" interests, Burke's conception of the national interest seems to overcome the potential weakness of earlier liberal theories that take into consideration only individual interests and the interest of society as a whole or the state.[71]

From the beginning, Burke's defense of the constitution as the product of tradition and history left itself open to attack as a form of prejudice or duplicity. If society was the result of convention, not of divine fiat, and the constitution was open to a certain amount of reform, how could Burke reject the claim that the people should have the right to rewrite the constitution entirely? Burke's defense of custom and hereditary rights depended first of all on the claim that custom was a more certain guarantee of rights than reason alone. Burke argued that no one should reject the time-honored custom known as the constitution because to do so would be to dissolve the contract at the basis of civil society: "If civil society be the offspring of convention, that convention must be its law" (p. 110). What radicals saw as merely customary, the result of prejudice rather than reason, Burke defended as the almost sacred product of historical processes. From this claim that people must obey convention for the sake of stability, it was not very far to a defense of prejudice on the grounds of utility. An irrational belief, according to this argument, is better than no belief at all – because the irrational belief will at least allow for a certain amount of stability. For such reasons, Burke argued, the English, in the "cold sluggishness of our national character,"

instead of casting away all our old prejudices . . . cherish them to a very considerable degree, and, to take more shame to ourselves, we cherish them because they are prejudices; and the longer they have lasted, and the more generally they have prevailed, the more we cherish them. We are afraid to put men to live and trade each on his own private stock of reason; because we suspect that this stock in each man is small, and that individuals would be better to avail themselves of the general bank and capital of nations, and of ages. (p. 138)

People's own unknowing, prejudiced, even irrational behavior can lead to a rational ordering of society more effectively than attempts to rebuild society wholesale on the basis of what appears to the current generation to be rational. Although such a conception of social processes would later appeal to those who espoused evolution, a secularized form of Providence, for Burke himself it is clear that the ultimate source of morality and of the social order was the real thing, divine Providence: "The law is not subject to the will of those, who by an obligation above them, and infinitely superior, are bound to submit their will to that law" (p. 147).

Burke's notion of national character, then, offers certain strengths lacking in either Locke or Rousseau. In particular, his theory of interests treats society neither as composed of atomized individuals nor as a monolithic "general will," but as a complex set of subordinate associations between the individual and the nation. His conception of Parliament as the site in which the national interest could be developed out of competing interests within society still resonates as a possible ideal for modern, pluralistic societies. In these senses, Burke is a true precursor of liberal nationalism, and it is not entirely incomprehensible that liberals like Leslie Stephen and Walter Bagehot felt they could learn something from Burke after evolutionary theory had challenged the individualist assumptions of utilitarianism. As Avrom Fleishman has noted in *Conrad's Politics*, many of Joseph Conrad's political ideas resembled Burke's. However, as I will argue in chapter 3, Conrad had far more egalitarian concerns typical of late nineteenth-century liberals. Burke's brand of the "theory of freedom" made practically no concessions to the demands of equality. Indeed, Burke defended inegalitarian social arrangements as desirable guarantors of liberty. He claimed that "in this partnership [of society] all men have equal rights; but not to equal things" (p. 110). So, when Leslie Stephen praised Burke for his "conception of a nation as a living organism of complex structure and historical continuity," and even more strikingly when John Stuart Mill envisioned a political ethology, "a science of national character," they seemed to a large degree to be abandoning the egalitarian principles of the utilitarian tradition.[72]

Many eighteenth-century thinkers, including Burke and Rousseau, had emphasized the influence of manners or mores (*mœurs*) on the development of political institutions, and Tocqueville had developed this conception of civilization. Over the course of the nineteenth century, however, this concept of mores influencing politics came to be replaced by a sense that the general laws of development of society made certain changes in politics inevitable. When political thinkers looked to the social sciences for guidance, they tended to assume that the laws of society resembled natural laws, and this caused some of them to despair of the traditional categories of ethical thought. It was in an atmosphere of lost religious faith and unbounded faith in science that theories about racial essences seemed to offer a meaningful alternative to liberal thought. Burke's notion of "inherited" liberty became especially problematic when it was considered analogous not to inheriting property but to inheriting a gene pool. "National character" came to mean not the "moral, civil, and social habitudes" of the people, but their biological essence. English superiority, then, seemed not just an accident of history but a physical fact that only miscegenation or the degeneration of English racial stock could change.

As John Burrow and George W. Stocking, Jr. have demonstrated, Victorian anthropologists and sociologists developed the theory of sociocultural evolution largely in the hopes of maintaining the Christian and Enlightenment view that people really, naturally were equal, in the sense of all sharing a common human nature.[73] The rise of evolutionary theory, comparative philology, and geological knowledge had undermined faith in the literal truth of the Biblical account of creation. Various theories of polygenesis claimed that the different races had separate origins or that they had developed so early in human history that racial differences were virtually as significant as differences among species. The champions of slavery and opponents of political liberalism had no difficulty drawing on racial theory to assert that the natural superiority of European races and of the upper classes proved the foolishness of liberalism. Some polygenist physical anthropologists, advocates of repressive policies towards "alien races," also doubted whether "our fellow countrymen [were] beings so advanced in the scale of humanity as to be able to be left to themselves."[74] However, when politics interested them, sociocultural evolutionists had quite the opposite concern: to show that all people, having fundamentally the same human nature, were capable of advancing high enough in the scale of humanity to be able to enjoy liberal institutions. Apart from physical theories of racial difference, the main challenge to the idea of a unified human nature came from the evident fact of the wide variety of human customs and the difficulty of accounting for the failure of "savage" races to develop civilized customs like those of the Europeans. All of this served to emphasize the limits of earlier liberal and utilitarian theories of a rational human nature. Bentham's calculus of pain and pleasure appeared increasingly naive, and various forms of evolution seemed to offer the promise of an alternative ethics, based on a science of social progress.[75]

Part of the solution of the evolutionists was, like Vico, Rousseau, and the other early philosophical anthropologists, to assume that Europeans themselves had at one time been "savages" and then to hypothesize a natural, and unidirectional, evolutionary process that would allow each society to develop to the heights of European (or, as the Victorians added, English) civilization over time. Evolutionists such as Edward B. Tylor attempted, in particular, to show that various social systems, such as the different forms of marriage and kinship, played useful roles in the specific cultures to which they belonged, although they emphasized the tendency of all such systems to develop toward the civilized practices that happened to be condoned by Christian morality.[76] From the point of view of political thought, sociocultural evolutionism amounted to yet another attempt to reconcile historicism – the theory that ideas are valid in relation to their own time – with a notion of moral and social progress. As Burrow and other historians of evolutionary social theory have observed, the evolutionists often relied on the tacit "identification of social evolution with progress," the assumption that whatever has evolved is good.[77] Thus, for example, Mill envisioned a science of national character, political ethology, which would reveal the basic unity of all human character, but explain its variation across time and culture: "the more highly the science of ethology is cultivated, and the better the diversities of national character are understood, the smaller, probably, will the number of propositions become, which it will be considered safe to build upon as universal principles of human nature."[78] Yet, as Mill himself seems to recognize in some passages of his *System of Logic*, his dedication to understanding all human society on the basis of the modern scientific principle of efficient cause undermines the practical political impact of his planned ethology. The notion of "character" could serve as a useful way of describing human development in the philosophy of Aristotle precisely because the standards of human conduct were taken to be relatively unproblematic; the *telos* of a thing was assumed to be inherent in its nature and if one could understand its character one also understood how it should behave. For Mill, who attempted to apply the modern scientific method with its determinism of efficient causes, the notion of "character" loses its status as a guide to human action and becomes merely an analytic concept, so that the ethology can give no guidance as to how one *ought* to act. Similarly, Leslie Stephen attempted to explain altruistic behavior towards other members of the same tribe in evolutionary terms in his *The Science of Ethics* of 1882. Morality, he argued, in terms that Nietzsche might have endorsed, was nothing more than the behavior that was well adapted to the needs of the race. As Stephen observes, "A man not dependent upon a race is as meaningless a phrase as an apple that does not grow upon a tree."[79] Unlike Nietzsche, however, Stephen did not seem to grasp that if morality was no more than the function of evolution it therefore ceased to mean what morality always had meant – namely a subjectively valid and binding reason for acting in one way as opposed to another.[80]

In the effort to explain the basic ontological unity of the human species, progressivist and evolutionary liberal thinkers in England generally ignored the arguments of Rousseau, in the *Discourse on the Origins of Inequality*, that natural inequalities (of ability, for example) should be distinguished from moral inequalities, and that it was only in society that differences of human nature take on moral significance.[81] Rousseau grounds his egalitarian politics in the notion that by virtue of membership in a society, people should be recognized as morally equal. Liberals like Mill, Walter Bagehot, Stephen, and Henry Maine revived much of Burke's thought, and particularly a Burkean conception of national character, and tried to graft it onto a conception of historical progress that relied on notions of secular historical forces rather than divine providence. In this attempt, they developed what might be seen as the "theory of freedom's" equivalent to the democratic confusion of "negative" and "positive" freedoms criticized by Isaiah Berlin. For, instead of seeing equality as a political concept, the sociocultural evolutionists attempted to ground equality metaphysically in a theory of human nature. As a result, their theory was open to objections on the grounds that people are not *really*, naturally equal (i.e., the same) and therefore that restrictions on traditional political liberty were desirable in order to create a national character that was more authentically capable of real liberty. The theory that apparent inequalities were simply the result of differential development of "national character" left English liberals open to the eugenicists' claim that people are not really equal but that character is innate and determined by heredity. Thus, whereas the French theory of the "freedom of the will" was vulnerable to attacks on deterministic grounds, the English theory, embracing determinism, was open to attack on the basis of very simple sociological evidence. The poor were poor, the savage races savage as a result of the natural forces of evolution. With the increasing identification of national character and race, the attempt to understand the development of nations gave way to the eugenic theories of Karl Pearson and others, modelled on the work of Francis Galton. An evolutionary ethics could not explain why anything should be done to contradict the processes of natural selection, or indeed why natural selection should not be helped along by programs of mass sterilization or in the extreme case genocide.

Fortunately, the Enlightenment notion that "all men are brothers" is scientifically correct in so far as we are all one species and share most of our genetic material and other biological characteristics. Yet, the principles of liberal democracy lie, as the voluntarist tradition recognized much more clearly than the utilitarians, not in people's natural equality but in their moral equality. The English liberal social Darwinists, while sharing the utilitarian tradition of treating "freedom" as a purely negative or political concept, rather than a positive or metaphysical one, nonetheless felt compelled to treat equality as a natural, rather than a conventional, concept. As a result, they reduced the problem of freedom to a problem of the natural, equal rationality of human beings and created a metaphysics based on the assumption of such equality. Philosophically, the sociocultural evolutionists' approach to politics maintains the major weakness of Burke's thought – its reliance on a teleological conception of history – but fails to maintain its characteristic strength, which was its capacity for accounting for the complexity of the various interests in society. Despite their Burkean conception of history, the sociocultural evolutionists fall back into the utilitarian trap of "not [taking] seriously the distinction between persons."[82] They treat the national character as a version of individual character writ large, and assume, like the utilitarians before them, that the common good will also be the good of every individual. In terms of race, what is remarkable about the discourse of national character is that it views the nation as a parallel category to the race, a smaller subdivision than the "great races of mankind," but a subdivision nonetheless. While not clearly differentiating "racial" from "cultural" differences, the discourse of "national character" treats both race and nation as essentially natural forces that can be analyzed with methods drawn from the natural sciences. Understanding the "nation" as akin to the "race" led the utilitarian theorists of national character to attempt to justify moral equality on the basis of natural equality, a project with inherently elitist and anti-democratic implications since it implied the possibility that a natural aristocracy could legitimately rule over a naturally inferior minority. Through its influence on the eugenics movement, this was English liberalism's contribution to organicist nationalism. It also led Joseph Conrad to wonder about the compatibility of the liberal "national idea" with imperialism, a problem he would address in his *Heart of Darkness*.

LITERARY FORM AND THE CRISIS OF LIBERALISM

The liberal compromise between character and will attempted by Mill began to collapse, then, in the last decades of the nineteenth century, partly as a result of the rise of scientific theories of society and the attempt to adapt concepts from a political philosophy that belonged to a teleological theory of nature to newer scientific models based solely on efficient cause. When "will" and "character" each claimed absolute priority in the definition of the nation, both "will" and "character" lost their usefulness as political concepts within the liberal framework and became unabashedly metaphysical principles. This intervention of metaphysical concepts in political thought led to the destruction of the liberal nationalist compromise. Will became a "spiritual principle" and character an inevitable product of the interaction of circumstances with "the laws of mind" largely as a result of a shift in discourse on the nation (and on politics more generally), first from "political" causes of nationality to social and cultural ones and later to "race and descent." When the idea that "all men are brothers" came to seem susceptible to scientific proof or falsification, it ceased to provide a convincing motive for political action. Both the discourse of national character and the discourse of national will attempted to guarantee the justice of the relationship among citizens as free and equal by appeals to the idea of the nation, which acted as a sort of metaphysical guarantee – of the equality of all Frenchmen for the discourse of national will and of the principle of English liberty for the discourse of national character. Such metaphysical appeals to the nation-state invited, however, counterattacks that claimed that people were not really equal or really free except inasmuch as their full membership in the nation made them so. Thus in the Dreyfus affair, the Jews appeared to Barrès's nationalists not to be really equal to other Frenchmen. This was what Arendt called the "perversion of equality from a political to a social concept." In the liberal justifications of imperialism, liberty appeared not as a political right of the English constitution but as a natural characteristic of Englishmen, and this justified not only denying liberty to non-Englishmen but eventually also the eugenic theory that one could breed a better English national character. The history of these discourses suggests that metaphysical guarantees of the principles of liberty and equality are not only logically problematic but ultimately also detrimental to liberty and equality themselves. The case of liberal nationalism suggests that the willingness to accept the notion that one's fellow-citizens are free and equal moral persons has depended on assumed agreement that they become so by virtue of being full members of one's own nation-state. This seems to be the nature of what Yael Tamir has called the "magic pronoun 'my'": a sense that something more than being merely human must unite people before they will accept that their relations among each other should be ruled by the requirements of liberal justice.[83]

Liberal conceptions of justice seem to assume a society of free and equal persons that is in important respects homogeneous. Notions of race change, of course, and – as an eloquent article of 1966 by Samuel Beer maintains – the hope of liberals who continue to embrace the national idea must be that it can overcome distinctions of race.[84] Strangely enough, however, there is an objection to liberal nationalism that in a sense runs deeper than race, and that objection has to do with what the twentieth century understands as "culture." As the comparison of Gellner's definition of nationality with John Stuart Mill's shows, the notion of "culture" plays something very like the role in contemporary thought that "character" did in nineteenth-century English liberalism. It seems inevitable that any liberal defense of the nation-state will cite the sense people have of sharing a culture with others as a central reason for the current organization of humanity into nation-states. This claim is not meaningless, for politics depends on communication and the attempt to arrive at a set of sufficiently shared values to allow the cooperative functioning of society. Without a shared culture, and in particular a shared language, it is very difficult to have a functioning liberal-democratic state. However, the idea that political organizations should foster a particular culture or cultures tends to encourage two extremes of political thought, cultural imperialism and cultural relativism. Contemporary forms of liberalism tend to rely on a notion familiar to nineteenth-century liberal nationalism, namely that one can only recognize as a truly free and equal moral subject a person with whom one shares values, or, at the very least, with whom one can communicate in one's own language. The problem of the liberal nation-state is precisely that, whereas a separation of church and state or a "color-blind" state is at least conceivable, it is impossible to imagine a separation of state and culture. The next three chapters will show how this sense of the weight of "culture" arises largely from experiences of life in a modern liberal nation-state that were of central concern to the modernists themselves. Arendt uses a number of references to Proust and Conrad as evidence for her analysis of the "decline of the nation-state," which I have summarized and amplified in this chapter. As I will argue in the following chapters, not only the content of their works but also their struggle with formal issues in the history of the novel involved a reconsideration of the status of the nation-state in the context of its crisis from the 1890s to the First World War.

The crucial weakness of both character and will nationalists was to ignore the political significance of the separateness of persons, to assume a unified national character or the possibility of achieving a unified national will that would make all citizens into a single unit. Thus, in the name of encouraging solidarity among individuals, the liberal nationalists of the nineteenth century attempted to overcome the conflictual nature of life in modern society by appeal to a larger whole – whether the race, the national culture, or the popular will. When this effort to reconcile the irreconcilable and to "displace" politics by appeal to the nation became dominant in liberal discourses – as in Renan's concept of the national will as a "daily plebiscite" or Leslie Stephen's idea of moral behavior as that which is useful to the race – it gave way to the anti-liberal rhetoric of organic nationalists and racial theorists and paved the road for the radical dissociation of liberalism and nationalism in the twentieth century. In these cases, the search to reconcile the ethical and the sociological perspectives on individual life – to overcome the animating conflict of modern, individualist society – though deeply seated in liberalism's conceptions of fraternity and justice, ultimately could be accomplished only by abandoning liberal principles and opening the way to totalitarian temptations.

For the first generation of modernist novelists, the conflict between ethics and sociology had come to seem so irreconcilable, and yet the need to overcome that conflict seemed so evident, that the conventions of the nineteenth-century novel appeared incapable of responding to the challenge. The development of literary modernism involved an attempt to refigure this conflict and to explain the possible role of the idea of the nation in overcoming it. In the context of this sense of the radical incompatibility of the roles of subject and object of historical processes, Walter Benjamin's statement about the novel in general, inspired by Lukács, comes to seem a specifically modernist theory of what the novel must do: "To write a novel means to carry the incommensurable to extremes in the representation of human life."[85] The modernists sought to carry the incommensurable to extremes, and then to make those extremes commensurate. The nation was the social unit in which this making commensurate of the incommensurable, this bridging of ethics and sociology, could move from literary form to social reality.

CHAPTER THREE

"His sympathies were in the right place": Conrad and the discourse of national character

The Englishman who tells the story of *Heart of Darkness*, and the four who listen to it, do not consider it a particularly English story. The "primary" narrator does not repeat for it what he has already said of another of Marlow's tales: "This could have occurred nowhere but in England, where men and sea interpenetrate . . ."[1] The action of *Heart of Darkness* takes place in the "centre of a continent" – Africa – and its main actors are employees of a European company – "a Continental concern."[2] Marlow comments that "all Europe contributed to the making of Kurtz," the novel's central figure, and most later critics have followed Marlow's lead in considering Kurtz's story one of European, not English, depravities (p. 50). Yet England has a special role to play in this story about the relations between Europe and Africa. Eloise Knapp Hay and Benita Parry have shown that England does not remain immune to criticism in *Heart of Darkness*.[3] It symbolizes the ideal of efficient, liberal imperialism worshipped by Kurtz's "gang of virtue" and the sense of common purpose shared by the friends aboard the *Nellie*. The brooding gloom of Africa hovers over England too. Marlow tells his story in an effort to stave off this darkness by explaining his own behavior in Africa in ethical terms. Yet his inability to give a rational account of his attachment to Kurtz points to the power that Kurtz's many appeals to England and Englishness have over Marlow. It suggests that Marlow's ethical framework fails to account adequately for a mysterious "hidden something," the power of national character that works on Marlow without his realizing it.

The contemporary crisis of liberal nationalism plays itself out in Marlow's problematic attempts to justify his actions in the Congo and especially his loyalty to Mr. Kurtz. Both Marlow and Conrad seem eager to defend the idea of England, which they associate with the values of a liberal, civilized society: "efficiency," "liberty," "sincerity of feeling," "humanity, decency, and justice."[4] Marlow is careful to distinguish the efficient and humane English, who rule by law and get "some real work" done in their possessions, from the other European imperialists, who plunder their dependencies purely for their own material advantage while treating all the natives indiscriminately as "enemies" and "criminals" (pp. 13, 20). Yet, in the 1890s, the values of English liberalism were under attack on two fronts. On the one hand, deterministic theories of national character, such as that hinted at by the Company Doctor, suggested that the values Conrad and Marlow associated with the "idea" of England were the result not of shared devotion to common beliefs (of what we today would call "English culture") but of essential physical differences among the various nationalities, of the brute fact of "Englishness." On the other hand, the growth of universalistic, democratic, and socialist politics, represented in the novel by Kurtz, threatened to level the cultural differences, the specifically English institutions and specifically English character, that Victorian liberals had prized. The Rights of Man threatened to efface the Rights of Englishmen. Within liberal politics, the two traditional strands, Whig and Radical, had re-emerged in the conflict between Unionists and supporters of Irish Home Rule in the 1880s. Among political theorists, the old Whiggish defense of specifically English liberties was to give way, on the one hand, to the crasser forms of social Darwinism, and, on the other, to the New Liberalism with its internationalist aspirations. *Heart of Darkness* enacts the conflict within English liberalism at the turn of the century between a traditional Whig defense of liberal values as reflections of the English national character not necessarily suitable for other nations and a growing aspiration toward a universalistic, international democracy. Conrad shows the impasse that English liberal nationalism has reached as it confronts the results of imperialism and social Darwinism. Marlow's perplexity suggests that English liberalism cannot offer an adequate account of the role of cultural differences in shaping political beliefs. Marlow senses the threat posed to his Victorian English liberal values, his ethos, by both the Company's vulgar materialism and Kurtz's unworldly idealism.[5] He rejects the Doctor's biological theory of national character, but he cannot hold out for long against Kurtz's appeals to "moral ideas," laden as they are with claims on Marlow's English sympathies. In the Congo, he faces a "choice of nightmares," and he chooses Kurtz, although he cannot say why.

Kurtz offers Marlow a vision of internationalist politics that appeals, strangely enough, to Marlow's specifically English values. The text alludes to the symbolic importance of England in motivating many elements of Kurtz's savage enterprise. Kurtz, having been "educated partly in England," claims to admire English values: "as he was good enough to say himself – his sympathies were in the right place" (p. 50). Indeed, Marlow tells his listeners, the "wraith" of Kurtz chooses to relate his story to Marlow "because it could speak English to me." "Sympathy" with the enlightened, English mode of imperialism marks Kurtz and his associates off from the Company's other employees, making them part of "the new gang – the gang of virtue," who see themselves, according to the brickmaker, as emissaries "of pity, and science, and progress, and devil knows what else" (p. 28). Whereas most of the other employees come from various countries in continental Europe, Kurtz and his two followers with non-African blood have strong biological or emotional connections to England: Kurtz himself has a "half-English" mother and his followers are "an English half-caste clerk" and a Russian who has "served some time in English ships" (pp. 50, 34, 54). None of these Kurtzians, however, is purely English. They are all products of biological or intellectual miscegenation: quarter-English, half-English, or merely anglophile. They suggest Englishness gone wrong, a misinterpretation of liberal English values. It is perhaps precisely Kurtz's imperfect Englishness that makes him such an extremist in the application of the putatively English values of pity, science, progress, and virtue.

Marlow himself appears to be the Company's first purely English employee. The Company Doctor, who measures Marlow's cranium "in the interests of science" before he leaves for Africa and asks him in French whether there has ever been any madness in his family, excuses himself: "Pardon my questions, but you are the first Englishman coming under my observation" (p. 15). Marlow's Englishness plays an important part in his Congo experience, differentiating him from all the other Company employees, linking him to his listeners on the *Nellie*, and eventually serving as the basis of an intimate connection between him and Kurtz. Kurtz and his admirer the Russian Harlequin continually address Marlow with attention to his nationality, interpellating him as an Englishman. Marlow appears only half-aware of the extent to which his Englishness defines him for those he meets. He inhabits the identity of a representative Englishman uneasily, eager to appear instead as a cosmopolitan cynic. He assures the Company Doctor, who hints that nationality may determine character, that he is "not in the least typical" of his countrymen: "If I were . . . I wouldn't be talking like this with you" (p. 15). The Doctor responds: "what you say is rather profound, and probably erroneous" (p. 15).

The problem posed by the Company Doctor will come back to haunt Marlow's narration. For Marlow finds himself unable to describe his motives for his own actions in Africa. He continually refers to the inexplicability of his attachment to Kurtz: "It is strange how I accepted this unforeseen partnership, this choice of nightmares forced upon me in the tenebrous land invaded by these mean and greedy phantoms" (p. 67). He can never quite adequately explain why he chooses Kurtz's nightmare over the Company's, why he admits to being Kurtz's "friend," or why he is willing to be considered a member of the "party of 'unsound method'" (p. 67). Yet this choice is the central ethical problem of the story's climactic final section. One force acts on Marlow, apparently without his realizing it. Throughout the story, and especially in the second installment (in which Marlow recounts his meeting with Kurtz), appeals to his nationality gradually draw Marlow into the "gang of virtue." Marlow's choice of nightmares shows the importance to him not only of Kurtz's claim to represent liberal, English values, but also of the more basic appeals to "partnership," "brotherhood," "friendship," and "sympathy" made by Kurtz and his ally the Russian Harlequin, always on the basis of their shared association with things English. Marlow never says that Kurtz's connection to England forms one of his attractions, makes him, in the words of *Lord Jim*, "one of us." Yet the many references to Marlow's Englishness provide an explanation of the choice of Kurtz over the Company for which Marlow himself cannot account. Whenever, in his nightmarish progression up the Congo, something reminds him of England, Marlow discovers a moment of truth or "reality" among the many lies and illusions of the Company. Whatever appeals to his basic humanity or to his English nationality, whatever is "meaningful," "natural," or "true," draws Marlow to Kurtz's side in the inexplicable "choice of nightmares."

Ever more frequent allusions to England and Englishness in the story's second installment suggest that Marlow has failed to see how his very Englishness is drawing him deeper into Kurtzian depravity. The references to England create a structural pattern of irony, in which Marlow's subjective perceptions – his belief in the universal validity of English values – fail to match his objective situation – the contingency and perhaps even hypocrisy on which these values depend. Marlow persistently sees more than the "typical" Englishman would see, but then turns out to be more typically English in his blindnesses than he would have expected. Joyce's Stephen Dedalus, a narrator-hero, had the ambition to embody the conscience of his race. Marlow, more diffident, expects to stand slightly apart from his race, but his Polish creator uses the Marlow stories to investigate those features of national belonging that Marlow himself fails to apprehend. The distance between Conrad and his narrator-hero is more evident than that between Joyce and Stephen. Conrad's work, less formally audacious, nonetheless uses the ambiguous status of the narrator or storyteller as a basis for examining the shaping function of national culture in the life of an individual. Marlow's dual role as participant in and teller of his story makes his own account of the motivations of his "choice of nightmares" suspect. Marlow tells his story to four English friends, and its "spokenness" is crucial, for it suggests the process by which Marlow attempts to make sense of what he has done. He seems to believe that "a man's character is his fate" (*"ethos anthropoi daimon"*),[6] and he tends to explain the events of his story in "ethical" terms, from the perspective of a participant.[7] He accounts for the various actions he describes by reference to the unique moral characteristics of the actors involved, and particularly to their possession or lack of "restraint," "innate strength," or "character." Of course, Marlow makes many remarks of a sociological or anthropological nature on the Company, its employees, and the Africans. Yet he seems unable to grasp completely the ways in which ineffable cultural forces have determined his own character (his *ethos*). He attempts to account to himself for Mr. Kurtz's actions and his own primarily on the grounds of morality and free will. He is eager to see the "restraint" exercised by the cannibals on board his steamer in the Congo as akin to the restraint of civilized Englishmen. He wants to believe that a good character can be measured by universally applicable standards, and thus that *ethos* is itself a universal measure rather than merely a product of accident.

Ironically enough, it is by an appeal to "Englishness" that Kurtz attempts to convince Marlow of the validity of Kurtz's own internationalist goals. Whereas Kurtz and Marlow are both attracted by the possibility of an international politics based on virtue and efficiency, Conrad seems to suggest that the very values they affirm are so dependent on a particular cultural framework as to be unsuitable for export. Perhaps partly because of his mixed parentage, Kurtz has carried his putatively English values to un-English extremes. It is Marlow's very susceptibility to the claims of "virtue," conditioned by his own Englishness, that makes him capable of being swayed by Kurtz's universalist appeal. What Kurtz presents as universally valid ideals – pity, science, progress – turn out to be culturally specific. Conrad presents the reader with the material for a "sociological" perspective on Marlow's and Kurtz's actions in which this paradox becomes apparent. The novel is a written document that contains Marlow's spoken story in crystallized form as well as the primary narrator's observations of Marlow. This written document, by showing Marlow from the outside, suggests the influence on Marlow of apparently irrational cultural forces. In the framing of Marlow's narrative, the novel takes on its significance as the story of the national idea, for it is the primary narrator who at the beginning of the novel apotheosizes the Thames as the river that has "known and served all the men of whom the nation is proud" and at the end observes that "the tranquil waterway leading to the uttermost ends of the earth flowed sombre under an overcast sky – seemed to lead into the heart of an immense darkness" (pp. 8, 76). The written frame suggests the limits of Marlow's perspective, his inability to explain his own actions. It shows how forces beyond his control shape his action and his character: "I did not betray Mr. Kurtz – it was ordered I should never betray him – it was written I should be loyal to the nightmare of my choice" (p. 64). Yet, unlike many realist novels of the nineteenth century, *Heart of Darkness* neither presents an omniscient narrator who can give a purely "objective" account of Marlow's character nor allows Marlow to achieve the final sort of maturity that would make all his mistakes and uncertainties clear to him. At the end of the novel, recounting his lie to the Intended, Marlow will be just as baffled about his own motives as he was when he set out to tell the story. No position outside culture is afforded the readers. Indeed, the novel calls attention to the fact that it is written in English and that it tells the story of five Englishmen discussing far-off events. At key moments of the story, Marlow points out that he speaks with most of the Company's employees in French. Marlow must make sense in English terms of what seems a very foreign story.

Occasionally, Marlow's "ethical" discourse breaks down and he becomes aware of the possibility of a sociological explanation of his actions. One such moment occurs after he proclaims his faith in the idea that redeems the conquest of the earth: "What redeems it is the idea only. An idea at the back of it, not a sentimental pretence but an idea; and an unselfish belief in the idea – something you can set up, and bow down before, and offer a sacrifice to . . ." (p. 10). After the ellipsis, the primary narrator announces, "He [Marlow] broke off." Here, Marlow glimpses the possibility that the idea he reveres may appear to his listeners as a type of cultural fetish, a product made by humans' own activities but worshipped by them as a god. He therefore breaks off uneasily, just as later in the story he will frequently cut short his narration while he attempts to think through the ethical consequences of his own or Kurtz's actions: "It is impossible to convey the life-sensation of any given epoch of one's existence – that which makes its truth, its meaning – its subtle and penetrating essence. It is impossible. We live, as we dream – alone . . ." (p. 30). Marlow's idiosyncratic mode of narration – his heavy foreshadowing and impressionistic accounts of his perceptions – calls attention to the possible inadequacy of his ethical explanation of events. It signals the development of a distinctively modern consciousness of the forces through which culture shapes character and of the inevitable lack of an Archimedean point from which to make either ethical or sociological judgments.[8] Marlow's perplexity results in part from a tension within his own liberal nationalism. Whereas he wishes to assert the universal validity of the values he embraces and associates with England, he also suspects that these values merely seem universal from a particular, idiosyncratic world-view, which is itself the product of historical accident. Marlow uneasily occupies the dual position of participant in and observer of English ideology.

It is the indeterminacy of Marlow's motivations that makes the text a crucial founding example of literary modernism. Yet, the text suggests that one of the most significant of the forces through which culture molds character is the mysterious power of nationality, that "hidden something" that works almost unnoticeably on Marlow and that he can never fully articulate.[9] The contemporary crisis of liberal nationalism plays itself out in Marlow's problematic attempts to justify his actions in the Congo and especially his loyalty to Mr. Kurtz. Scholars of Conrad's politics have developed two opposing accounts of his world-view: the "organicist-nationalist" and the "liberal-individualist." Avrom Fleishman, for example, attributes to Conrad three "guiding principles": "organic community, the work ethic, and the critique of individualism."[10] Yet Ian Watt rightly objects that Conrad held to "basic social attitudes which, though certainly not democratic, were in many ways deeply egalitarian and individualist."[11] Conrad himself expressed sympathy with liberal politics, asserting for example that his mind "was fed on ideas, not of revolt but of liberalism of a perfectly disinterested kind, and on severe moral lessons of national misfortune."[12] He claimed in particular that England and the English system of government were uniquely well suited to the development of individual liberties. Both Marlow and Conrad seem eager to defend the idea of England, which they associate with the values of a liberal, civilized society. The fact that Conrad's primary political commitments were to a form of liberal individualism and to nationalism has been one source of the extended debates over Conrad's politics, largely because critics in the late twentieth century tend to see liberalism and nationalism as conflicting systems of belief. However, a strong nationalistic current within English liberalism, from Edmund Burke to Leslie Stephen, had venerated English institutions as especially suited to the development of liberty and had even associated the unique character of English institutions with the unique character of English people. Conrad spoke the language of this English liberal nationalism, treating faith in the nation-state as the necessary corollary of a belief in the fundamentally egoistic and individualistic character of human nature.

CONRAD'S "IDÉE NATIONALE" AND ENGLISH LIBERAL NATIONALISM

Conrad expressed many of the concerns of English liberal nationalists in a letter that he wrote to his friend R. B. Cunninghame Graham, the socialist and Scottish nationalist, the day after sending his publishers the manuscript of the final two installments of *Heart of Darkness*.[13] In this letter, Conrad thanks Cunninghame Graham for his compliments on the first installment of *Heart of Darkness*, but warns him that in the remainder of the novel, the "note struck" may no longer "chime in with [his] convictions." Critics generally agree that whereas Cunninghame Graham admired the anti-imperialist tone of the first installment, Conrad thought him less likely to endorse the dark vision of human nature portrayed in Kurtz. Conrad also warns his friend that "the idea [in the rest of the book] is so wrapped up in secondary notions that You – even You! – may miss it." In the remainder of the letter, switching from English to French, Conrad attacks his friend's faith in social democracy, arguing that the "idée nationale" is preferable to the "idée démocratique" as the basis for a political system, rejecting fraternity and internationalism, and defending egoism and nationalism.

Conrad's critics have studied the letter, but have failed to make the connection between Conrad's comments on the novel he was just completing and the remainder of the letter, in which Conrad draws attention to the centrality of the "national idea," an "idea without a future," to his political world-view. He calls the democratic idea "a very beautiful phantom" in the service of "the shades of an eloquence that is dead precisely because it has no body." On the other hand, he defends the national idea by suggesting that it at least is "a definite principle." He writes in a tragic vein, with the sense that the "idée nationale" is under attack, threatened perhaps by the forces of history. Conrad's statement of faith in the national idea seems to echo Marlow's. Conrad's concern for the health of the national idea results in part from his fear that social-democratic movements in Poland will undermine the nationalist movement, for which his parents had suffered. (The final partition of 1795 had removed Poland as a sovereign state from the map, and Conrad's father was imprisoned for his part in the Polish nationalist movement. Conrad's given name, Konrad, which he chose as his English surname, was that of a legendary Polish national hero. His ambivalence about having left Poland remained a source of concern for the rest of his life.) Yet the letter also makes sense in an English context. Upon being naturalized as an Englishman, Conrad transferred much of his love of country to England, of which he considered himself a "spoiled adopted child."[14] This letter points to a crucial justification of the "national idea" that Conrad shared with the English liberal tradition: the importance of the nation-state as a source of solidarity that could channel the fundamentally egoistic drives of individuals into the development of civil society. Throughout this letter, Conrad draws on a recurrent trope in English political thought that can be traced back, as Avrom Fleishman has noted, at least to Edmund Burke's response to the French Revolution, namely the danger that democratic ideals of international fraternity will undermine the true source of solidarity in the shared national character.[15] He argues, however, not (as Fleishman suggests) against individualism but in favor of nationalism as a form of super-individualism, which appeals to the egoistic impulses essential to human nature. Conrad's defense of the "idée nationale" echoes many of Marlow's comments on social and political matters in *Heart of Darkness*, and the echoes link them both to the English liberal tradition and to the turning-point at which it had arrived by the 1890s.

Ultimately, Conrad's letter to Cunninghame Graham shows that, as he was finishing *Heart of Darkness*, Conrad was attempting to come to terms with the potential conflict between liberalism and nationalism. Throughout the nineteenth century, the two forces had gone hand in hand, as liberal movements sought to replace multinational empires within Europe with self-governing nation-states. Conrad still wants to hold to the old faith in the national bond as the source of "sympathies" that can bind together free and equal individuals within an increasingly competitive and atomized liberal society. Yet, tendencies within both liberalism and nationalism threatened to destroy this faith. In particular, the principle of nationality could not be extended outside of Europe without threatening the interests of European imperialists. The optimistic, liberal idea that a world of nation-states could embody the principles of freedom, equality, and justice had motivated the founding of the Congo free state. Thus, the explorer Henry Stanley had written,

On the 14th of August, 1879, I arrived at the mouth of this river [the Congo] to ascend it, with the novel mission of sowing along its banks civilised settlements, to peacefully conquer and subdue it, to remould it in harmony with modern ideas into National States, within whose limits the European merchant shall go hand in hand with the dark African trader, and justice and law and order shall prevail, and murder and lawlessness and cruel barter of slaves shall for ever cease.[16]

The nation-state was to serve the liberal goals of rule by law and peaceful competition among individuals. Mid-Victorian liberals, such as John Stuart Mill, defended imperialism as a stage on the road to representative government and a world of liberal nation-states. The most evident political theme of *Heart of Darkness* is, of course, the utter failure of the Congo Free State to live up to this propaganda. Conrad's loss of faith in the liberal idea of the nation resulted in part from this failure. In the wake of Darwinism and the disillusionments of the scramble for Africa, however, nationalism and liberalism came increasingly to appear as opposed principles, with nationalists embracing theories of racial determinism and liberals looking toward a future of universal government.

Conrad invokes a "possessive individualist" psychology in the English empiricist vein when he writes in the letter that "Man is a wicked animal. His wickedness must be organized." By reference to Cain and Abel ("that's your true fraternity"), he suggests that the state of nature was no paradise. He goes on to argue that "it is egoism that preserves everything – absolutely everything – everything we hate and everything we love," showing a Hobbesian understanding of the motivation for the formation of civil society in self-defense, or what might be called unenlightened self-interest. In his more conservative accounts of the sources of human solidarity, such as *Typhoon* and *Nigger of the "Narcissus,"* Conrad seems to echo Hobbes's worship of authority's ability to check instinctive human selfishness and laziness. However, Conrad's appeals to "self-sacrifice," "abnegation," and "fidelity" point to a more positive conception of human nature and society. For Conrad, the "national sentiment" can cultivate these qualities by encouraging solidarity among individuals. (On the other hand, the "idée démocratique," by falsely assuming the basic goodness of all people, and by competing with the "idée nationale," threatens social revolution and the destruction of these noble values.) This belief corresponds to the positive side of the English liberal tradition's conception of the nation-state. Recent historiography has called into question the notion that Victorian liberalism subscribed to the ideal of *homo economicus*.[17] Far from endorsing the cash nexus as the sole desirable relationship among people, many late Victorian liberals turned to the shared sense of nationhood as a source of forms of sociability that would mitigate the potentially anti-social effects of an economic and political system based on competition. They described such forms of sociability with words like "altruism," "sympathy," "character," "culture," and "civilization."[18] Like Burke and his many Victorian admirers, Conrad rejects the attempt to create a political system based purely on rationality and equality but suggests that in the context of a cohesive civil society, inspired by the idea of the nation, people are capable of overcoming their more brutish instincts and creating a meaningful social order.

Marlow understands his own story in *Heart of Darkness* in terms of a similar antithesis between the evil of which people are capable in a state of nature and the more noble sentiments and actions that society and the devotion to an idea can develop in them. Like Conrad, he seems to speak in favor of a Hobbesian, individualist interpretation of human nature when he comments to his listeners:

You can't understand? How could you – with solid pavement under your feet, surrounded by kind neighbours ready to cheer you or to fall on you, stepping delicately between the butcher and the policeman, in the holy terror of scandal and gallows and lunatic asylums – how can you imagine what particular region of the first ages a man's untrammelled feet may lead him into by the way of solitude – utter solitude without a policeman – by the way of silence – utter silence, where no warning voice of a kind neighbour can be heard whispering of public opinion. (pp. 49–50)

The trappings of civil society and the state – neighbors, public opinion, and especially the legal and penal systems – contain people's fundamentally egoistic and hostile energies and channel them into productive pursuits. Yet Marlow in *Heart of Darkness*, like Conrad in the letter to Cunninghame Graham, also offers a more positive conception of human nature and of society. After his comments about the policeman and the butcher, Marlow goes on to say that

These little things [the social institutions he has just mentioned] make all the great difference. When they are gone you must fall back upon your own innate strength, upon your own capacity for faithfulness . . . And there, don't you see, your strength comes in, . . . your power of devotion not to yourself but to an obscure, back-breaking business. (p. 50)

Innate strength, faithfulness, and devotion play little role in Hobbes's political theory. They correspond to the values that Conrad expects the national sentiment to implant in the individual. These are also the values that Victorian liberal nationalism associated with the power of institutions to shape "national character."

Conrad alludes in the letter to his devotion to "an absolutely lost cause – an idea without a future." While he is referring in part specifically to the idea of Poland, he seems also to suspect that the idea of nationality in general is in danger of becoming outmoded. The two concerns that motivate Conrad's defense of the "national idea" – an individualist conception of human nature and an emphasis on the ways in which social institutions contained the potentially destructive impulses associated with individualism – became, in post-Darwinian England, the focus of a debate about the sources and nature of national character. Evolutionary thought encouraged many social thinkers to understand the characters of various peoples as resulting from the historical development of their cultures and institutions. These thinkers often expressed skepticism about the possibility of exporting English institutions, such as rule by law and representative government, to other nations. Almost all English liberals and other writers on the subject agreed that the English had a propensity for liberty that other nations lacked. The main source of disagreement was the question of whether people of other nationalities, from the French to Indians and Africans, could eventually benefit from English institutions and customs or whether elements of their "characters" made them permanently unsuited for liberty.[19] Evolutionary thought had at first assisted liberals in making the case that even primitive cultures were capable of developing the character necessary for self-rule. Towards the end of the nineteenth century, however, the idea of "national character" began to harden in political discourse. Rather than referring to what the twentieth century has come to call "culture," "national character" increasingly meant what the twentieth century calls "race." Whereas Burke's primarily political conception of national character had emphasized the importance of English institutions, some of Burke's later admirers attributed the unique character of English liberty not to England's constitutional arrangements but to the physical constitution of Englishmen. Eventually, the claim that the English had a privileged national relationship with liberty became part of chauvinist propaganda, exemplified by the argument that British imperialism derived from the "desire of spreading through the habitable globe all the characteristics of Englishmen – their energy, their civilization, their religion, and their freedom."[20] Conrad's defense of England's conduct in the Boer War contains the distant echo of Burke's faith in "the rights of Englishmen": "That they [the Boers] are struggling in good faith for their independence cannot be doubted; but it is also a fact that they have no idea of liberty, which can only be found under the English flag all over the world."[21]

By the 1890s, the discourse of "national character" faced a crisis. The growing eugenicist movement treated character as strictly a result of biological heredity. Eugenics already had a strong following in England by the time that Karl Pearson argued, in 1901, that in England "the feckless and improvident . . . have the largest families . . . at the expense of the nation's future. . . . [We] cannot recruit the nation from its inferior stocks without deteriorating our national character."[22] The notion of a distinctive national character in such theories implied the opposite of liberalism. Rather than foster the natural, progressive development of character through liberal institutions, eugenicists proposed forms of social engineering that would ensure the reproduction of the "superior stock" among the English. Traditional individualist and ethical notions of behavior were irrelevant to such projects. Some important, liberal Darwinists, such as T. H. Huxley, objected to such uses of Darwinism, recognizing that the so-called "evolution of society" was "a process of an essentially different character" from that of the "evolution of species."[23] In his lecture "Evolution and Ethics" (1893), Huxley argued that the ethical standards by which people in society decide how to act are and should be diametrically opposed to the processes by which the fittest survive in the state of nature, and that the development of human societies could no more be understood as the result of natural selection than could the growth of a highly cultivated garden.[24] From the perspective of the evolutionary social sciences, however, such an "ethical" stance could not claim scientific validity. Rather, it appeared to be a last-ditch effort to maintain the worn-out categories of liberal thought against the onslaught of a more rational biological determinism that seemed to hold the true key to history. Because of the continuing strength of positivism, social theory in late Victorian England generally did not confront the problems of cultural relativism and pluralism or the intellectual limitations of biological determinism that concerned contemporary continental thinkers such as Durkheim and Weber.[25] As a result, the discourse of "national character" tended to fade into a strict determinism with distinctly pro-imperialist and authoritarian overtones. Meanwhile, on the political left, democrats and Fabian socialists generally maintained their

faith in the rationality of human nature and paid relatively little attention to the problems of cultural difference and historicism associated
with the notion of "national character" and its Burkean heritage. Both
Conrad and Marlow are stuck between the two extremes of racial determinism and an unbounded faith in the universality of human nature.
Conrad offers an almost allegorical account of the conflict between the
two perspectives on human nature. What makes Conrad such a complex
figure, however, is that he endorses neither racial determinism nor internationalist democracy, but presents liberal values as the fragile products
of historical accident that seem destined to develop successfully only in
a particular cultural context.

KURTZ AND THE PHANTOM OF INTERNATIONAL DEMOCRACY

Seen as, in part, the story of the "national idea," *Heart of Darkness* participates in contemporary debates about "national character" and the
capacity of particular cultures for "civilization" and "progress." One
target of Conrad's critique, as Ian Watt has shown, is the extreme optimism of those advocates of progress, like Kurtz, who maintain a sort of
mid-Victorian faith in the ultimate triumph of civilized values.[26] When
Conrad rejects the "idée démocratique" as "un très beau phantôme"
and prefers the "idée nationale," which he considers a "principe défini,"
he resembles Burke, first of all in his emphasis on the nation as an idea
that consecrates the social bond, making it more than a simple contract.
Fleishman rightly observes the basic similarity of Conrad's and Burke's
views of society as what Conrad elsewhere calls a "common conservative principle."[27] Victorian social thought tended to a certain skepticism
of claims for political rights on the basis of universalistic *a priori* theories
of human nature. Burke had argued that the English constitution was "a
vestment, which accommodates itself to the body" of the nation.[28]
Conrad's complaint that the eloquence that serves social democracy is
dead "precisely because it has no body" contains an echo of Burke's
skepticism of the "rights of man." For Conrad, as for Burke, the concrete, bodily reality of the nation-state could foster civilization, including individual liberties, whereas a revolutionary and democratic
conception of society depended on the empty abstractions of a disembodied ideal. Both Burke and Conrad conceive of the embodied nation,
rather than ghostly international fraternity and equality, as the source of
social order. Both rejected the most optimistic conclusions of the French
Enlightenment. Fleishman has represented the echoes of Burke in

Conrad's political writings as aligning Conrad with both the left- and right-wing critics of Victorian liberalism.[29] In Conrad's case, however, these echoes do not suggest a disdain for liberal individualism so much as a typical late Victorian sense of the importance of having a cohesive civil society in which individualism can attain its full positive potential. Nationalism appears as a corollary of liberalism, not an alternative to it.

Heart of Darkness describes a similar polarity between what Conrad, in the letter, calls "the shades of a dead eloquence" (social democracy) and a "definite principle" (the nation). Kurtz exemplifies the internationalist attitude that Conrad criticized in Cunninghame Graham and his social-democratic friends. His politics are not specifically social-democratic, but he has the character of a demagogue, as his colleague's comment to Marlow shows: "The visitor informed me that Kurtz's proper sphere ought to have been politics 'on the popular side . . . He would have been a splendid leader of an extreme party . . . Any party . . . He was an – an – extremist'" (p. 71). Kurtz serves "the shades of a dead eloquence" – his own. His vision of imperialism in the service of civilization has made him the favorite of the "International Society for the Suppression of Savage Customs." In the first lines of his report for this Society, Kurtz has written that "we whites . . . 'must necessarily appear to them [savages] in the nature of supernatural beings. . . . By the simple exercise of our will we can exert a power for good practically unbounded'" (p. 51). Kurtz echoes the most optimistic conclusions of the Enlightenment, such as Rousseau's claim that "he who could do anything would never do evil."[30] This, says Marlow, "was the unbounded power of eloquence – of words – of burning noble words" (p. 50). Yet, the optimism of Kurtz's opening paragraph seems to lead inexorably to the insanity of his postscript to the report: "Exterminate all the brutes!" (p. 51). In his letter, Conrad uses a similar phrase to describe the position of the extreme anarchists: "Je souhaite l'extermination générale" ["I hope for general extermination"]. Conrad respects this statement because it is just, or perhaps simply accurate ("juste"), and straightforward ("clair"). His respect for the extreme anarchist resembles Marlow's for Kurtz: "he had summed up, he had judged."

Conrad implies, in a confused way in the letter, but more clearly in *Heart of Darkness*, that Kurtz's belief in international fraternity and the basically good nature of all people leads logically in the end to hatred of everyone and desire for their destruction. What connects the two positions is the failure to admit the involvement of one's own ego, or in political terms, one's interests. By claiming to represent perfect virtue,

Conrad suggests, people wind up justifying their own most savage lusts for power and blood as the emanation of idealism and rationality ("We make compromises with words"). Kurtz's eventual savagery, then, is a natural extension of his internationalism and optimism, just as (a Burkean might argue) the Reign of Terror is a natural extension of the Revolution. Kurtz has allowed himself to be worshipped at "certain midnight dances ending with unspeakable rites" (p. 50). As Marlow notes in describing his final struggle with Kurtz,

I had to deal with a being to whom I could not appeal in the name of anything high or low. I had even like the niggers to invoke him – himself – his own exalted and incredible degradation. There was nothing above or below him – and I knew it. He had kicked himself loose of the earth. (p. 65)

By believing in himself and his rationality alone, by abandoning the body and the earth, by serving the shades of a dead eloquence, Kurtz has been led to a vision of himself as God,[31] and this is in effect the mistake made, in Conrad's view, by the social democrats. Conrad's defense of egoism as the basis of human society suggests that by recognizing the fact that selfish interests motivate our behavior, we can escape Kurtzian self-delusion.

If Conrad and Marlow are both skeptical of the optimism of the Enlightenment, neither embraces the opposite extreme within the Victorian debate over national character, namely the racial determinism that saw differences among various human societies as directly reflecting underlying biological differences among the races. The Company Doctor represents one pre-Darwinian variant of racial determinism, the polygenetic tradition that had produced such monuments of Victorian physical anthropology as Bernard Davis and Joseph Thurnam's *Crania Britannica* (1865).[32] He has a "little theory" that somehow correlates size of cranium, nationality, and ability to survive in Africa:

I always ask leave, in the interests of science, to measure the crania of those going out there . . . Ever any madness in your family? . . . It would be . . . interesting for science to watch the mental changes of individuals on the spot, but . . . [He breaks off.] I have a little theory which you Messieurs who go out there must help me to prove. This is my share in the advantages my country shall reap from the possession of such a magnificent dependency. The mere wealth I leave to others. Pardon my questions, but you are the first Englishman coming under my observation. (p. 15)

Marlow rejects the application of a physical, scientific theory of national character to his own case. The claim that merely physical characteristics differentiate the Englishman from other Europeans or Africans seems to

offend him because it does not leave room for the "idea." If this biological theory of national character were correct, Marlow senses, human
autonomy would be a sham, for each person would pursue his or her
own lusts without any enlightenment, driven on by material interest and
without any moral purpose. The Company's bureaucracy epitomizes
such a potential future world, in which the social bond that makes the
nation strong has been degraded to a pact among thieves for the distribution of the booty of imperialism. In a world dominated by a struggle
among the races, the strongest race would win, regardless of ideals. As
Marlow observes near the beginning of the novel, "[The Romans] were
conquerors, and for that you want only brute force – nothing to boast of,
when you have it, since your strength is just an accident arising from the
weakness of others" (p. 10). All conquests would result from a similar
accident if the Doctor were right in attributing national character simply
to biological difference.

Marlow particularly dislikes the use of such "scientific" methods on
himself. Yet the possibility the doctor suggests – that some fundamental
racial difference, correlated with biological inheritance, shapes the
actions of various national groups once they get to Africa – haunts
Marlow. On his trip up to the Central Station, Marlow makes "a speech
in English with gestures" to the sixty Africans under his command, and
when they continue to disobey him, he begins to doubt his own sanity and
remembers his conversation with the Company Doctor: "'It would be
interesting for science to watch the mental changes of individuals on the
spot.' I felt I was becoming scientifically interesting" (p. 24). Marlow's
admission that he himself could be scientifically interesting leaves open
the possibility that the actions of the various characters in *Heart of
Darkness* reflect such underlying racial differences. Yet Marlow rejects this
mode of explanation. Kurtz's idealism about human nature, even carried
to horrible extremes, seems more congenial to him than the crass materialism of the Company and its philosophical expression in the Doctor's
"little theory." Yet other factors, apparently not understood by Marlow
himself, seem to contribute to Marlow's choice, most notably a long series
of appeals to his nationality made by Kurtz and his associate the Russian
Harlequin. These factors also point to a different understanding of
human nature and politics than either the racialism of the Company
Doctor or the extreme historical optimism of Kurtz. For Conrad, cultural factors – speaking the same language, smoking the same tobacco,
shared attitudes to work – and the habits of mind associated with them
play a fundamental part in the make-up of the individual. The success of

a liberal political organization seems to depend, for Conrad, on the for-
tuitous combination of such ineffable cultural factors.

The novel's opening pages establish two competing versions of a historical explanation of the cultural differences among various human
societies, both inspired by the meeting of Marlow and his listeners
aboard the *Nellie* and each suggesting an alternative explanation of the
origins of noble sentiments in the idea of the nation. At first, Conrad
seems to be presenting a fairly conventional picture of the English
nation, or at least its adult, male, middle classes, as the embodiment of
liberal ideals. As Hunt Hawkins has pointed out, however, Conrad both
"makes and unmakes" the idea of Englishness in his works.[33] *Heart of
Darkness* presents a competition among differing conceptions of precisely
where English greatness lies. The only cohesive community that *Heart of
Darkness* offers as an alternative to Kurtz's disembodied dreams is the
friendship of the five men aboard the *Nellie*, the cruising yawl on which
Marlow tells the stories of "Youth" and *Heart of Darkness*. These stories
revolve around the nature of relationships among Englishmen aboard
merchant ships. The characters aboard Marlow's ship *Judea* in "Youth"
are "Liverpool hard cases," whereas the crew on the real ship *Palestine*,
on which Conrad based the *Judea*, included four non-Britons. (Conrad
had similarly anglicized and fictionalized the real-life crew of the
Narcissus in *The Nigger of the "Narcissus."*)[34] Conrad originally planned to
have the first three Marlow stories appear together in *"Youth" and Other
Stories*.[35] The volume as planned begins with the statement by the
primary narrator of "Youth":

> This could have occurred nowhere but in England, where men and sea inter-
> penetrate, so to speak – the sea entering into the life of most men, and the men
> knowing something or everything about the sea, in the way of amusement, of
> travel, or of bread-winning. (*Works*, XVI, p. 3)

What could have occurred nowhere else is the gathering of Marlow and
his four friends to share Marlow's story of his first command – the same
friends who later, aboard the *Nellie*, listen to Marlow's account of his
journey to the Congo. "We all began life in the merchant service," the
primary narrator of "Youth" observes. "Between the five of us there was
the strong bond of the sea." At the beginning of *Heart of Darkness*, he
comments again, "Between us there was as I have already said somewhere, the bond of the sea" (p. 7). This bond of the sea, forged in the
merchant service, and the narrator's comment that in England "men
and sea interpenetrate" suggest that the friendship of the five men has

about it something typically English – that their society is a microcosm of the English nation, the island that another Conradian narrator describes as "A great ship! . . . A ship mother of fleets and nations! The great flagship of the race; stronger than the storms! and anchored in the open sea."[36] On board the *Nellie*, just a few miles from the open sea, at the gateway from England to the rest of the world, Marlow and his four listeners seem to carry on this function of symbolizing the English nation in *Heart of Darkness*.

The primary narrator tells the first, unabashedly heroic version of this collective story. The Thames, "after ages of good service done to the race that peopled its banks," causes the five men on the *Nellie* to "evoke the great spirit of the past," a history of conquest and commerce that has, without any conscious plan on the part of men but as if by divine providence, spread around the world "spark[s] from the sacred fire." The primary narrator thinks of English history as running in an unabated upward movement from the Elizabethans to the Victorians, spurred on by commerce and conquest. Marlow offers an interpretation of English history slightly at odds with the primary narrator's. The process of civilization appears to him as a mere flash of light intervening between prolonged periods of darkness. Only after describing the times when Britons were savages and the wilderness exercised the "fascination of the abomination" on the first Roman conquerors does Marlow, as if embarrassed, distinguish himself and his English listeners from the Romans (and from the pre-Roman Britons as well): "Mind, none of us would feel exactly like this. What saves us is efficiency – the devotion to efficiency" (p. 10). Marlow goes on to utter his famous statement about the idea that redeems the conquest of the earth. The narrator's "great spirit of the past" transforms itself into Marlow's "idea," which differentiates the British from the Romans and from other conquerors but has, as it were, an intellectual rather than a spiritual reality.

The primary narrator views English history with reverence, and sees in it a quasi-divine "spirit of the past," uniting "all the men of whom the nation is proud." Marlow considers the conquest of the earth "not a pretty thing" and recognizes that before the Roman conquest the Britons too were "savages." Whereas the narrator sees in the national life a hallowed tradition at the root of England's ability to bear the light of civilization out to the rest of the world, Marlow seems uncomfortably aware that the idea is something closer to mere custom, a mental habit resulting from a series of more or less chance events that happens to have given the English a devotion to efficiency that other nations lack. Despite his inability to account for his own behavior from anything but an ethical standpoint, Marlow takes a somewhat more detached, sociological attitude to the nation than the primary narrator. We need the idea, he suggests, because in this age without idols we need something to worship, something that can redeem our otherwise selfish and meaningless acts. Whereas the primary narrator is a willing participant in English history who unselfconsciously records his observations on it, Marlow is an observer who wishes to take a skeptical, objective stance, but whose scientific credentials are undermined by his evident emotional need to participate in the national myth. Just as Marlow will later feel himself unaccountably drawn towards Kurtz, in these opening pages of the story he already feels his objectivity to be compromised by too close an identification with his subject.

Heart of Darkness has become one of the most famous examples of "the ambivalence of colonial discourse"[37] largely because, at the end of Marlow's story, the primary narrator comes to see the Thames as resembling the Congo. Such doublings occur frequently in Marlow's narrative, with actions or appearances in Africa mirroring those on board the *Nellie*, as when the primary narrator describes Marlow's "worn, hollow" face and Marlow, in turn, describes Kurtz as "hollow at the core" (pp. 48, 58). They contribute to the ironic representation of the English friends as more like Kurtz and his disciples in Africa than they realize. What does the map in the sepulchral city have to do with the map in Fleet Street? One crucial similarity between Marlow and Kurtz is their faith in the power of ideas to redeem even base actions. Even before Marlow relates Kurtz's appeals to his Englishness, he refers to the curiosity that the stories he has heard about Kurtz have provoked in him: "I wasn't very interested in [Kurtz]. No. Still, I was curious to see whether this man who had come out equipped with moral ideas of some sort would climb to the top after all and how he would set about his work when there" (p. 33). As Kurtz is being taken down the river near the end of the story, he protests, "I'll carry out my ideas yet" (p. 61). This devotion to ideas, and particularly to those picked up as part of his English education, distinguishes Kurtz from the Company's other employees and perhaps even makes his savagery possible. Burke had observed that "[We English,] in the cold sluggishness of our national character, instead of casting away all our old prejudices . . . cherish them to a very considerable degree, and, to take more shame to ourselves, we cherish them because they are prejudices."[38] Marlow's attraction to Kurtz suggests that one such English prejudice is devotion to universalistic ideas that are unsuitable for export.

MARLOW'S THEORY OF CHARACTER

Marlow's only partial submission to the primary narrator's providential account of English history corresponds to his general sense of the importance of accident or mere contingency in political affairs. His ethical stance towards the events of his story reflects his primary concern with the unique individual rather than the broader movements of history. He remarks near the end of his story, "Destiny. My destiny! Droll thing life is – that mysterious arrangement of merciless logic for a futile purpose" (p. 69). Marlow's attitude to the stories he tells is a bemused fatalism. This fatalism leads him to place enormous stress on the notion of character in his analysis of events. As an alternative to Kurtzian idealism about human nature, Marlow continually speaks of the importance of "character," "innate strength," and internal "restraint." He respects the accountant's "starched collars and got-up shirt-fronts" as "achievements of character," and these achievements seem to enable the accountant to maintain not only his appearance but also his integrity "in the great demoralisation of the land" (p. 21). Marlow is satisfied that his English listeners possess character and restraint, which they have learned as members of a developed civil society: "What saves us is efficiency – the devotion to efficiency" (p. 10). He is less certain, however, about which other groups possess the virtues necessary to the development of civilization. The lack of "external checks" in Africa puts a high premium on internal "restraint" (p. 25). Marlow is disturbed by Kurtz's lack of "restraint" and amazed to find the hired cannibals aboard his steamboat possessed of it. They exercise restraint by not eating their white masters, although they outnumber them thirty to five (pp. 42–43). Even the hollow Manager, whom Marlow despises, "would wish to preserve appearances. That was his restraint" (p. 43).

Marlow finds the qualities of character and restraint to be unevenly distributed among individuals, probably at birth ("innate"). Despite his reputation as a racist, however, he does not find any particular ethnic group to have a monopoly on "restraint" (although the English do well in his account). In fact, he frequently notes the common humanity of Africans and Europeans. He draws attention to the potentially disturbing possibility that "savage" customs originate in the same impulses as "civilized" ones, for example in his reference to "the tremor of far-off drums, sinking, swelling, a tremor vast, faint; a sound weird, appealing, suggestive, and wild – and perhaps with as profound a meaning as the sound of bells in a Christian country" (p. 23). Like many a Victorian anthropologist, Marlow has an abiding faith in the unity of human nature despite the diversity of its manifestations. In this respect, Marlow resembles others of Conrad's English heroes whose idealism blinds them to the effects of cultural differences, such as *Lord Jim*'s Jim and *Nostromo*'s Charles Gould. His experiences in the Congo temper this faith, but it never leaves him entirely and indeed it seems to motivate his attachment to Kurtz.

Just as Marlow's own musings on the savagery of pre-Roman Britain seem to call into question the fairly conventional nationalism and historical optimism of the primary narrator, Marlow's account of his "choice of nightmares" in the Congo will itself problematize even Marlow's more skeptical account of English culture. For, as it turns out, even the devotion to efficiency and the other saving graces of civilized life nearly desert Marlow in the Congo. Strangely enough, it is Marlow's very faith in civilization, progress, and especially the English way of doing things that seems to lead him to make what he himself calls his "strange" and "unforeseen" choice of nightmares. It is in the story's second installment that Marlow becomes irrationally attached to Kurtz, the man whose "moral ideas" had already made him curious in the first installment. Appeals to his nationality mark every stage of Marlow's recruitment to the "gang of virtue." Overhearing a conversation between the Manager and his uncle about Kurtz, Marlow learns of Kurtz's assistant, the "English half-caste clerk," whose "great prudence and pluck" in carrying out his mission Marlow admires, while the Manager and his uncle consider him a "scoundrel" (p. 34). Marlow soon heads up the river, with several of the Company's pilgrims. As he gets closer to Kurtz, Marlow, "travelling in the night of first ages," contemplates his distant kinship with the savages who dance on the shore (p. 37). He meets what he takes to be his first sign of a nearer kinsman when he comes across a hut recently inhabited by a white man, the Russian Harlequin – known to the Manager only as a trader who has intruded on the Company's protected interests. Marlow discovers the Harlequin's copy of

An Inquiry into some Points of seamanship by a man Towser, Towson – some such name – Master in His Majesty's Navy . . . The simple old sailor with his talk of chains and purchases made me forget the jungle and the pilgrims in a delicious sensation of having come upon something unmistakably real. (pp. 39–40)

Marlow experiences his encounter with the English sailor's book as a brief contact with the "real" in the midst of his dreamlike voyage. When he has to leave off reading the book, Marlow assures his listeners, "it was like tearing myself away from the shelter of an old and solid friendship" (p. 40). The original owner's fascination with the *Inquiry* impresses Marlow, especially when he mistakes the marginal notations in Russian for cipher. He considers the use of cipher "an extravagant mystery," and comments aloud that the book's owner "must be English." The Manager responds to this observation with hostility: "It will not save him from getting into trouble if he is not careful" (p. 40). Marlow reports to his listeners: "I observed with assumed innocence that no man was safe from trouble in this world." Marlow feels a bond of national solidarity with the imagined English trader, who has thwarted Belgian protectionism and devoted himself to studying the work of an English sailor. The shared text of Towser or Towson helps to cement the gang of virtue's claims on Kurtz's new recruit. It is at this point in the story that Marlow breaks off his narrative to recount the most spectacular appeal to nationality in Kurtz's own claim to kinship with him and his assurance that "his sympathies were in the right place." Marlow apparently treats Kurtz's appeal to his sympathies with some irony of his own, prefacing it with the remark, "as he was good enough to say himself," which seems to distance Marlow from the content of Kurtz's claim, yet the remainder of the story will show Marlow himself developing unexpected sympathies for Kurtz.

After having related Kurtz's appeals to their shared English "sympathies," Marlow describes the final stretch of the journey to the inner station. When he arrives and finally meets that other admirer of Mr. Kurtz, the Russian Harlequin, the question of nationality arises again almost immediately: "The harlequin on the bank turned his little pugnose up to me. 'You English?' he asked all smiles. 'Are you?' I shouted from the wheel. The smiles vanished and he shook his head as if sorry for my disappointment" (p. 53). The Harlequin immediately takes to Marlow, just as he admires all things English. Marlow and the Harlequin seal their friendship by sharing some of Marlow's "excellent English tobacco," for which the Russian thanks him: "Now, that's brotherly. Smoke! Where's a sailor that does not smoke?" (p. 54). This act, mirroring the frequent sharing of tobacco on board the *Nellie* on the Thames, seems to complete Marlow's induction into the "gang of virtue" (p. 28). He has unwittingly become, at least in the eyes of the European pilgrims, a "partisan of methods for which the time was not ripe . . ." Marlow later comments, "it was something to have at least a choice of nightmares" (p. 62).

Marlow never offers an adequate account of his reasons for remaining loyal to Kurtz, for what he calls his "choice of nightmares" in the story's final installment. His reasons remain unclear to him until the end, but it seems that the appeals to national sympathy and solidarity made by the Harlequin and Kurtz lead him to side with Kurtz after the struggle between his disgust at Kurtz's barbarism and his hatred for the Company's hypocrisy. By the time Marlow has arrived at Kurtz's station, he has, almost inadvertently, cast his lot with the gang of virtue. He tells the Russian Harlequin, "As it happens, I am Mr. Kurtz's friend – in a way," and when the Harlequin appeals to him as a "brother seaman" to protect Mr. Kurtz (just before disappearing into the wilderness with one final handful of "good English tobacco"), Marlow makes the promise, "Mr. Kurtz's reputation is safe with me" (pp. 62–63). Later on, when Kurtz's Intended again appeals to Marlow's love for Kurtz, she says to him: "You were his friend . . . His friend" (p. 73). Although he hesitates, Marlow accepts the designation. Yet why Marlow pronounces himself Kurtz's friend remains obscure, and the lie he tells the Intended about Kurtz's final words has become a crux of Conrad criticism. Marlow offers a quasi-sociological explanation of the lie, claiming that to reveal Kurtz's words ("the horror, the horror") would have been "too dark – too dark altogether" (p. 76). While Marlow's general concern for the workings of civilization certainly explains this decision in part, his loyalty to Kurtz's memory seems also to result from his sense of their kinship. Marlow lies because he has allowed the sentiments of "brotherhood" and "friendship" to obscure his dedication to the truth. His sympathy for Kurtz and for the Intended blinds him. Conrad observed in the letter to Cunninghame Graham, "There is already as much fraternity as there can be – and that's very little and that very little is no good." In Marlow's lie to the Intended, Conrad shows how the dream of fraternity can stand in the way of justice and truth. Kurtz and the Harlequin have succeeded in their appeal to Marlow's "sympathies" as an Englishman. Without his recognizing it, they have interpellated him – "brother seaman" – and made him their own.

There is, then, one force that molds character and that Marlow seems unable to analyze to his own satisfaction. In "Youth," he wonders aloud what made a crew of apparently undisciplined English sailors obey him, a twenty-year-old second mate, when they knew that the ship they were trying to save was doomed to sink. Help was nearby, so the sailors' lives did not depend on their success. Marlow denies that a sense of duty or a desire for glory or financial reward could have driven them:

No, it was something in [the English sailors], something inborn and subtle and everlasting. I don't say positively that the crew of a French or German merchantman wouldn't have done it, but I doubt whether it would have been done in the same way. There was a completeness in it, something solid like a principle, and masterful like an instinct – a disclosure of something secret – of that hidden something, that gift of good or evil that makes racial difference, that shapes the fate of nations.[39]

The sailors' very Englishness, a force beyond their understanding or control, makes them act nobly in an emergency. Yet here Marlow's belief in the existence of a "hidden something" does not amount to any sort of racial theory of history. The uneven distribution of character appears to him as an inexplicable secret, and it just so happens that the English have more of it than other peoples. Marlow's pride in his Englishness does not lead him to pronounce race a "key to history."[40] Even Marlow feels threatened by the biological definition of national character when the Company Doctor tries to apply it scientifically to Marlow himself. This threat reflects the degeneration of the English liberal discourse of national character in the 1890s. Both Conrad and Marlow are stuck between the two extremes of racial determinism and an unbounded faith in the universality of human nature.

CONRAD, CHARACTER, AND CULTURE

Marlow has proven unable to find a middle way between the idealistic theories of human nature espoused by Kurtz and the racism of the Company Doctor. He cannot account for the logic of the "hidden something" that has shaped his character and made him susceptible to the appeals of the gang of virtue. Conrad himself, in the author's note to his autobiographical *A Personal Record* (1912), refers to a force that seems to have molded his "character" and that is superficially similar to Marlow's "hidden something":

The impression of my having exercised a choice between the two languages, French and English, both foreign to me, has got abroad somehow. That impression is erroneous . . . I have a strange and overpowering feeling that [English] had always been an inherent part of myself. English was for me neither a matter of choice nor adoption . . . it was I who was adopted by the genius of the language, which directly I came out of the stammering stage made me its own so completely that its very idioms I truly believe had a direct impact on my temperament and fashioned my still plastic character.[41]

Marlow attributes the English sailors' uniqueness to an innate "racial difference," relatively untouched by cultural and educational forces, whereas Conrad claims that, despite his Polish birth and ancestry, the English language, a product of English history and culture, has decisively influenced the development of his character. Marlow's creation seems to result largely from Conrad's desire to portray his own life experiences through the filter of an English version of himself. Most of Marlow's experiences originate in Conrad's autobiography, but Marlow's Englishness marks him off from his Polish-born creator. The Marlow stories investigate the question of the transferability of cultural values and assumptions. Marlow, in his remarks about the "hidden something," identifies nationality closely with race and therefore puts an unbridgeable gap between each nation and her neighbors; Conrad implies that nationality, while it determines character and is beyond the conscious control of the individual, can be acquired, and is thus primarily a matter of upbringing, nurture rather than nature.

The distinction between the cultural and the biological explanations of character corresponds to a broader distinction between two types of explanation of the motivations of an individual's behavior. In the quotation above, Conrad expresses the subjective sense that he cannot imagine himself as he was before the English language influenced his character. He has a "strange and overpowering feeling" that English has always been a part of him, but it clearly has not objectively always been so. There was a time, "the stammering stage," before he knew English. It is only in retrospect, from his own perspective as a fully formed subject, that his development as an adoptive Englishman seems to have made English "an inherent part" of himself. This retrospective sense of the necessity of character – that is, the sense that his character has been formed almost automatically and without any conscious choice on his part – resembles Marlow's own sense, in *Heart of Darkness*, that he could not have chosen to act differently than he did in Africa. It is the sort of optical illusion that makes the forces by which culture shapes the individual inexplicable by the individual in her own ethical terms. The individual, whose character has been formed by the contingencies of birth and upbringing, senses that despite the conscious workings of her mind, some greater forces have shaped her destiny. Yet the nature of this necessity is not such as to allow of formulation as a universal, sociological law. The almost mechanistic claim that all people of a given nationality will necessarily act in a similar way in given circumstances coarsens the sense of retrospective necessity felt by the individual subject who attempts to explain her own actions with attention to the complex interpenetration between consciousness and circumstance. As an observer, Marlow blithely asserts the existence of a "hidden something" that motivates the sailors, but when the Company Doctor tries to make a similar claim about Marlow's own experience – that his nationality has determined it in a way beyond his control – he objects. He turns to the mode of auto-biographical storytelling that allows him to assert his status as a unique individual, not simply a representative of a given type: "I hastened to assure him I was not in the least typical." Conrad gives the reader reason to doubt Marlow's claim, and the tension between Marlow's own account of his behavior and the possible deterministic reading of it suggested by the Doctor is a crucial element in the novel's irony.

Heart of Darkness, with its exploration of imperialism, racial difference, and subconscious motivations, and with its intensely modern irony and ambivalence, is a favorite text of those who interpret Conrad's modernism politically. I have focused on this novel here for its emphasis on the perilous implications of the discourse of national character, but Conrad's other novels also richly explore the ironies of Englishness. The heroes of Conrad's next major novels, Jim in *Lord Jim* and Charles Gould in *Nostromo*, are deracinated Englishmen who attempt to unify small, multi-ethnic nations (Patusan and Costaguana), but who are unable to make their moral principles stick in their new, racially diverse communities. They both ultimately find that their political projects are at the mercy of "material interests," whose laws and justice are "inhuman."[42] In *Under Western Eyes*, a teacher of languages of ambiguous national allegiances rejects the spiritualist aspirations of a Russian nationalism that, like Kurtzian internationalism, concerns itself more with the unbridled popular will than with the difficulties of shaping a national character. Avrom Fleishman has described Conrad as "skeptical of the exclusive rightness of any ideology or class but unstinting in the hope that they may complement each other in a unified whole – the organic community of the nation" (p. 48). Yet, while the ideal of an organic community may appeal to Conrad, it is the inorganic elements of most existing communities – the role of chance, material interests, and ideology in their formation – that seem to interest Conrad most. His heroes do attempt to redeem their national communities, but they often wind up disillusioned and aware of the weakness of the individual, whatever his or her devotion, in the face of the historical forces of accident, greed, and prejudice. Though perhaps more attached emotionally than Joyce to the idea of the nation, Conrad, perhaps through having meditated so extensively upon the structure of political communities, seems far more pessimistic than Joyce about the possibility of achieving that moral unity of the nation which, for both of these exiles, seems a nostalgic ideal.

The narrative method of *Heart of Darkness*, which has made it a classic of English "modernism," emphasizes Marlow's location within a culturally specific set of assumptions that he cannot escape. This method also suggests a certain pessimism about liberalism and the idea of the nation. Unlike Stephen Dedalus's diary, Marlow's lie to the Intended and the primary narrator's summing up offer no sense of ultimately resolving the problems of the narrative. Marlow and his four English listeners cannot say clearly what it is about Marlow's story that has caused their unease, but they feel their optimistic outlook on English civilization to be threatened. Incapable of explaining his actions when confronted with the non-English in Africa, Marlow tells his story to four fellow Englishmen, and although telling his story seems to him the best way to lay the soul of Kurtz to rest, the storytelling does not result in a neat conclusion or solution. By making Marlow so incapable of explaining his own attachment to Kurtz, Conrad suggests that the liberal English nation-state represented by Marlow and his listeners faces a crisis it cannot comprehend. Its values – humanity, decency, justice, efficiency, liberty, devotion to ideals – are culturally specific and on the verge of being outmoded. Since they depend so completely on a particular English character, which is the product of historical accident (or good luck), they are incapable of being exported to the rest of the world. When the devotees of an English-style liberalism attempt to apply it to places and peoples unsuited by character to liberal self-government, the result is either a fanatical idealism tinged with egalitarianism *à la* Kurtz that tears down all institutions or a bureaucratic and hypocritical nightmare like the Company's in which the strongest take advantage of the weakest while cloaking their motives in the forms of law and liberalism. The difficulty is that even the best-willed of imperialists seem condemned to apply their own ethnocentric standards to the societies they encounter, and Conrad seems to find little reason to trust that even the most noble-sounding of these standards, "humanity, decency, and justice," can really be applied impartially except, perhaps, within the context of a nation-state as fortunate as Conrad does seem to believe England has been in the history of its constitutional arrangements and the development of its civil society. Even among this happy breed of men, it may be that the ideals of a neutral justice, rule of law, and universal standards of right conduct are little more than the totems of a particularly successful cult whose time is running out. At any rate, Conrad would like to believe that he, a stateless Pole, has successfully become an Englishman, but in *Heart of Darkness* he expresses a profound skepticism about whether Africans, or even Belgians and Frenchmen, can do the same. For this reason if for no other, Conrad's "national idea" has no future.

CHAPTER FOUR

Citizens of the Plain: Proust and the discourse of national will

The most famous image of Marcel Proust seems the archetype of modernist isolation from political concerns – the neurotic novelist writing all night and sleeping all day in a cork-lined room, from which he attempts to exclude any sound or light that could distract him from remembering the intimate experiences of his youth. Proust's focus on the nuances of intimate relations, memory, and personal identity seems far removed from the problems of the nation-state. Despite his reclusiveness, however, Proust was not indifferent to politics: his most thorough statement of his aesthetic theory occurs in a political context and responds directly to the "relativism" of the nationalist Maurice Barrès. Towards the end of *Le Temps retrouvé*, the final book of *A la recherche du temps perdu*, the narrator discovers the principle of involuntary memory that will allow him to begin writing the novel he has long been planning. Through a series of sudden recollections, he finds that certain types of memories and certain sensations function as signs in his mind, that he must interpret them through his art, and that "the essential character [of these signs] was that I was not free to choose them, that such as they were they were given to me. And I realized that this must be the mark of their authenticity."[1] The narrator submits himself to the effort to make an authentic account of the "inner book of unknown signs" of his unconscious, a difficult task which he must undertake without help from anyone else:

How many for this reason turn aside from writing! What tasks do men not take upon themselves in order to evade this task! Every public event, be it the Dreyfus case, be it the war, furnishes the writer with a fresh excuse for not attempting to decipher this book: he wants to ensure the triumph of justice, he wants to restore the moral unity of the nation, he has no time to think of literature. But these are mere excuses, the truth being that he has not or no longer has genius, that is to say instinct. For instinct dictates our duty and the intellect supplies us with pretexts for evading it.[2]

The most evident suggestion of this passage – that the novelist's primary duty is to the inner book of unknown signs in his or her unconscious – chimes in perfectly well with the image of Proust in the cork-lined room. The narrator defends the autonomy of art. Yet, the temptation to turn away from this duty offered by great public events in the life of the nation, while dismissed as a "mere excuse," also appears as a strong counter-claim on the novelist's attention. The narrator presents his position as a response to that espoused at the beginning of the war by Maurice Barrès, who "had said that the artist . . . must first and foremost serve his country." Ultimately, in fact, the narrator's justification for the autonomy of art is oddly utilitarian. He sees the artist as serving the nation (the *patrie*) precisely through dedication to the work of art. He says that in order to serve his country properly, the artist, like the scientist, must "think of nothing – not even his country – but the truth which is before him" (III, 917). The cork-lined room perhaps becomes necessary precisely because the countervailing demands of "justice" and the "moral unity of the nation" offer such a powerful motivation to regard something other than obedience to the novelist's instinct as the primary duty. It is through the authenticity of its account of experience that art achieves its claim to freedom from political demands. This mimetic relationship to life, art's ability to bear witness to a particular truth, requires that the artist reject political propaganda. This is an autonomy dependent on an appeal to a higher, universal demand: the demand for truth.

The language of the passage also suggests what much of the novel will confirm: that what appears most intimate and private, the "inner book of unknown signs," is itself something not chosen by the subject but impressed upon it from outside: "such as they were they were given to me." If this is true, then the problem of authenticity or truth to oneself turns out to be a problem of choosing among a variety of standards (truth, justice, moral unity), each of which comes from outside oneself. This paradox will prove crucial to Proust's conception of involuntary memory. Like Conrad and Joyce, Proust calls attention to the interpenetration of the private realm of ethical values and the public realm of social values. He does not, however, find in this interpenetration the possibility of a liberation. Rather, he reinstates a dualism between private and public values partly through a re-examination of the dualistic tradition of Western thought. Whereas the voluntarist tradition from Rousseau to Renan emphasized the possibility of an act of purely free will outside of time and space which could unify the "will of all" and the "general will," Proust doubts the freedom of the will, and finds in the effects of time and history the existential limit of any such pure self-presence. Ultimately, the notion of involuntary memory will underwrite for Proust not only a radically deconstructed notion of personal identity, but also a fairly conventional liberal politics, which defends a private realm of individual autonomy without embracing the more optimistic hopes of liberalism for a future of social justice. It is a rather tragic form of liberalism, which treats truth, justice, and the moral unity of the nation as potentially in perpetual conflict. With Tocqueville and Renan and against Rousseau, Proust emphasizes the need to maintain the autonomy of the private realm as a defense against the potentially homogenizing forces of a mass, egalitarian society.

Proust presents his theory of art as a response to the nationalism of Maurice Barrès. Barrès, who was for many years the deputy for a part of Lorraine that had not been annexed by the Germans, concerned himself largely with revenge for the defeat of 1871 and with the forging of national unity on a secular, but authoritarian, basis. Nationalism, a term which Barrès himself is credited with having given its modern right-wing authoritarian associations, involved for Barrès "the acceptance of a determinism," the acknowledgment that one's moral perspective is necessarily shaped not by appeal to universal principles but by the circumstances of one's birth.[3] Criticizing the belief in universal laws of Hugo, Michelet, Taine, and Renan, Barrès argued that "we are not the masters of the thoughts that are born in us" (p. 31). The only true source of ethics is submission to the moral perspective with which we are born:

I must seat myself at the exact point that my eyes themselves, as they have been shaped by the centuries, demand, at the point from which all things can be situated in relation to a Frenchman. The totality of these just and true relations between given objects and a determined man, the Frenchman, that is French truth and French justice; to find these relations, that is French reason. And nationalism is simply nothing other than to know that such a point exists, to seek it out and, having attained it, to keep ourselves at that point in order to take from it our art, our politics, and all our activities. (p. 27)

Here, Barrès enunciates the purest form of nationalist determinism in a mode remarkably similar to that of Joyce's Stephen Dedalus. Barrès calls this attitude relativism (pp. 73ff.). The artist and the politician are to express the national consciousness in every action. The route towards this perspective has been decisively prepared by the notion, in Rousseau and Renan, that the citizen finds true freedom only by achieving unity with the general or national will. Yet, in Barrès, the will itself is nothing. The history of the French people purely determines every aspect of the individual's perspective. As I argued above, the voluntarist tradition makes this argument from pure determinism seem more plausible precisely because it emphasizes so thoroughly the pure freedom of the will in strict opposition to all external determinations. The freedom of the will is no more than an article of metaphysical faith that Rousseau and Renan retain, and when this metaphysical faith is rejected, the moral subject of the voluntarist tradition becomes nothing more than the purely passive nexus of historical forces. The hostility of the voluntarist tradition to anything but a unitary conception of the will worsens this situation, for instead of an active, worldly process of transforming reality through *praxis*, the will in Rousseau and Renan is a purely spiritual force outside of matter and with which matter can quite easily dispense. Within the voluntarist tradition, the alternative to an absolute dualism of spirit and matter is what Tocqueville called "a sort of predestination [that] is a close relative of the purest materialism."[4] The elect of nationalism are predestined not by an otherworldly grace but by a purpose imagined to be inherent in material processes.

Proust's narrator accepts Barrès's theory that truthfulness can only be truth for us. He conceives of what recent ethical philosophers have called a "radically situated" self, a self largely constituted by its contexts, such as that Barrès described with the words, "we are not masters of the thoughts which are born in us" (p. 31).[5] Proust denies, however, that this radically situated self must reflect only a national perspective. Truth is relative not just to one's nationality but to all other aspects of one's personality. In his response to Barrès, Proust's narrator attempts to rescue the voluntarist conception of society by developing a new account of human freedom, according to which the self, without transcending the determinations in space and time of its personality, can nonetheless achieve a measure of universalization of its experience and thus of ethical autonomy through the process of interrogating its unique historical and social location. For Proust, the self becomes a site of competing social roles and identifications, and it is the conflict generated by the conception of the self as fragmentary that allows for ethical development. Proust treats life in society as what Renan called a "daily plebiscite," but he emphasizes the mutability implicit in this conception of social belonging and the pernicious effects of the "forgetting" that constitutes the nation.[6] More importantly, he describes the life of the individual herself as a sort of daily plebiscite with only one voter, or rather with a different voter at each moment. This rethinking of the category "individual" or "self" – Proust uses the term "*moi*" – helps to rescue the voluntarist tradition from the relativism of a Nietzsche or a Barrès,

which threatens to undermine the voluntarist emphasis on the normative notions of duty and justice. Proust jettisons the notion of free will as
consisting in an absolute overcoming of all determinations, and in this
he largely agrees with the English character tradition, but with the voluntarist tradition he emphasizes the active role of the subject in arriving
at standards of conduct and truth, and thus the possibility of achieving
intersubjective forms of social knowledge and action. For Proust, as for
the political philosopher Michael Sandel, the self "comes by" its ends or
purposes in at least two ways: by choice and by discovery.[7] Proust thus
offers intimations of a universalistic conception of justice that could co-
exist with a perspectivist critique of human understanding.

On the level of real-world politics, Proust's narrator, like Proust
himself, holds the value of national unity in high esteem and hopes that
it can correspond with a universalistic sense of justice. He also inherits
from the voluntarist tradition a skepticism of subordinate social identifications, and particularly a sense of the conflict between racial difference
and social and political equality. He thus accepts the Barrèsian premise
that the existence of racial differences poses a radical limit to the possibility of universal justice and to the moral unity of the nation, and it is
this animating tension between race and nation that leads Proust to his
pessimistic conclusions about formal politics. Proust's own reaction to
the two great public events the narrator mentions suggests that, like his
narrator, he was at least strongly tempted to try to reconcile the two types
of duty with one another – to use the novelist's instinct to restore justice
and the moral unity of the nation. For, during the war, as Proust radically revised the novel whose first volume had been published in 1913, he
increasingly applied his insights into the nature of personal identity to
the problem of the nation-state, and thus developed a social psychology
of democratic experience. The most well-known of Proust's revisions
during the war was to move the narrator's childhood home of Combray
from the district around Chartres, where its counterpart in Proust's own
life, Illiers, is actually located, to the vicinity of Rheims, on the front
lines.[8] This change in his fictional landscape allowed Proust to have the
war impinge on the lost paradise of his childhood. It was also during
the war that Proust greatly expanded the role that the Dreyfus affair of
the 1890s would play in his novel.[9] The expanded presentation of the
affair and the war suggests that the problems of "justice" and "the moral
unity of the nation" became increasingly central to Proust's endeavor,
even while he sought to submit himself more completely to his "instinct"
and to the task of reading his "inner book of unknown signs."

Although a number of critics have concerned themselves with Proust's attitudes to society, the Dreyfus affair, the aristocracy, or homosexuality, they have often taken Proust's observations on his times either as simple representations of the material of social history or as indictments of the homogenizing forces of society in general. Even those who treat Proust with considerable historical specificity tend to find in him an outright rejection of politics and the social sphere in favor of the intimate. Leo Bersani, for example, finds in Proust's analysis of "the anticommunitarian impulses . . . in homosexual desire" the material for a radically deconstructed conception of the person that could usher in a new type of politics, dependent not on ideology or faith but on narcissism.[10] However, seen as interventions in the struggle to define and defend the Third Republic, Proust's central formal and psychological concerns – particularly his idea of involuntary memory and his model of a fragmentary personal identity – seem more than a general rejection of society and politics as artificial constructs. If Conrad concerned himself with what Acton called the "claim of national liberty," for Proust, it is national unity and the consequent equality of all citizens that are in question and in need of defense. Proust's analysis of the self responds not just to general existential conditions of life in society but in particular to life as a citizen of a modern, liberal nation-state, which is in the throes of an attempt to transform itself from a hierarchical social structure to one ruled by what Tocqueville called "equality of condition."[11] Like Tocqueville, Proust represents the tension between universality and particularism as animating specifically modern societies and perhaps especially as a product of the condition of equality in liberal democratic society. In his conception of involuntary memory, he presents a model of membership in such a society that, while pessimistic about formal politics, does attempt to reconcile the normative demands of justice with the existence of a heterogeneous population. Both Conrad and Joyce, I have argued, sought to reconcile their sense of the individual's having been shaped by forces external to herself with the notion of individual ethical freedom. Although Proust seems tempted by such a utopian project, what he eventually offers instead is a conception of the ethical individual as a site of competing forces that can never achieve absolute integration.

COMBRAY: SITE OF THE UNIFIED SELF?

Before turning to Proust's revision of the voluntarist tradition and his attitude to political problems and social change, it is worth considering the common conception of Proust's narrator that underwrites the image of Proust as entirely apolitical. In the first volume of *A la recherche du temps perdu*, Proust sought, like other early modernist novelists, to reconcile two selves, the remembering "I" and the remembered "I," the narrator and the protagonist of his story. Like Joyce's *A Portrait of the Artist as a Young Man*, and with even more explicit references to Balzac, *A la recherche* recasts the disillusionment plot structure.[12] The site of the potential unification of remembered and remembering selves in Proust is the lost memory of his childhood in Combray, a small town apparently isolated from the forces of society at large. Proust's narrator attempts to re-integrate his personality in memory. He understands the conflicts within his personality to result from historical forces and seeks in his country, and particularly in the French middle ages, a model of an integrated personality. The town of Combray functions as a sort of pre-modern society that the later history of the Third Republic will destroy. In the later volumes of *A la recherche*, the two great public events intervene in the story, as "the waves of the two currents of Dreyfusism and anti-Dreyfusism [divide] France from top to bottom" and then the war uproots all the accustomed hierarchies of society (II, pp. 306–307). While these events will later make the faultlines of French society evident, the narrator's own descriptions of Combray of his childhood already ironically point up the tensions that underlie the apparent tranquillity of the town. The narrator is often seen as deeply nostalgic for the lost paradise of his childhood, the family home in Combray which he describes in the first chapters of the novel.[13] Yet, like Joyce, Proust presents childhood itself and the supposed site of the integrated personality as traversed by political and historical conflicts.

In Combray, the narrator's family knows everyone, and they therefore mistakenly assume that they know everything about everyone. They fail to comprehend the high social position achieved by Charles Swann, an old friend of the family whose bourgeois origins they know well and whose aristocratic connections they cannot imagine. This conflict between the reality of Swann's social life and the narrator's family's conception of it leads to one of Proust's first observations about the complexity of social life:

But then, even in the most insignificant details of our daily life, none of us can be said to constitute a material whole, which is identical for everyone, and need only be turned up like a page in an account-book or the record of a will [*testament*]; our social personality is a creation of the thoughts of other people. (*Remembrance*, I, p. 20; *Recherche*, I, pp. 18–19)

The will and the account book, emblems of the individual as a legal or economic entity, do not offer a complete account of the social personality; indeed, they distort the social personality by reducing a complex set of relations to a simple, self-identical unit. Remarkably, the fiction of the legal individual, normally associated with industrial society and modern economic life, functions quite successfully in Combray itself, which the narrator represents as a sort of pre-modern society. The individual is a fairly fixed quantity and the narrator's family cannot accept the existence of people in Combray whom "one didn't know at all" ("on ne connaissait point"). Whenever such a person is sighted, the servants must scurry to find out his or her origins, and they always manage to prove that the foreigner really is "someone one knows," such as a relative of one of the town's residents. As a result of this rigid social structure in which everyone has a place,

middle-class people in those days [*les bourgeois d'alors*] took what was almost a Hindu view of society, which they held to consist of sharply defined castes, so that everyone at his birth found himself led to that station in life which his parents already occupied, and from which nothing, save the accident of an exceptional career or a "good" marriage, could extract you and translate you to a superior caste. (*Remembrance*, I, pp. 16–17; *Recherche*, I, p. 16)

The rigid world of the bourgeois of Combray thus forms a traditional order, with its own rituals, such as having lunch early on Saturdays, that create a sort of "patriotic" spirit among the members of this "closed society" (I, p. 119). For the narrator, it seems, it is life in the "world," outside Combray, that will unravel the fiction of the stable individual with a fixed social position. Underlying the bourgeois society of Combray and reinforcing the sense that its laws are permanent and fixed is the society of the peasantry, and particularly the servant Françoise. As her name suggests, Françoise seems to belong, with the rest of her class, to the eternal France, or more specifically to the France of the middle ages. However, there are signs in Combray itself, despite its medieval associations, its elaborate caste system, and the absence of people that "on ne connaît point," that the French social order is less stable than middle-class people in the early days of the Republic ("les bourgeois d'alors") imagine. Combray is already a site of competing social and psychological forces which threaten to destroy the narrator's peace of mind, just as the family arguments over Parnell disturb the young Stephen Dedalus.

A recurrent analogy between the self and the French nation helps Proust to develop his psychology. The self in Proust bears a certain resemblance to the ego in Freud, a sort of battlefield where, as in trench warfare, the combattants cannot achieve resolution, but only, at best, a balance of powers. Proust first presents the self as a type of battlefield in the third sentence of the novel, when the narrator observes that, awaking after half an hour's sleep, "I had gone on thinking, while I was asleep, about what I had just been reading, but these thoughts had taken a rather peculiar turn; it seemed to me that I myself was whatever the book was describing: a church, a quartet, the rivalry between François I and Charles V" (I, p. 3). As the first metaphor of the divided self in the novel, this reference to French history is remarkable, for the rivalry between King François I and Emperor Charles V largely determined the borders of modern France and allowed the rise of the early modern sovereign state through the king's consolidation of his powers at the expense of the feudal nobility. François Mignet's history of this rivalry, which probably inspired this allusion of Proust's, ends with the Treaty of Cambrai, of 1529, between François I and Charles V, a treaty that in its humiliation of the French king seems, especially in Mignet's account, to prefigure the terrible defeat of 1870–71.[14] Cambrai was on the Habsburg side of the border between France and the Habsburg low countries in 1529, and became part of France under Louis XIV in 1679. It seems likely that Proust associated Cambrai with his Combray, an association strengthened by his later decision to move "Combray" from the neighborhood of Chartres to that of Rheims in order to have the war impinge on it directly. The hero thus describes an imagined conflict between two parts of himself as a re-embodiment of a crucial struggle in French history, a struggle that reached its conclusion in a treaty that helped to establish the modern French state. Proust will return to this analogy between his personality and the borders of the French state in his description of the effects of the First World War on Combray. In the novel's final volume, *Le Temps retrouvé*, Combray will similarly become a battleground, partially occupied by the Germans, as Gilberte de Saint-Loup informs the narrator: "[The places of our childhood] have become a part of history, with the same claim to glory as Austerlitz or Valmy . . . For a year and a half [the Germans] have held one half of Combray and the French the other" (III, p. 778). The story of the battle of Combray emphasizes the element of political or military struggle involved in the forging of identity. Even in the first years of the Republic, the Combray that the narrator remembers was itself a paradise only to the extent that it embodied a temporary truce in the self's attempt to define itself against others, just as the borders of the French state result from a particular peace signed long ago with a neighboring country but always open to revision or renewed hostilities.

Among the most flexible of borders in the novel is that between France and Germany, represented both by the Emperor Charles V and by the Emperor William (Kaiser Wilhelm). The Germans are, in Proust's novel as in modern French history, the archetypal "others." Throughout the novel, the characters whose patriotism is suspect, whether the Dreyfusard Jews like Swann and Bloch at the time of the Dreyfus affair or the anti-Dreyfusard aristocrats at the time of the war, are accused by the patriotic French of having German blood or German allegiances. Indeed, the Guermantes, whose ancestress Geneviève de Brabant the narrator associates with the medieval past of Combray, are more suspect than anyone else because of their links to various German aristocratic houses and to the Kaiser, to whom the Baron de Charlus respectfully refers as "l'Empereur Guillaume." Yet the history of Combray emphasizes the role of the German others in shaping the French self. The narrator mentions that Combray church itself houses, along with the tombs of the counts of Brabant, that of the sons of Louis the Germanic, grandson of Charlemagne and the first king of Germany after the division of Charlemagne's empire by the Treaty of Verdun in 843 A.D., which gave rise to the very existence of a distinct political entity known as Francia or France (I, p. 65). The German king's sons buried in the French church call attention to the historical intertwining of the two nations. The story of Geneviève de Brabant herself "seemed to emanate from a Merovingian past," the era of the Frankish kings prior even to this division (I, p. 10). What the historical associations of Combray and its aristocratic patrons the Guermantes suggest is that the French nation itself is not an eternal spiritual essence but a temporary product of a history of social conflict. For Proust, it is almost a running joke that even the site of the narrator's memories of a structured and stable French past was not itself French until relatively recently. Proust's presentation of the self and the nation seems to echo Renan's claim that "The nation, like the individual, is the culmination of a long past of endeavours, sacrifice, and devotion."[15] Yet, writing after the Dreyfus affair, Proust is particularly aware of the prospect of ancient divisions rising to the surface. The waking self, like the nation at peace, maintains an uneasy truce with the outside world and among its own conflicting impulses. When the self falls asleep, these divisions resurface.

PROUSTIAN AND CARTESIAN DOUBT

In describing the divisions within the self, Proust often refers to philosophical concepts, and although he of course does not present a systematic philosophy, he seems eager to make sense of his models of the self in relation to the voluntarist tradition. Two ideas, that the will is not free and that the self is not unitary or indivisible, develop in tandem throughout the novel. They are not original with Proust, but Proust makes use of them in a way that helps to revolutionize novelistic form and also suggests possible ways of rescuing elements of voluntarist ethics from the critiques of a Nietzsche or a Barrès. Proust first introduces the problem of the will's dependence on that which it receives from outside itself in terms of the relationship of the self to others in the family. The narrator's family is concerned to prevent him from recognizing his own "lack of will-power" ("manque de volonté"), which they consider detrimental to his mental and physical health (*Remembrance*, I, p. 13; *Recherche*, I, p. 12). For much of the novel, the narrator believes that his own lack of self-control results from this lack of will, which he considers peculiar to himself and connected to his "neurasthenia," an imprecise medical name for his neurotic anxiety. Gradually, however, through the course of the novel, it becomes evident that the will's reliance on what is outside itself is typical not only of the narrator but of many other figures in society, and perhaps of people in general. In the first chapter of the novel, the narrator's parents, fearful for their child's neurasthenia, fail to punish him for his misbehavior when he sends Françoise to interrupt their visit with Swann in order to deliver a note asking his mother to come kiss him goodnight. For several pages, the narrator anticipates his punishment for transgressing the rules of the household in this way. When his parents finally do come upstairs from their visit, the father unexpectedly tells the mother to stay with the child, who cannot sleep without her. The narrator describes his recognition of the crucial unfreedom as it then occurred to him:

And thus for the first time my unhappiness was regarded no longer as a punishable offence but as an involuntary ailment [*un mal involontaire*] which had been officially recognised, a nervous condition for which I was in no way responsible; I had the consolation of no longer having to mingle apprehensive scruples with the bitterness of my tears; I could weep henceforth without sin . . . I ought to have been happy; I was not. It struck me that my mother had just made a first concession which must have been painful to her, that it was a first abdication on her part from the ideal she had formed for me, and that for the first time she who was so brave had to confess herself beaten. (*Remembrance*, I, p. 41; *Recherche*, I, pp. 37–8)

The fact that there are elements of his personality for which he cannot reasonably be held responsible both comforts and depresses the narrator, for it is no longer to be expected that he will be the author of all his own states of mind. On the other hand, this recognition both destroys the ideal of self-sufficiency that the mother cherishes for her son and requires the son to enjoy his lack of responsibility at the expense of his mother.

In describing his lack of responsibility, the involuntary character of his states of mind, Proust's narrator is laying the groundwork for his theory of involuntary memory. He does so in a way that calls attention to analogies between the intimate life of the narrator's family and the concerns of the political realm, analogies that will loom larger in later volumes of *A la recherche*. It is his father who tells his mother to stay with the narrator on this occasion, and the narrator observes: "My father used constantly to refuse to let me do things which were quite clearly allowed by the more liberal [*larges*] charters granted me by my mother and grandmother, because he paid no heed to 'principles,' and because for him there was no such thing as the 'law of nations' [*Droit des gens*]" (*Remembrance*, I, p. 41; *Recherche*, I, pp. 37–38.) As a result, the father, who is generally much more strict than the mother, will occasionally, as on this memorable night, allow his son undreamt-of privileges. The world of Combray is, as René Girard has noted, patriarchal, not only in the general sense of being ruled by men, but also in the more specific sense of being ruled by a single male head of the household.[16] In such a society the "law of nations," the shared international code of civilized behavior, does not apply, for the law is no more than the will of the patriarch. It is in the world outside the family, the world of adults, that relations of equality prevail and the problems of friendship and justice arise. However, just as the existence of involuntary ills will carry over to life outside the family, there is a sense in which this patriarchal society remains the norm. For, just as the father makes his judgments "for an entirely contingent reason or for no reason at all," the characters in *A la recherche* are born within given social relations and with given abilities that depend not on reason but on custom, prejudice, or accident of birth (I, p. 38). In this sense, even the society of equals outside of Combray remains continually in tension with the patriarchal origins of society as a whole, and questions of status remain influential in the midst of an

egalitarian state. It is always the case, and associated in Proust specifically with the rule of the father, that the individual is born not only as a
human being but also as one expected to fulfill certain roles which, from
the perspective of adulthood and universalizing rationality, can only
appear contingent and unreasoned.

The narrator's description of the process of recovering lost time
traces the problem of the discovery and choice of ethical standards
appropriate to a self that is both radically situated and practically
free:

I put down the cup and turn towards my mind [*esprit*]. It alone can discover the
truth. But how? What an abyss of uncertainty, whenever the mind feels over-
taken by itself; when it, the seeker, is at the same time the obscure country
through which it must go seeking and where all its equipment will avail it
nothing. Seek? More than that: create. It is face to face with something which
does not yet exist, to which it alone can give reality and substance, which it alone
can bring into the light of day. (*Remembrance*, I, p. 49; *Recherche*, I, p. 45)

Proust extends the Romantic idea that the senses both perceive and "half
create" what they find in nature precisely by internalizing it.[17] The self,
human nature, is for Proust at once a conscious invention and a bundle
of instincts given to the individual "as such" ("telles quelles").[18] The
creation of the self that is to be presented to the world therefore involves
a process of objectifying oneself, for the self creates a personality for
itself by interacting with others, by developing the potentialities given it
through the formation of habits, and by the act of discovery involved in
recognizing itself. In Proust, the self is no longer, as in Descartes, an indivisible unit outside of space. Instead, it is understood in spatial terms as
an obscure country ("pays obscur"). The process of searching takes
place, however, in the dimension of time, so that the decipherment of
the "inner book of unknown signs" mentioned later in *Le Temps retrouvé*
can be truly authentic only in the instant of the self's emergence into the
light of day. The created, narrated self cannot – or can only momentar-
ily – be identical with the instinctual self glimpsed in involuntary
memory. Proust transforms two typical attributes of the individual in the
voluntarist tradition and in realistic convention – the conception of the
self as an indivisible mental substance and the idea of a pure free will.
These two attributes of the self are central to the Cartesian dualist tradition. According to Descartes, the most certain truth is that "I am a
mind, or intelligence, or intellect, or reason."[19] The thinking thing, or
mind, is indivisible, while the body is divisible, and the mind consists of
a faculty of knowledge and a faculty "of choice or freedom of the will,"

which is "not restricted in any way" (pp. 39, 59). Unlike Barrès, and with Descartes, Proust maintains that the individual has a form of freedom and a unique identity, but he also sees these forms as the product of a personal history that is only partly controlled by the subject and that cannot be transcended. These transformations of the notion of identity justify, in turn, Proust's most celebrated innovations in narrative form: the replacement of chronological time by the interior time of the narrator, and the emphasis not on the external events of the plot but on the effects these events have on the mind of the narrator.

Proust's narrator is, of course, fascinated with the lack of certainty of his own perceptions. The novel begins with a scene that seems to echo Descartes's *Meditations*, an echo of which Proust's commentators have taken surprisingly little notice, although Georges Poulet mentions it briefly.[20] This famous opening suggests a radical doubt about the capacity of the mind to achieve absolutely certain knowledge and the reliance of all knowledge on the notoriously unreliable faculty of memory.[21] Descartes's first meditation begins: "Il y a déjà quelque temps que je me suis aperçu que, dès mes premières années, j'avais reçu quantité de fausses opinions pour véritables" ["It has been some time since I noticed that, ever since my first years, I had accepted a large number of false opinions as true"].[22] Descartes's narrator/thinker goes on to doubt everything that he has learned from his senses on the grounds that it is impossible to distinguish waking life from a dream. Similarly, Proust's first sentence consists of a memory of a time when knowledge was uncertain to his narrator: "Longtemps, je me suis couché de bonne heure" ["For a long time, I used to go to bed early"].[23] Both first sentences describe an event in the past, using the passé composé tense, but Proust's adverb of time ("Longtemps") shows that he is describing a repeated occurrence, whereas Descartes's adverbial phrase ("Il y a déjà quelque temps") designates a single moment in the past. Whereas Descartes's text will lead to a moment of absolute rhetorical self-presence ("I am, I exist"), Proust's construction of the self must take place in memory and therefore in the past, and furthermore in a past that is in an important sense indefinite, for even such objective markers of time as dates disappear from Proust's narration.

In the next few sentences of Proust's novel, the narrator describes the repeated experience of mistakenly believing that he himself is the subject of the book he has been reading just before falling asleep. This first set of illusions is followed by a long series of similarly confused impressions typical of the narrator's consciousness in the moments

between sleep and wakefulness. It is a closely related problem, of distinguishing between dreams and wakefulness, that causes Descartes's
thinker in the *Meditations* to doubt all his previous knowledge. As
Descartes observes, even his sense of his current physical condition may
be a dream: "How often, asleep at night, am I convinced of just such
familiar events – that I am here in my dressing-gown, sitting by the fire
– when in fact I am lying undressed in my bed!" (p. 13). Precisely such
are the fantasies of Proust's half-awakened narrator, who imagines
himself in a series of familiar rooms from his childhood before settling
on the room in which he is actually lying. Indeed, both Proust and
Descartes liked to lie in bed and think, and it is said that the need to rise
early for his morning sessions tutoring the queen of Sweden contributed
to Descartes's untimely death.[24]

Descartes moves from the simple past tense of his first sentence to an
ideal present in which he attains certain knowledge: "Maintenant donc
que mon esprit est libre de tous soins . . ." ["Now then that my spirit {or
mind} is free of all cares . . ."].[25] Proust originally sketched an opening
for *A la recherche* that would specifically fix his memory of his half-wakeful
state on a particular day: "Au temps de cette matinée dont je voudrais
fixer le souvenir . . ." ["Around the time of that morning, of which I
would like to fix the memory . . ."].[26] In the published version of the
novel, however, it is not one specific moment of waking but an indefinite
series of similar moments that the narrator remembers, and he uses the
imperfect tense: "le sujet du livre se détachait [not '*se détacha*'] de moi,
j'étais libre de m'y appliquer ou non" ["The subject of the book would
detach itself from me, leaving me free to apply myself to it or not"].[27]
The detachment of the book that the narrator has been reading from
himself resembles, of course, the detachment of the book he is currently
writing from himself. It is in the process of writing that his mind becomes
separate from the book, and this process of separation again resembles
that of Descartes, who asks whether there are not things that cannot be
doubted, "for example, that I am here, seated near the fire, clothed in a
dressing-gown, having this paper between my hands, and other things of
this nature" – only in order immediately to deny the certainty of this self-
presence. Drawing on Hegel's *Phenomenology of Spirit*, Judith Butler has
argued that the act of writing creates for Descartes an "I" that seems separable from its narrator. The writing "eclipses its own bodily origins"
through a "grammar of severable parts" in which not only the body of
the thinker, but various faculties of his mind, including memory, are imagined as separable from his thinking essence.[28] "Sum res cogitans,"

Descartes concludes – "I am a thinking thing" – but only by virtue of having been able to separate his body from his thought through the act of writing.

Proust's text foregrounds the production of an "I" that can be "detached" from its body in the moment of self-contemplation. For Proust, it is in the state of partial wakefulness that the self is in a sense detached from all its previous assumptions, for it does not know where it is located and has only the dim memories of various previous awakenings to set it right:

> [My mind] lost all sense of the place in which I had gone to sleep, and when I awoke, in the middle of the night, as I could not tell where I was, I did not even know who I was; I had only the most rudimentary sense of existence, such as may lurk and flicker in the depths of an animal's consciousness; I was more destitute than the cave-dweller. (*Remembrance*, I, p. 5)

> [Mon esprit] lâchait le plan du lieu où je m'étais endormi, et quand je m'éveillais au milieu de la nuit, comme j'ignorais où je me trouvais, je ne savais même pas qui j'étais; j'avais seulement dans sa simplicité première, le sentiment de l'existence comme il peut frémir au fond d'un animal; j'étais plus dénué que l'homme des cavernes. (*Recherche*, I, p. 5)

In the moment between waking and sleeping, Proust's narrator achieves the detachment from all his own faculties that Descartes seeks, although he loses the power of rational thought along with everything else. Two interrelated questions await answers. The word "even" ("même") suggests on the one hand that the question of *who* he is appears in some sense epistemologically prior to the question of *where* he is. Yet, the relationship of the two clauses suggests that the question of identity ("who") depends for its answer on the question of location: "as [*comme*] I could not tell where I was [*où je me trouvais*; literally, where I found myself]. . . ." The conjunction "comme," like its English equivalent "as," suggests both causal dependence and temporal simultaneity. Both causally and temporally, the knowledge of who he is relies on, or perhaps parallels, the knowledge of where he is. The two questions are separate but the relationship between them is undecidable. The problem posed by Proust's novel is, in a sense, whether the self is anything more than a place-holder, a marker of a given location traversed by various desires and experiences coming from outside itself. Proust ultimately refuses to answer this question.

Descartes faces a similar problem. In order to overcome his doubt, Descartes decides to withhold his assent from any beliefs that are at all questionable, but he observes: "My habitual opinions keep coming back, and, despite my wishes, they capture my belief, which is as it were bound over to them as a result of long occupation and the law of custom" (p. 15). However, through a continual effort to liberate himself from these habitual opinions, Descartes's thinking thing convinces itself that it has detached itself from all such memories. On the basis of this radical process of doubting, Descartes develops a new foundation for knowledge in the indivisibility of the thinking thing which is the essence of the "I," the idea of God, and the freedom of the will. Descartes refuses to accept any knowledge from memory and attempts, in fact, to establish his thinker as a subject who, like Proust's awakened narrator, lacks any attributes at all, except of course for the ability to think, which in Descartes is not strictly an attribute but the essence of the "I." It is not until he has proved God's existence, and on the basis of God's goodness the reliability of memory, that Descartes is willing to admit the contents of memory as evidence, for without the knowledge of a benevolent God it remains quite possible that an evil genius has provided him with all the memories that appear to be his own. Proust's narrator, on the other hand, does not seem to have the option of excluding all his memories, and at any rate he does not make any appeal to an omnipotent God who could guarantee the validity of his perceptions, however clear and distinct. The world returns to the mind (as in Descartes's French, "esprit") of the awakened subject, not as in the *Meditations* by a conscious act of the intellect, but as a result of the functioning of memory. Memory itself is a lesser type of god, and it simply comes to him as he lies awake and uncertain of his own identity:

but then the memory – not yet of the place in which I was, but of various other places where I had lived and might now very possibly be – would come like an aid from on high [*un secours d'en haut*] to draw me up out of the nothingness [*néant*], from which I could never have escaped by myself: in a flash I would traverse centuries of civilisation, and out of a blurred glimpse of oil-lamps, then of shirts with turned-down collars, would gradually piece together the original components of my self [*les traits originaux de mon moi*]. (*Remembrance*, I, p. 5; *Recherche*, I, pp. 5–6)

The instant following the self's total deprivation, in which memory supplies the needs of the dislocated subject, provides a paradigm for the whole novel. Proust will concern himself with the ethical problem of reconstructing the personality out of memory in the context of a radical rejection of all attempts to ground judgment in a conception of the self as capable of achieving absolute self-presence or of guaranteeing the correspondence between consciousness and reality by an appeal to a force outside consciousness. There is nothing except the internal consistency of the narrator's consciousness, the fact that his memories make sense to him and that, as Descartes himself puts it, most of his opinions are "highly probable" (but not certain), to convince Proust's narrator of the reality of the world around him. Not only is there no appeal to God as the cause of the narrator's being. Even the feature of the "I" that Descartes takes as most certain is in doubt for Proust, namely that it is "one and the same I who is now doubting almost everything, who affirms that this one thing is true, denies everything else, desires to know more, is unwilling to be deceived, imagines many things even involuntarily, and is aware of many things which apparently come from the senses" (p. 19).

It is apparently from the memories that Proust's narrator pondered on those evenings in an indefinite past that he constructs his novel. *A la recherche* offers a phenomenology of moral experience, akin in inspiration if not in form to Husserl's contemporary philosophical efforts.[29] The problem of arriving at appropriate norms for his behavior depends for Proust's narrator on the act of interpreting the contents of his consciousness, which are the only traces available to him of an outside world. As the narrator's theory of involuntary memory shows, it is truthfulness to the "inner book" that he takes to be the measure of his art. This apparent concession to "subjectivism" or "relativism," more perhaps than his descriptions of the aristocracy or of homosexuality, has disturbed some Marxists and many moralists.[30] Although there are a variety of events in the novel, such as the Dreyfus affair itself, the war, and a number of political and cultural trends, that can easily be confirmed by reference to other works on the same historical period, or that Proust's first readers could have remembered for themselves, Proust's ultimate appeal for the validity of his observations is, like that of Descartes, to his readers' capacity for introspection. Descartes expects only a small group of readers to be "able and willing to meditate seriously with me, and to withdraw their minds from the senses and from all preconceived opinions" (p. 8). Similarly, Proust appeals to that small group of readers of whom,

it seemed to me that they would not be "my" readers, but the readers of their own selves, my book being merely a sort of magnifying glass like those which the optician at Combray used to offer his customers – it would be my book, but with its help I would furnish them with the means of reading what lay within themselves. So that I should not ask them to praise me or to censure me, but simply to tell me whether "it really is like that," if the words they read within themselves are the same as those which I have written. (*Remembrance*, III, p. 1089)[31]

Where Descartes is assured that his readers will, if they only pay close enough attention, come to subscribe to his proof of God, Proust merely hopes that a sort of dialogue with his readers will lead to a shared self-knowledge.

PROUSTIAN ETHICS: INVOLUNTARY MEMORY AND SOCIAL ROLES

When the narrator recalls how, upon awakening, "as I could not tell where I was, I did not even know who I was," he hints at some of the problems that his epistemological "perspectivism" will pose for his ethics. The fundamental ethical problem for Proust is the fact that the self, the "obscure country" of memory and desire, is not transparent to that other self, the seeker after truth. The possibility frequently arises that what the narrator or another character believes about his or her own motives is a mere projection. The "self" loses its substantiality and its ability to make rational decisions on the basis of free will when it appears as nothing more than a place-holder, a projection of unconscious forces and desires. Paul de Man has demonstrated the centrality of the act of reading as an allegory of the incommensurability between language and its referents in Proust's text.[32] The first illusion described in the text is the narrator's impression that he himself is the subject of the book he has been reading just before falling asleep. In another particularly important scene of reading, analyzed at length by de Man, the narrator considers the significance of the novel as a genre, which results from the first novelist's recognition that the "image" of other people's joys or misfortunes, rather than those joys or misfortunes themselves, is what moves us, so that "the simplification [of our complicated structure of emotions] which consisted in the suppression, pure and simple, of real people would be a decided improvement" (I, p. 91). In the course of reflecting on his reading, the narrator comes to understand his own consciousness as a limit beyond which he cannot pass in any attempt to achieve an immediate perception of external reality. He observes:

When I saw an external object, my consciousness that I was seeing it would remain between me and it, surrounding it with a thin spiritual border that prevented me from ever touching its substance directly; for it would sometimes evaporate before I could make contact with it, just as an incandescent body that is brought into proximity with something wet never actually touches its moisture, since it is always preceded by a zone of evaporation. (I, p. 90)

As part of the summary of the path he takes to the discovery of involuntary memory, in *Le Temps retrouvé*, the narrator recalls this recognition: "For between us and other people there exists a border [*liséré*] of contingencies, just as in my hours of reading in the garden at Combray I had realized that in all perception there exists a border as a result of which there is never absolute contact between reality and our intelligence [*esprit*]" (*Remembrance*, III, p. 1023; *Recherche*, IV, p. 553). Typically, Proust here transforms the observation made in the first-person singular into a conclusion expressed in the first-person plural. He thus transforms what might have been a statement of a psychological order about the narrator's own peculiarities of thought into something more like a general epistemological claim about the possibility of humans' attaining an immediate intuition of other human beings or indeed of the material world generally. The problem posed by uncertainty about one's own perceptions of the world is ultimately akin to that of Sartre's existentialism, namely how to live an authentic and moral life when one inherits one's prejudices and assumptions, if not from an evil genius, then at least from a society whose values may well be hypocritical.

The cornerstone of Proustian ethics is the claim that despite its radically subjective perceptions of reality, the self is capable, through a sort of dialogue among its component parts, of overcoming Barrèsian "relativism" to establish a more satisfactory relationship with the "images" of other people that inhabit, and in a sense haunt, its consciousness. It is the fragmentary conception of identity as a series of roles inhabited successively by the individual but not ultimately detachable from the individual's essence that makes possible the overcoming of relativism without appeal to free will. The competing elements of the personality, while not susceptible to being chosen freely, nonetheless interact with one another in ways that lead the self to a higher level of awareness and to a greater peace with the others who inhabit its consciousness. Enlightenment is possible for Proust's characters individually (if not for society as a whole), but it depends, as de Man might put it, on the acceptance of a blindness, the recognition of one's limited capacity for insight into oneself.[33] The characteristic moments of recognition of the self's blindness do, however, lead in Proust's novel to greater self-knowledge, and that self-knowledge permits action that is more, rather than less, ethically desirable, if it cannot necessarily be said to be simply "morally right." Ultimately, then, Proust's ethics appear more Aristotelian than Kantian, for they rely for the possibility of ethical development on the characteristic tendencies of the self and its susceptibility to training or formation by way of habit, rather than on the self's ability to abstract itself entirely from its interests and position to pursue a course of action that is right in the abstract. Unlike Aristotle, though, Proust shares the modern, non-teleological view of both nature and human nature, and therefore does not take the natural capacities of the human being as a guide to what is right. Left without either "natural" or "transcendental" norms by which to guide his action, the narrator is forced to invent such norms for himself, and he does so through the process of interaction with other characters and reflection on that interaction.

Like Conrad's Marlow, Proust's narrator is fascinated by the figure of the fetish, the product of people's own activity that they worship as a God. In presenting his theory of involuntary memory, he calls attention to the "fetishistic attachment" that the mind forms to objects (he is concerned with once-fashionable hats) in which it had once placed its faith (I, p. 460). There is a sense throughout *A la recherche*, that the self, the "moi," is just such an object of fetishistic attachment. The various impulses, desires, and sensations successively experienced by the thinking "I" are only unified in recollection, but this recollection endows the remembered self with a sort of magical power. The fact that this "I" or "me" can be decomposed into a series of social roles or a series of instantaneous impressions does not deprive it of its magical powers, of the sense that the individual has of a unique and ordered experience that presents to the self of the current moment a set of memories and a duty which it is not free to reject. One of Proust's most typical rhetorical techniques consists in using two rather different metaphors to describe the same object. The difference between the two metaphors leaves open a recurrent Proustian question, namely whether identities are best understood as agglomerates of discrete fragments or as organic unities. For example, in *Le Temps retrouvé*, the narrator will distinguish between the cinematic and writerly conceptions of reality, claiming that

what we call reality is a certain connection between these immediate sensations [of phenomena] and the memories which envelop us simultaneously with them – a connection that is suppressed in a simple cinematic vision, which just because it professes to confine itself to the truth in fact departs widely from it – a unique connection which the writer has to rediscover in order to link for ever in his phrase the two sets of phenomena which reality joins together. (III, p. 924)

In this recapitulation of the theory of involuntary memory, the narrator clearly prefers the writerly conception of reality as a series of experiences linked together by the subjective impulses of memory. The cinematic, or merely objective, account of reality, which fails to provide the subjective element of experience linking together the various "facts," is less true because it attempts to be purely factual. However, the recurrence of similar dual perspectives throughout the novel suggests that the narrator's strict preference for the writerly over the cinematic conception of reality has an element of arbitrariness in it. The writerly, subjective perspective is most adequate perhaps to the task of art, which is truthfulness to individual experience, but the cinematic and theatrical representations of reality seem just as valid for exploring the realm of interaction among individuals, and the gap between these two perspectives is apparently unbridgeable.

The narrator's investigations into his own lapses in judgment show the active role that the self must play in constructing its own moral standards. The artist must ultimately decipher the private "inner book of unknown signs," but this decipherment in itself brings the signs to the surface of the self and in this sense makes them public and shared. As in Descartes's meditations, it is a sort of dialogue with the self, in particular a dialogue between voluntary and involuntary memory, that provides Proust with his standards of knowledge and conduct. Thus, whether or not we are born with a given set of predispositions ("instinct," as Proust calls it) does not seem ultimately to prevent us from judging more or less objectively the contents of our consciousness, which are the only evidence we have of the world outside ourselves. Proust's theory of involuntary memory does not preclude the possibility that the standards by which the artist judges the world are ultimately unique, incommunicable and perhaps even the product of an accident of birth. While accepting the basic premise of Barrès's relativism, that "I must seat myself at the exact point that my eyes themselves, as they have been shaped by the centuries, demand" in order to find the truth for myself, Proust does not assume that it is impossible to progress from this historically located position to something akin to a universalistic perspective on "my" experiences. Unlike Descartes, however, Proust never embraces the notion of an absolute standard outside the self (Descartes's God) that will guarantee the correspondence between what the self thinks it perceives and the things in themselves outside consciousness. Proust does, however, accept that there are standards within the self for what it ought to accept as real in judging its perceptions. Descartes too believed that we judge the contents of our consciousness on the basis of ideas which are innate in us, although unlike Barrès he believed that the same ideas are innate in everyone. It is significant that the only explicit mention of Descartes in the novel is the narrator's endorsement of the statement from the beginning of the *Discourse on Method* that "Good sense is, of all things among men, the most equally distributed."[34] No more than Descartes does Proust claim that no world outside of consciousness really exists. Proust even claims that people are endowed with reason or good sense capable of helping them to judge the contents of their consciousness, but he doubts even more radically than Descartes whether consciousness can achieve a clear and distinct picture of the world outside itself.

THE WAR: THE MORAL UNITY OF THE NATION AND THE GENERAL WILL

Proust seems to present his response to the dualistic and voluntarist tradition of thought in universalistic terms – as a psychology that is valid across all cultures. Yet, in the later volumes of *A la recherche*, the experience of living in a society "divided from top to bottom" by the Dreyfus Affair and then later a society entirely focused on a single goal, the defeat of the Germans, leads him to a new set of observations about individual psychology that turns out to be crucial to his theory of involuntary memory. Nationality turns out to be the most general of roles, short of that of "human being," and the most unconsciously inhabited. It thus plays a fundamental part in situating the self and poses a serious obstacle to ethical development. Furthermore, like Renan, the narrator represents the "racial" heterogeneity of the French nation as a destabilizing force in his ethical system, which may even undermine the possibility of a universalistic sense of justice. The two public events reveal what Proust's narrator takes to be the arbitrariness of social identifications, the disjunction between role and essence, but they also reveal the close interpenetration between role and essence, the importance of such social categories as "Frenchman," "Jew," "aristocrat," or "homosexual" in the formation of individual identities. To use a trope that is common in Proust, there is at the same time a distance and an intimate connection between the "name" and the "place," between the signifier of a given social role and the signified, the person who fills that role. This odd, intimate relationship calls attention to the fetish-character of the "self," the power of a given place-marker, the "I," or the proper name, to crystallize social relations.[35]

The narrator himself locates the development of his theory of involuntary memory in relation to his experiences in wartime Paris. In *Le Temps retrouvé*, Proust specifically relates the problem of the moral unity of the nation and of the self to the role of historical conflicts in forging the unitary nation with which Proust's narrator identifies himself. Throughout the description of the war, the narrator calls attention to what might be called the fiction of the "we" whereby citizens of the nation identify themselves with the nation as a whole. Thus, he notes that when speaking of the French position in the war, Mme Verdurin would "say 'we' when she meant France. 'Now listen: we demand of the King of Greece that he should withdraw from the Peloponnese.'" Similarly, but with greater self-reflexiveness, Françoise, inspired by the pacifist butler, observes of the French government's military pressure on the same (pro-German, but officially neutral) King Constantine of Greece, "We are no better than they are. If we were in Germany, we would do just the same" (III, p. 875). In the course of the war, precisely as a result of his conversations with the defeatist Baron de Charlus, the narrator himself becomes increasingly aware of the limits of his own attitude of moral neutrality. What this discovery also allows him to undertake is a revaluation of the traditional analogy, found first in Plato's *Republic*, between justice in the state and justice in the soul. Whereas this analogy traditionally suggests that the overcoming of internal conflict in the state as in the soul permits the achievement of an equilibrium dependent on a hierarchy of classes and of passions, Proust transforms the analogy to suggest that it is precisely the struggle among competing and incommensurable forces within the state, as within the soul, that allows for moral and political transformation and maintains the health of the body and the body politic. Conflict is crucial to Proust's model of the self. The fiction of the "we" turns out to be a magnified form of the fiction of the "I."

When the narrator returns to Paris from his sanatorium in 1916, he discovers that a major reversal of the political order has taken place as a result of the war. Anti-Dreyfusard aristocrats such as the Baron de Charlus have become suspect as pro-Germanist, while old Dreyfusards like the fictional M. Bontemps and the historical Georges Clemenceau have become the backbone of the "party of social order" (III, p. 750). This turning of the "social kaleidoscope" has allowed Dreyfusard Jews to be embraced by the patriotic right wing (I, pp. 554–557). During the Dreyfus affair, Charlus had claimed to doubt the nationality of the narrator's friend Bloch, a young Jewish intellectual, observing, "It is not a bad idea, if you wish to learn about life, to have a few foreigners among your friends." The narrator informed Charlus that Bloch was French, to which Charlus replied, "Oh, I took him to be a Jew" (II, p. 297). During the war, it is the Baron himself, with his various German allegiances, whose patriotism has become suspect. Madame Verdurin, who has ousted him from her "little clan," asks with feigned confusion, "What is his nationality exactly, isn't he an Austrian?" (III, p. 788). The Baron becomes a principle of anti-patriotism, unable to believe any "good" news of French victories. Although he pretends to the narrator (and perhaps to himself) that he is entirely pro-French, his pessimistic predictions concerning the course of the war show his true sympathies. He continually expects the worst for France. Of the French optimists, who expected to win the war in the first two months, he observes, "They did not know as I do the strength of Germany, the courage of the Prussian race!" (III, p. 821). The presence of such a defeatist in one of the oldest aristocratic houses of France teaches the narrator a lesson about what he takes to be the arbitrariness of social identifications. The narrator's experience of spying on the Baron also leads him to discover a model of an alternative public sphere and an image of international fraternity in the form of the homosexual brothels to which the Baron repairs at night, along with soldiers of all the allied nations.

Although the war itself was of course not part of the original (pre-war) plan for the novel, Proust makes it a crucial phase in the narrator's arrival at his theory of involuntary memory. Charlus's criticisms of Barrès during the war prepare the way for the narrator's repudiation of Barrès's nationalist prescriptions in the final, post-war section of the novel (III, p. 822–823). More importantly, his recognition that an intelligent man like the Baron de Charlus could share none of his own opinions about the war helps the narrator to understand the idea of the nation as a sort of limit of one's ability to see the world objectively. While listing the stages of his discovery of the idea of lost time, the narrator observes:

Finally, to a certain extent, the germanophilia of M. de Charlus . . . had helped me to free myself for a moment, if not from my germanophobia, at least from my belief in the pure objectivity of this feeling, had helped to make me think that perhaps what applied to love applied also to hate and that, in the terrible judgement which France had passed against Germany – that she was a nation outside the pale of humanity – the most important element was an objectification of feelings as subjective as those which had caused Rachel and Albertine to appear so precious, the one to Saint-Loup and the other to me. (III, p. 951)

The most unconscious of social roles seems to be that of belonging to a nation, and the fact that to be part of another nation appears to put another person outside the pale of humanity emphasizes the nation as perhaps the highest level of abstract identification short of universality.

The broader question of the moral unity of the nation as a particular barrier to human understanding that needs to be examined becomes apparent, however, as the narrator's discussion of Charlus's Germanophobia continues:

[J]ust as I as an individual had had successive loves and at the end of each one its object had appeared to me to be valueless, so I had already seen in my country successive hates which had, for example, at one time condemned as traitors – a thousand times worse than the Germans into whose hands they were delivering France – those very Dreyfusards such as Reinach with whom to-day patriotic Frenchmen were collaborating against a race whose every member was of necessity a liar, a savage beast, a madman . . . (III, p. 952)

There could be no better illustration of Renan's claim that it is forgetting that constitutes the nation, but what Proust has added to this claim is the recognition that a similar sort of forgetting structures the individual. Ultimately, however, the narrator seems to have a typically liberal faith in the ability of the individual to overcome his or her prejudices, a faith which he does not have for the nation as a whole.

What is most interesting about the narrator's observations on the "nation-individual," finally, is the reversal of the traditional analogy between the soul and the state. In *The Social Contract*, Rousseau had argued that the general will, or what is right, conflicts with the will of all, or what the people want, only "when the social bond begins to relax and the state to grow weak, when private interests begin to make themselves felt and small societies begin to influence the large one."[36] For Proust, on the other hand, such a conflict between the general will and the will of all is in fact the usual course of events. Indeed, a similar conflict takes place within the individual. The narrator offers a theory of the individual's relationship to the nation that seems, once again, close to the "relativism" of Barrès:

Now within a nation, the individual, if he is truly part of the nation, is simply a cell of the nation-individual. Brain-washing is a meaningless expression. Had the French been told that they were going to be beaten, no single Frenchman would have given way to despair any more than he would if he had been told that he was going to be killed by the Berthas. The real brain-washing is what – if we are genuinely a living member of a nation – we tell ourselves because we have hope, which is a form of a nation's instinct of self-preservation. To remain blind to the unjustness of the individual "Germany," to recognize at every moment the justness of the cause of the individual "France," the surest way was not for a German to be without judgment, or for a Frenchman to possess it, it was, both for one and for the other, to be possessed of patriotism. (III, p. 798)

In this passage, the narrator seems to be endorsing the perspective of Barrès by suggesting that anyone who is a French patriot will continually be assured of the justice of the French cause. More interestingly, he also implies a theory of ideology, for he argues that "Brain-washing is a meaningless expression" and that one's beliefs depend not on rational judgment but on the projection of one's own interests as the measure of justice. He attempts to show that judgment in itself has nothing to do with justice and everything to do with prejudice. Ultimately, however, what is most important for the narrator's theory of involuntary memory in this passage is his analysis of the fiction of the "we," which is analogous in its effects to the more general fiction of identity that is that fetishistic object known as the self, or "*moi*." He observes that he himself cannot really imagine the Baron's perspective. Patriotism is simply the quality of identifying oneself entirely with the nation, and it is a quality that the Baron de Charlus lacks but the narrator possesses, so that

after all, I can only conjecture what I might have done if I had not been an actor in the drama, if I had not been a part of the actor France in the same way as, in my quarrels with Albertine, my sad gaze and the choking feeling in my throat had been parts of the individual "me" [*moi*] who was passionately interested in my cause; I could not arrive at detachment. (*Remembrance*, III, p. 799; *Recherche*, IV, p. 353)

Again, as in the opening scene of the entire novel, it is the problem of arriving at "detachment" that poses the limit to the narrator's self-understanding. The war makes the ethical and sociological individuals somehow one, in the sense that the individual who is truly patriotic is incapable of detachment from the mass of the nation. At the outside limit, the war provides evidence to Proust's narrator of a type of hermeneutic circle, according to which the self as it currently exists can only grasp its own history from within the language that it has inherited, along with a set of ideologies. The nation is the particular form of the fiction "we" that claims to define the self through and through.

Throughout the novel, it seems an existential condition, either of consciousness or of language, that a conflict analogous to that between the "will of all" and the "general will" animates the individual's own self-awareness. At the same time, it is within the power of consciousness to grasp this inevitable conflict and to understand the impossibility of an exhaustive account of the contents of consciousness itself. This structure, analogous to what Derrida has called "difference," seems ultimately in Proust to offer the materials for a defense of a fairly traditional sort of liberalism. The public face of the individual is nothing but the series of discrete aspects of the social personality she presents to the world. It is to a purely interior and private realm that the experience of organic unity belongs, and while this inner realm turns out to contain above all traces of the other public realm, it remains nevertheless decipherable by the individual only in the moment of retreat from the public world, which is tainted by fashion, propaganda, and the inevitably inadequate perspective of the will of all rather than the general will. Even the encounter with the other ultimately takes place in such a private realm. It is in his retrospective consideration of his conversation with Charlus that the narrator converts it into a basis for judging his own perspective. The first interview itself is merely the occasion for the narrator's later revision of his theory of involuntary memory, which takes place in the library of the Guermantes household, as he casts his mind back over the war.

It is precisely the fact of the basic incommunicability of this moment of subjective self-presence that seems in Proust to justify the separation of private and public realms. Barrès would make the recognition of one's irredeemably subjective perspective on reality the basis of a rejection of the liberal ideals of universalism, equality before the law, and human rights. For Proust, on the other hand, the inevitable gap between each person's subjective perspective on her own experience and the objective, external perspective makes the existence of an autonomous private realm necessary. It is only in the private realm that one encounters the inner book of unknown signs, but it is only in the conversation with others, in a separate public realm, that one can make sense of what is found in that private realm. Unlike the thinkers in the liberal tradition whom he resembles in other respects, Proust hopes for very little from the formal public sphere of politics *per se*, but he understands the encounter with others in society, or even in private conversation, as a form of political encounter in which the private is made public.

THE DREYFUS AFFAIR: THE ACCURSED RACES AND THE NATION-STATE

If Proust's narrator sees an extreme limit to the ability of the self to overcome its own prejudices or to communicate with others, it has to do with what he calls "race." The narrator uses the term to describe a category of social roles that are apparently intractable. Jews, homosexuals, aristocrats, peasants, and inhabitants of provincial towns are all described as belonging to "races." The word seems to refer throughout the novel to those social roles whose fetish-character is so pronounced that they appear to limit the ability of the self to perform the process of self-interrogation that is the central task of Proustian ethics. Because of their power, these social categories take on, in Proust's novel, the appearance of "natural" forces that threaten to undermine the process of enlightenment. Proust's narrator continually rejects outright racism, and reveals racial identities to be structured by social forces, but he still sees in these particularly powerful categories of identitarian thought a potentially unbreachable limit to the self's capacity to universalize itself. In the context of his description of the role Charlus's Germanophilia played in his own discovery of involuntary memory, the narrator complains that people, unable to comprehend the subjective character of their own judgments of reality, continually devise theories to explain the validity of their prejudices. He lists several examples of such theories: "that it is against nature to have schools directed by the religious order, as the radicals believe, or that it is impossible for the Jewish race to become part of the nation [*se nationaliser*], or that there exists an undying hatred between the Teutonic and the Latin races, the yellow race having been temporarily rehabilitated" (*Remembrance*, III, p. 952; *Recherche*, IV, p. 492). Yet, despite his continual rejection of racial theories from Gobineau to Barrès, the narrator does frequently treat race as a limit of ethical development. Even this passage, with the implicit suggestion that the desirable solution to the problem of anti-semitism is the assimilation of the Jewish race into the French nation, draws on the traditional voluntarist discourse of liberal nationalism with its suspicion of loyalties other than those to the nation as a whole.

The problem of racial identities for Proust seems to be that the modern nation-state demands the suppression of those very differences among people that have the most formative effect on their conceptions of their own identities. In his descriptions of the Dreyfus affair, the narrator's attitude to the problem of the "nationalization" of the Jewish race is much less sanguine than in his remarks in the post-war section of the novel. In describing the beginning stages of the affair, he suggests, for example, that those who imagined they were following rational arguments concerning Dreyfus's guilt or innocence were perhaps at root submitting to atavistic racial tendencies: "Bloch believed himself to have been led by a logical chain of reasoning to choose Dreyfusism, yet he knew that his nose, his skin, and his hair had been imposed upon him by his race. Doubtless the reason enjoys more freedom; yet it obeys certain laws which it has not prescribed for itself" (II, pp. 306–307). Proust's narrator refers here, as frequently throughout the novel, to Kant's ethics, and to the categorical imperative that Barrès had criticized in *Les déracinés*, namely the conception of the human as a rational being who must regard itself as establishing a universal law through all the actions of its will. Kant's conception of autonomy is precisely that the reason must obey only those laws which it has prescribed for itself. It is here, with the question of the racial inheritance involved in the functioning of the reason, that Proust's narrator explores what he takes to be a serious limit to the ability to interpret reality objectively. The question of race is the ultimate form of the mind/body problem for Proust. For Proust's narrator agrees with Barrès that the reason is not capable of such universalizing, autonomous moral reflection, since the reason cannot prescribe all its laws for itself but must, at least to a certain extent, follow the laws of merely physical nature.

The narrator seems here and elsewhere to adopt the language of Darwinist character-determinism in describing this condition of what Kant would call heteronomy. Indeed, the narrator extends Barrès's theory by treating the Jews as akin to other races, notably the race of "men-women," or homosexuals, but also the "races" of aristocrats and peasants who fail to incorporate themselves into the modern nation of equal citizens/bourgeois. The word "race" seems to apply to whatever group fails to be assimilated into the nation and maintains a distinctness the narrator associates with echoes of a distant past. He does not, however, wholeheartedly subscribe to the Barrèsian view that the reason is irreducibly different for each race. He allows that the reason enjoys more freedom than the body, and, against racial theorists of the nation, he explicitly claims that the Jews are capable of "nationalization." Ultimately, he presents the cases of Swann and Bloch, whose "Jewishness" determines their attitudes to the Dreyfus affair, as akin to his own involuntary illness. This underlying analogy seems to structure his views on race. "Jewishness" turns out to be a form of theatricality, in which the Jew plays a role assigned to him by history and/or nature.[37] This role, however, seems destined to conflict with the narrative of nationhood, which claims to overcome all subordinately assigned roles and to create a "moral unity," a "we" that is subjectively unified. On the one hand, the Jews are the ancient race that must be assimilated into the modern nation, the irrational body to be overcome by rational mind. On the other hand, they are a sort of anti-identitarian principle that undermines the fiction of stable social identities, just as the fact of the self's radical situatedness or embodiment continually undermines its attempts

to achieve autonomy, "detachment," and universality. These two perspectives on race are as irreconcilable as the "organic" and "geometric"
views of the nation. The nation understood as organic unity requires the
assimilation of the Jews. Seen as a geometrical construct, the nation's
attempt to incorporate the Jews amounts to a fantasy of an unrealizable
organic unity, which the Jews themselves, and all the other "accursed
races," will continually undermine.

The question of race thus poses the problem of whether social roles
depend on intractable, natural forces. What Proust's analysis of the
question of racial identities eventually suggests is that it is the logic of
the nation-state, with its demand that nationality be the measure of citizenship and ultimately of humanity, that makes the existence of "races"
appear to threaten the ethical process. In other words, the nation-state's
hostility to subnational and international groups and its demand for a
homogeneous "we" make the pseudo-natural qualities associated with
race into central political problems for modernity. In the context of a
society in which "Jewishness" and "Frenchness" appear to be mutually
opposed categories, the nation-state presents itself as hostile not only to
Jewishness but to whatever other social roles make compelling demands
on the loyalty and desires of its citizens. It is the homogenizing logic of
the nation-state, which demands that all citizens deny whatever distinguishes them from their fellows, whatever makes them unlike others, and
demands moral unity in place of fragmentation, that makes the "curse"
of racial identity appear incompatible with full citizenship.

Hannah Arendt has drawn on Proust's descriptions of the Dreyfus
affair to demonstrate the "perversion of equality from a political to a
social concept" attendant on the Dreyfus affair. Morris B. Kaplan has
recently shown the centrality of this reading of Proust to understanding
Arendt's theory of politics in the liberal nation-state.[38] I will argue here
that Proust depicts the hysteria of the affair particularly in terms of the
irreconcilability of political and social equality with the heterogeneity he
associates with the term "race." Making use of Arendt's analysis of the
close relationship between modern anti-semitism and the rise of the
liberal nation-state, I will suggest that Proust himself found the competing demands of "Jewishness" and "Frenchness" to be irreconcilable and
thus that, while he criticized the pure racialism of Barrès, he ultimately
established a position very close to that of Renan, namely that national
unity demanded the suppression of racial difference. His theories of
involuntary memory and ethical development reveal the profound
assimilationist bias Proust derived from the voluntarist tradition, but

they also point the way to a new sort of liberalism, based on the conception of the self as multiple and radically situated. These other possible
relationships I will summarize by the expression "equality of condition
and multiplicity of selves."

It is particularly in the volume *Sodome et Gomorrhe* that Proust addresses
himself to the problem of the two "accursed races" ("races maudites"),
to which he belonged, the race of Jews and that of men-women or
homosexuals. Arendt argued, in *The Origins of Totalitarianism*, that Proust
bore witness to the passage from a religious anti-semitism directed
against the "crime" of "Judaism," which consisted in belief in the Jewish
religion, to a modern, "scientific" anti-semitism directed against the
"vice" of "Jewishness," which consisted in having Jewish "racial"
origins. As Arendt observes, "Jews had been able to escape from their
Judaism into conversion; from Jewishness there was no escape. A crime,
moreover, is met with punishment; a vice can only be exterminated"
(*Origins*, pp. 83, 87). Arendt also contends that this transformation of the
crime of Judaism into the vice of Jewishness resulted in part from the
demands of the nation-state for "social" as well as "political" equality.
Modern anti-semitism resulted from the situation in which "Jews
received their citizenship from governments which in the process of centuries had made nationality a prerequisite for citizenship and homogeneity of population the outstanding characteristic of the body politic"
(p. 11). In such a context, various social groups within the triumphant
liberal nation-states of the last third of the nineteenth century could not
accept at the same time Jewish difference from the national norm and
the Jews' political equality with other citizens. Arendt, who greatly
admires Proust's description of the Dreyfus affair, claims that Proust
"mistook" his private obsession with Jewishness, which resulted from the
social impact of the Dreyfus affair, for an actual "racial predestination"
– an expression the narrator does indeed use (p. 84). I will argue instead
that, while Proust himself represented the conflict between social heterogeneity and political equality that Arendt makes the centerpiece of
her history of anti-semitism, he did not subscribe to theories of "racial
predestination" *per se*. However, he found the contradictions of minority
status in the modern nation-state to be so powerful that he was highly
skeptical of the possibility of justice on the terms prescribed by liberal
nationalism. His theory of "involuntary memory," like his discussion of
"racial predestination," emphasized what he treated as the inevitable
conflict between citizenship in a liberal nation-state and membership in
the "accursed races." In the Dreyfus affair, the nation demanded that the

Jew cease being a Jew and become instead a Frenchman, just as later, during the war, it would demand that the aristocrats abrogate their relationships of caste in favor of the moral unity of the nation. It was the contradiction between Jewishness and Frenchness, as it manifested itself in the social pressures of the Dreyfus affair, rather than any belief in the actual theories of racial predestination of a Gobineau or a Barrès, that made Proust so pessimistic about liberal-democratic politics.

The narrator concerns himself with a general historical transformation that he witnesses in the Third Republic. The major social reversal of the novel is that the bourgeois and Dreyfusard salon of Mme Verdurin first attracts the aristocracy and then essentially becomes aristocratic when, after the death of the Duchesse, Mme Verdurin marries the Duc de Guermantes. This transformation in "high society" is not an autonomous development, but a result of political changes and the breakdown of the caste system in which the bourgeoisie of the narrator's youth had such faith. As the narrator observes, "In society as it exists today a single generation suffices for the change which formerly over a period of centuries transformed a middle-class name like Colbert into an aristocratic one" (III, p. 1003). A little bit like the pigs who become indistinguishable from human beings at the end of Orwell's *Animal Farm*, the haute bourgeoisie of the 1870s have mixed almost entirely with the aristocracy by the end of the war. "The most characteristic feature" of post-war society, the narrator notes, "was the prodigious ease with which individuals moved up or down the social scale" (III, pp. 1003–1004). At this level, all that has happened is that processes that once took generations have sped up considerably. Yet the narrator also foresees the possibility that the increasing rapidity of social change could lead to a world in which differences of social class would indeed cease to mean anything: "Not only does snobbishness change form, it might one day altogether disappear – like war itself – and radicals and Jews might become members of the Jockey" (III, p. 1003). At a lower level of society, too, the caste system is being replaced by a mobile, and kaleidoscopic, class system. Thus the daughter of Françoise has none of her mother's countrified manners or ways of speaking. Instead, she speaks in a Parisian argot and despises the country where she was brought up (II, pp. 149–150 and *passim*). The mind of Françoise, with its traces of "an ancient French past, noble and little understood," seems headed for extinction as, in Eugen Weber's phrase, the republic turns "peasants into Frenchmen."[39] Similarly, the elevator-operator at the Grand Hotel at Balbec, touched by the spirit of the age, refers to himself and others of his class as "employees" rather than "servants" (I, pp. 857–8). Proust of course does not concern himself with the question of what precisely caused the increasingly egalitarian ideologies he encounters, or of which came first, the superstructure or the base. As far as he is concerned, the processes of transformation in society that he describes may be rooted in the growth of capitalist modes of exchange, in industrialization and urbanization, or in more or less cultural developments. However, it is certain that politics themselves play a decisive role in establishing the situation in which the caste system disintegrates. The memory of the ideals of the French Revolution is alive and well among the lower classes in Proust. When the Baron de Charlus offers his lover Morel one of his titles, Morel prefers to keep his own plebeian name. To the Baron's remark that "there was a time when my ancestors were proud of the title of chamberlain or butler to the King," Morel replies: "There was also a time when my ancestors cut off your ancestors' heads" (II, p. 1097).

It is in this sort of society, in which the ideal if not the reality of "equality of condition" is gaining ascendancy, that Proust depicts the consequences of the Dreyfus affair. It is in such a society that "role" and "essence" seem most eminently detachable. Since each person is formally equal before the law, the actual differences arising from their different historical situations, or even from physical differences among individuals, come to seem increasingly arbitrary. The apparent arbitrariness of social identities seems in fact peculiarly dependent on the increasingly egalitarian character of French society. Once deprived of their traditional content, markers of difference such as aristocratic birth or Jewish origin become almost free-floating signs, whose meaning can change radically from one moment to the next, as the "social kaleidoscope [turns] and . . . the Dreyfus case [precipitates] the Jews onto the lowest rung of the social ladder," or later the kaleidoscope turns again and casts down the Baron de Charlus (II, p. 194). The Dreyfus affair is a case of an event in the political realm affecting the development of society. As Proust repeatedly observes, when Dreyfus's innocence becomes increasingly apparent, "anti-Dreyfusard opposition . . . greatly increased in violence, and from being purely political [became] social" (II, p. 704). Stuck with an indefensible political position, the anti-Dreyfusard forces become increasingly intolerant socially. To their chagrin, however, the affair only speeds up the process of social leveling which has undermined their position, and the anti-Dreyfusard aristocrats complain that while they can no longer enjoy the company of their witty Jewish friends, they are expected to patronize the anti-Dreyfusard politicians, no matter how low their social origins. While the Dreyfusards themselves, defenders of the ideals of 1789, manage to triumph in the political realm, the narrator observes that in the stage immediately after Dreyfus's pardon, "Dreyfusism was triumphant politically but not socially," a fact that accounts for the Dreyfusard Madame Verdurin's sudden interest in social acquaintances who are anti-Dreyfusard (II, p. 914). Ultimately, it is the war that will reunite the two halves of the country by giving them a common enemy. In the meantime, however, the Jews in the novel are hardly considered Frenchmen. Swann, an entirely assimilated Jew, is exiled from society by his old friends the Guermantes, who view his political opinions as a form of personal betrayal. "Until today," observes the Duc de Guermantes, "I have always been foolish enough to believe that a Jew could be a Frenchman, I mean an honorable Jew, a man of the world" (II, p. 703). Not only does Charlus argue that Bloch is a foreigner; he also claims that "[Dreyfus's] crime is non-existent. This compatriot of your friend [Bloch] would have committed a crime if he had betrayed Judaea, but what has he to do with France," an opinion which does not reduce, but perhaps increases, the erotic charge he finds in the exoticism of Bloch's Jewishness.

Proust's own psychological theories seem to owe a great deal to his observations of society under the Dreyfus affair. It is the "social kaleidoscope" of the Dreyfus affair that makes the narrator aware of the mistake of believing that "one's position is an integral part of [*fait corps avec*] one's person." (*Remembrance*, I, p. 554; *Recherche*, I, p. 505). More than any of the other roles played in the novel – Professor of the Sorbonne, lover, artist, schoolboy – those roles associated with the term "race" draw attention to the "situatedness" of the self. They are roles that one has not chosen and is not free to renounce, as even the assimilated Jews discover. The very theatricality of the roles of Jewishness and homosexuality, what Sedgwick has called the "spectacle of the closet," testifies not only to the artificiality of these roles but also to the immense power that they hold over the people who play them; in other words, their theatricality emphasizes their fetish character. Early in the Dreyfus affair, the narrator notes Bloch's tendency both to call attention to his own Jewish origins and to downplay their importance, a combination which indicates Bloch's obsessive concern with what gentiles will think of him. Bloch remarks to the narrator, "I rather like to take into account the element in my feelings (slight though it is), which may be ascribed to my Jewish origin." The narrator comments: "he made this statement because it seemed to him at once clever and courageous to speak the truth about his race, a truth which at the same time he managed to water down to a remarkable extent, like misers who decide to discharge their debts but cannot bring themselves to pay more than half of them" (I, p. 802). The homosexuals, too, are obsessed with their "vice" (as the narrator calls it "for the sake of linguistic convenience"), which structures all their relationships with others (II, p. 635).

The narrator claims that Bloch and Swann are uncritical Dreyfusards because of their Jewish inheritance, just as Saint-Loup, who had been a Dreyfusard while he was in love with the Jewish actress Rachel, reverts to hereditary anti-Dreyfusism as soon as Rachel abandons him on the grounds that she cannot have sympathy with the "scion of an alien race" (II, p. 720). All these references to hereditary political opinions could be taken to be metaphorical, in the sense that these opinions might result not from an actual innate tendency but from the fact that society has placed these characters in a position that makes it inevitable that they will sympathize with others in their own group (Jews, aristocrats, etc.). Whether understood as the result of "nature" or of "nurture," however, or of a complex mixture of the two, the political opinions of the various "racial" and class groups in the novel are ultimately akin to the narrator's own "involuntary illness" and his theory of involuntary memory. For the outstanding characteristic of these opinions is that they are "given such as they are" to the characters, whom all the reasoning in the world will not dissuade from their belief in the righteousness of their cause, just as later the French will be unable to imagine that there could be any justice on the German side in the First World War. Ultimately, all of the characters share in varying degrees the peculiarity of the narrator, who frequently compares both himself and Swann to lunatics, drug addicts, and consumptives, who imagine they are on the verge of being cured when in fact they are entirely in the control of their disease. The implicit analogy between racial predestination and mental illness draws of course on traditional racial prejudices, but it also subverts them.

In the famous section of the novel known as the "races maudites" ("the accursed races"), Proust develops at length an analogy between Jews and homosexuals that, while not endorsing Barrès's racism, does embrace some of Renan's arguments about the nature of race, notably the interplay between physical or bodily and moral or spiritual characteristics of a race. The narrator observes Jupien and Charlus meeting in his courtyard, and remarks of their courtship ritual, "one does not arrive spontaneously at that pitch of perfection except when one meets in a foreign country a compatriot with whom an understanding then develops of itself, the means of communication being the same and, even though one has never seen each other before, the scene already set" (II, p. 627). In what follows, the homosexuals, like the Jews, appear as strangers in a strange land, whose only true compatriots (other homosexuals) are distasteful to themselves. Some recent critics have shown the tendency of Proust's text to deconstruct the "naturalizing" tendencies of Darwinist and other biological discourses on sexual and racial identity.[40] Drawing on Arendt's analysis of Proust, Morris Kaplan has demonstrated that Proust's analogy between the two accursed races shows the "complex genealogy of the production of 'natural' identities [homosexuality, Jewishness] as an attempt to stabilize an order disturbed by tensions between equality and difference."[41] The late nineteenth century created both Jewishness and homosexuality as categories revealing the essence of a person's identity, their "vice," and these essentialized identities replaced the older conception of Judaism and sodomy as "crimes," or specific acts that, while punishable, were not constitutive of the identity of the actor. Proust describes the transition to the modern "scientific" discourse and also shows, as Kaplan puts it, that the "'innate disposition' results in 'Jewishness' or 'homosexuality' only under social conditions of Christian orthodoxy or compulsory heterosexuality." Kaplan shows how apparently "natural," biological forces turn out, in Proust, to be constructs of historical and social discourses. Proust's account of this "naturalizing" process is appropriate to modern liberal-democratic conceptions of the individual that attempt to escape the trap of "exclusive identification," which reduces the person to membership in a given category, such as "homosexual" or "Jew."[42] One problem posed by Proust's text, it seems to me, is that despite its deconstruction of the "natural" categories of race-based thinking, these categories seem to maintain an immense power over the characters who are marked by them. They are roles whose fetish-character is so strong that their apparent "naturalness" seems unlikely to yield to attempts to find a common, universal humanity underlying these roles. This situation seems to me to result from Proust's eagerness to defend a liberal conception of the nation-state in the voluntarist tradition stretching from Rousseau to Renan against Barrès's nationalistic "relativism." Proust shares much of the voluntarist tradition's suspicion of loyalties to groups and identities other than the nation. He thus represents "natural," racial identities not only as historical constructs but also as primitive forms of social organization which are in continual conflict with the hegemony of the modern liberal nation-state. In Proust's portrayal of "racial" minorities, the conflict between heterogeneity and equality appears as an essential and inescapable feature of membership in the modern nation-state.

The narrator neither embraces the theory of "racial predestination" wholeheartedly nor rejects it as a mere ideological construct. Rather, he sees the tension between race and nation in a light similar to that suggested by Renan's "What is a Nation?" With Rousseau, Kant, and Renan, Proust treats whatever belongs to the private realm of intimate attachments, and whatever is not chosen by the will, as at odds with the demands of justice and moral unity. Renan had distinguished between two forms of "race," the race studied by historians and philologists that could be "made and unmade" and the race studied by anthropologists: "real descent, a blood relation."[43] Renan's main argument was that national groups belong in the former category, not the latter, and that race must be irrelevant to politics. Yet, Renan supported this claim with a theory of the "forgetting" necessary to ensure the unity of the national will, which suggested that in fact he saw race as highly relevant to politics – and saw in it a barrier to the equal participation of all in the cult of the nation, a barrier that must be overcome by assimilation. Proust develops a similar conception of the conflict between race and nation. In pursuing his extended analogy between Jews and homosexuals, the narrator observes that the Sodomites, "having been finally invested, by a persecution similar to that of Israel, with the physical and moral characteristics of a race . . . while steadfastly denying that they are a race (the name of which is the vilest of insults), readily unmask those who succeed in concealing the fact that they belong to it" (p. 639). On the one hand, the various "racial" identities, Jewishness, homosexuality, even aristocratic birth, are not "natural" categories but products of historical memory and forgetting. It is persecution that creates the "race." On the other hand, the fact of unmasking the situation in which races are "made and unmade" does not in itself "unmake" those very races: the "homosexual" or the "Jew" is a powerful social category precisely because of the imbrication of what appear to the narrator to be "natural" categories (race, descent, and heredity) with more evidently cultural categories, such as religious belief or laws regulating acceptable sexual behavior. The narrator seems, indeed, to suspect that a "natural" or biological fact underlies the socially constructed identities of "Jewishness," "homosexuality," and aristocratic blood. His theory that the inhabitants of Sodom escaped from God's angels by lying about their sexuality and then engendered a "numerous progeny" and his description of the "innate disposition" of the Sodomites do not seem merely poses to be deconstructed. It is true that the narrator disclaims any scientific status for his observations, but he continually observes traits that he takes to be inherited, as for example Robert de Saint-Loup's homosexuality which he considers to be the result of some sort of recessive trait that has also appeared in Saint-Loup's uncle Charlus.

While it is possible to see the narrator as a sort of stooge of gentile and heterosexual ideology and thus to discredit his observations, ultimately the author (by way of the plot he creates) seems to suggest that a kernel of biological heredity underlies the admittedly contingent constructions of homosexual or Jewish identity. Whatever Proust's or the narrator's position on the question of heredity, however, the narrator clearly shares with Renan the assumption that identities of this sort are detrimental to the cause of the "moral unity of the nation." Proust describes a form of social life in which each person is both an individual citizen and a member of various subnational or international groups, which may depend on affinity or indeed on such contingent facts of "racial" inheritance as the color of one's skin, and he treats this conflict as undermining both unity and the possibility of justice. In an almost tragic vein, undoubtedly made more poignant by Proust's own "Jewishness" and "homosexuality," the narrator refers to the Sodomites as

a race upon which a curse is laid and which must live in falsehood and perjury because it knows that its desire, that which constitutes life's dearest pleasure, is held to be punishable, shameful, an inadmissible thing; which must deny its God, since its members, even when Christians, when at the bar of justice they appear and are arraigned, must before Christ and in his name refute as a calumny what is their very life; sons without a mother, to whom they are obliged to lie all her life long and even in the hour when they close her dying eyes. (p. 637)

Even their friends, the narrator continues, misunderstand the homosexuals, "just as certain judges assume and are more inclined to pardon murder in inverts and treason in Jews for reasons derived from original sin and racial predestination" (p. 638). In this passage, the narrator explicitly criticizes the theory of "racial predestination," but he does subscribe to the view that, as a result of the opprobrium with which homosexuals, like Jews, are treated, they are under a curse that determines their fates. It is not entirely ironically that the narrator describes homosexuality as an "incurable disease" (p. 639). These identities, furthermore, create a significant barrier to the achievement of a shared sense of justice, for justice seems to assume a norm which reflects the hegemonic culture. It is not that Proust or the narrator accepts at face value the racialism of a Barrès, but that the "races" themselves, caught between dispositions that the narrator assumes are real and probably natural and a society that treats them as outcasts, form small societies within the larger one, and that the members of these societies seem incapable of directing their own destinies. The members of the minority races themselves are also afraid or incapable of being transformed from members of a given race into citizens of the nation, of being "nationalized."

Thus, the fate of the accursed races in Proust is to be rejected from the society of the modern nation-state with its demands for social homogeneity to accompany political equality. If the races are to be accepted, then it is apparently only through assimilation or "nationalization," that is, by lying to the dominant society which judges them according to the idiosyncratic standards that it disguises under the name of neutrality. The case of the "accursed races" suggests an almost tragic conception of the nature of identity in modern society, namely that a lie, a renunciation of one's own intimate life, is necessary to permit the minority group to belong to the nation of equal citizens with their increasingly homogeneous social system. At the same time, Proust's text also seems to offer the possibility of a conception of the "accursed races" that avoids the prospect of assimilation, namely the idea that the existence of large racial minorities implies the instability of the nation-state's own categories. The accursed races, then, could be considered a radically anti-identitarian principle that undermines the conventional conception of the nature of the self in modern society. As Kaplan puts it, they may problematize the nation-state's demand for "exclusive identification." This alternative is posed when the narrator rejects the "national" model itself as a possibility for overcoming the agonistic character of minority identities in modern society. Thus, the narrator observes that "I have thought it as well to utter here a provisional warning against the lamentable error of proposing (just as people have encouraged a Zionist movement) to create a Sodomist movement and to rebuild Sodom. For, no sooner had they arrived there than the Sodomites would leave the town so as not to have the appearance of belonging to it, would take wives, keep mistresses in other cities . . . In other words, everything would go on very much as it does today in London, Berlin, Rome, Petrograd or Paris" (II, p. 656). Both men-women and Jews undermine the stability of identitarian thought, but for Proust this position of being outside the identitarian logic of modern society is a tragic one. The nation, whether

French, Sodomitical, or Zionist, relies on the stable identity and devotion of its citizens. What the existence of races indicates, however, is that
such loyalty must always be gained at the expense of more private concerns. In a reverse image of the racism of a Barrès, the Sodomites and
the Jews in Proust function as signs of that which cannot be universal-
ized. Ultimately, the case of the Jews and the homosexuals suggests a
radical instability of political identity in modern society, an instability
not based on some essence of Judaism or homosexuality which resists
the "communitarian" logic of mass or democratic society, but based on
the existence of differences within such a society that cannot be easily
homogenized. As Bersani suggests, the Jews and the homosexuals form
a sort of "queer nation" within the nation, but this position does not
seem to have all the positive connotations Bersani associates with it.
Queerness, racial identity, is a curse in Proust, but a curse that is at any
rate truer than the fictional identity, equality, and moral unity of the
nation-state.

THE POSSIBILITY OF JUSTICE: EQUALITY OF CONDITION AND MULTIPLICITY OF SELVES

In his descriptions of the Dreyfus affair and the war, Proust offers a
defense of the particularities of the individual's life that rejects the
demand that such particularities be effaced by the overriding loyalty of
the "we," devotion to the nation-state above all else. Proust's description
of the ethical process, I have argued, seems closer to Aristotle's than to
Kant's, in as much as it treats the notions of free will or of an absolute
transcendence of one's location in history and society as impossibilities,
and emphasizes instead the role of habit in the ethical process and the
importance of shaping the pre-given dispositions of the self rather than
radically overcoming them. Yet, a number of features of Proust's ethical
views show the influence of the voluntarist tradition of Rousseau and
Kant not so much as a philosophy to which Proust or his narrator sub-
scribes but as an unrealizable ideal against which the world of French
society can be measured. Thus, the ideal of "detachment" from one's
desires and inclinations, in Proust frequently associated with the processes of reading and writing and the attempt to come to terms with the
radically other, seems to echo the forlorn Kantian ideal of autonomy.
Similarly, although the images of justice in the novel all point to the arbitrariness and falsehood of actually existing claims to establish norms for
human behavior, the ideal of a justice that would treat all people equally

remains in the background of the narrator's moral reflections, and is associated in particular with the image of his grandmother. While society in general may treat justice (what is right) as no more than utility (what is good for society), a few characters keep alive the conception of duty and justice as something prior to and transcending mere utility. Finally, the narrator's own attempts to give an adequate account of the ethical process that could be universalizable point to the hope for standards of judgment and action that would do more than reproduce the prejudices of society. Thus, his continual elevation of observations about his own psychology into general theories about human nature – the shift from the "I" to the "we" – contains the promise of a community of readers who could, by reading in their own inner books of unknown signs, create a Kantian kingdom of ends.

Almost every reference in the novel to the question of justice describes it as a sort of ruse perpetrated by the majority in a community on the minority. Thus, "justice" is a distraction from the novelist's true duty, the search for authenticity; the "justice" or "injustice" of the French cause in the war is entirely unrelated to the beliefs of Frenchmen and Germans in the justice of their causes; the narrator's father has no conception of justice or the law of nations, but acts for a contingent reason or for no reason at all; and even before God, the homosexual in search of justice must lie. The first reference to justice in the novel is perhaps the most pessimistic. When the narrator's great-aunt is teasing his grandmother at Combray by letting his grandfather drink brandy (which is bad for his health), the narrator observes, "as soon as I heard her 'Bathilde! Come in and stop your husband drinking brandy,' in my cowardice I became at once a man, and did what all we grown men do when face to face with suffering and injustice: I preferred not to see them. I ran up to the top of the house to cry by myself" (I, p. 13). For Kant, enlightenment was man's emergence from his self-imposed immaturity. For Proust, maturity is a self-imposed willingness to accept injustice.

Yet, the narrator maintains his belief in a justice which seems nowhere accessible in the society he describes. In particular, justice in the soul seems more attainable than justice in the state. Proust's own statements on political matters indicate that he shared many of the ambivalences of the narrator and that he sought in a liberalism that would protect a private sphere of individual autonomy a solution to the incapacity of the liberal state to meet the ideal of equality it had established for itself. The nation-state might offer the best opportunity, in a world of "radically situated" selves, for political justice, but Proust ultimately doubted its capacity to deliver on the promise of equality and instead sought in an ethical and psychological theory of the fragmentary nature of identity a solution to the problems which the political realm had been unable to answer. Furthermore, it was in a sense the nature of the political and social transformations of modernity that made necessary such a psychological or ethical theory. Just as it apparently did for Joyce's Stephen Dedalus, "race" represents for Proust's narrator the attachments and dispositions with which or into which the subject is born and raised. Unlike Stephen, Proust's narrator does not see in the embracing of the race a solution to the problem of the "radically situated" self. Rather, he adopts a tragic world-view according to which one must reject the attachments of race in order to become capable of fulfilling the more universalistic, or impersonal, demands of the nation. A full overcoming of such attachments, which would depend on an act of free will by which the reason could establish a universal law for itself, is impossible, so life for Proust's narrator – or, at least, the only life he knows, namely life in a society dominated by belief in the equality of all citizens and the moral unity of the nation – demands a constant and unresolvable struggle between the universal and the particular, the nation and the race, the willed and the given. The realm of private, intimate experience, in which the narrator deciphers his inner book of unknown signs, may offer an opportunity for personal ethical development, but Proust seems far less optimistic about the potential of the political realm.

At a biographical level, the reasons for this pessimism surely lie in the experience of the Dreyfus affair. "I was the first Dreyfusard," Proust claimed, "for it was I who went to ask Anatole France for his signature" on the petition of the intellectuals.[44] It is not the case, as is sometimes alleged, that Proust never became involved in politics.[45] Rather, at this one stage of his life which was also to prove crucial to his later literary project, Proust, then twenty-six years old, followed the events of the affair very closely, attending the sessions of the trial of Zola (for defaming the officers who had condemned Dreyfus). He also participated in organizing the petition demanding revision of Dreyfus's condemnation. Yet, the only echo of this political commitment in *A la recherche* is the narrator's passing reference to the fact that he had "fought more than one duel fearlessly at the time of the Dreyfus case," without any account of these duels or indeed any explicit reference to which side he took in them (II, p. 631) (although, given his acquaintances and his liberal frame of mind, it is probably safe to assume that the narrator is Dreyfusard). In the novel, Proust transfers his own fascination with the Dreyfus affair to Bloch, who, like the historical Proust, attends all the sessions of the trial of Zola.[46] It is almost as if Proust had separated his own personality among a number of characters, Bloch representing his Dreyfusism, Charlus his homosexuality, and the narrator his "lack of will-power" and the personal relationships within his family.

Whether this parcelling out of his personality constitutes a politically significant move on Proust's part seems open to debate. Proust's mother was Jewish, and although Proust himself was christened and raised Catholic, and continually denied any particular sympathy for the Jews, to the point even of repeating anti-semitic caricatures, he was also fascinated with "Jewishness" and its social manifestations, as his portrayal of Swann and the Bloch family in *A la recherche* shows. Proust removed all trace of Jewish ancestry from his narrator. Although he based many of the characteristics of the narrator's relatives on his own family, there is nothing to indicate that the narrator's mother and grandmother are anything but Catholic. It is remarkable, then, that Proust in a sense impersonates the gentile French position when he describes the situation of Jews during the Dreyfus affair. What are the implications of this impersonation? Why would Proust project his own experiences onto a narrator who is neither Jewish nor homosexual? Is Proust taking on a "dominant" position in order to subvert it? Is he, on the contrary, attempting to "pass" as a gentile just as, it is sometimes said, he attempted to "pass" as a heterosexual?[47]

It would be too simple to describe these maneuvers as a form of "passing," an attempt simply to escape from the condition of Jewishness or partial Jewishness or from his homosexuality.[48] For if Proust wanted simply to "pass," he could avoid all reference to homosexuals or Jews. Proust's narrator frequently observes, however, the thrill that those who are passing seem to derive from drawing attention to others who have failed to "pass," especially among homosexuals. The Baron de Charlus goes on at great length about the sexual proclivities of various acquaintances of his, never suspecting that anyone knows of his own "inversion," or perhaps suspecting it but unwilling to confront the possibility. The narrator's grandfather, although in the novel a gentile, enjoys playing a similar game by guessing the Jewish origin of the narrator's friends. He sings airs from well-known operas about "the chosen race" whenever Bloch comes to visit. Although his grandfather does not object to Jews in principle, the narrator relates that he "found that the Jews whom I chose as friends were not usually of the best type."[49] The fascinating effect of all these references to the secret lives of Proust's Jewish and homosexual characters is not to make Proust's narrator appear more convincingly heterosexual and gentile, but to reveal a sort of fiction underlying social life, in which each person presents himself or herself as an "unmarked" individual like every other, but everyone also knows the open secret that all people, or perhaps only very many people, have origins and proclivities which they are forced to repress. Proust's conceptions of habit and forgetting call attention to this act of repression of difference involved in social life.

As Walter Benjamin observed, when Proust sought to represent the moment that was most his own, the moment between sleep and wakefulness, he did so by choosing a moment "that everyone can find . . . in his own existence."[50] The way to universality, for Proust, is through immersion in subjectivity and particularity, and yet this very immersion seems to demand the rejection of all social identities. The construction of the narrative voice in Proust reveals the central paradox of the problem of justice of *A la recherche*, that the attempt to arrive at an objective reality must begin from a given social position. This position is what Proust's narrator describes as "instinct," what is given to him as such, is authentic, and cannot be chosen. The problem for Proust, which becomes particularly apparent in the revisions of the novel undertaken during the war, is whether or not justice and the moral unity of the nation are compatible with truthfulness to this given "instinct," to that which is particular to each individual and resists homogenization. To a certain degree, perhaps, Proust saw his project as requiring not simply a truthfulness to his own inner experience but also a suppression of that experience: a suppression that consisted in his "universalizing" his experience by projecting many of his own most intimate concerns onto a narrator who has neither Jewish ancestry nor homosexual desires. The Dreyfus affair and the war made this problem remarkably evident because they posed the question crucial to modern liberal nationalism, whether such partial identities, identities that are not shared by all people or even by all members of a given nation, are irreducibly in conflict with citizenship in the modern state. They posed this problem because they made one's identification with a given social group the crucial measure of one's citizenship.

The narrator's theory of art seems to demand for the artist the rejection of the very universalization that is at the basis of the ethical process he describes. For the artist must be concerned not with justice or with moral unity but solely with a strict truthfulness to the apparently unique experience of the individual. Yet Proust's practice suggests that it is only through the suppression of the markers of social difference that the individual becomes uniquely an individual; it is only by not being a Jew or a homosexual that the narrator becomes a representative Frenchman. This becomes the case as a result of the demands of the "moral unity of the nation" and the national conception of "justice," according to which one's subsidiary identifications are in necessary conflict with one's central, national identification. The novel itself reveals the central contradictions of the narrator's quest for authenticity and it reveals these contradictions as belonging to particular historical moments – the Dreyfus affair, the war – in which the demands of the state come to replace all subsidiary identifications, in which the fiction of the "we" overrides all private concerns. The nation becomes a sort of plain on which all differences among citizens have been levelled out, and it is only on this plain that citizenship seems to demand the rejection of whatever marks the individual off from his or her fellow-citizens. Authenticity to experience comes to appear radically opposed to the demands of national unity and justice in precisely such historical circumstances.

Proust offers a model of the relationship of self to society that resembles that of the novel of disillusionment, but is skeptical of the possibility of achieving a social consensus such as that embodied in the omniscient narrator of the novels of Balzac. The ethical process, which consists in conversation with the other, or with the image of the other, offers the promise of some form of immanent development of the powers of personality towards greater equilibrium, or perhaps simply towards a truce with the outer world. The nation seems to offer the promise of overcoming this dynamic and restoring a moral unity in which not only would the self overcome its fragmentation but it would also become integrated with the others that surround it. Ultimately, however, this is a false promise, both because the tensions between subjective and objective, ethical and sociological, perspectives on the individual are irreducible and because the national solution to these oppositions demands the suppression and forgetting of race, family, and other allegiances that make the individual something other than just an individual or just a Frenchman. Proust's perspectivism itself, then, far from supporting a nihilism or fatalism, serves as the support of a liberal conception of politics, albeit one that hopes for little from the public sphere or from the moral unity of the nation. It is a liberalism profoundly at odds with the desire for moral unity implicit in Rousseau's conception of the general will or Renan's of the national will.

Proust's narrative technique calls attention to the exigencies of citizenship in the modern state by emphasizing the particularity of the individual's life and its irreducible difference from all other lives. The narrator at least seems to find this demand for truthfulness incompatible with the quest for justice. One question posed by Proust's work is whether justice requires a similar forgetting. Would a social order that achieved justice demand that a person abandon all particularities and present himself or herself as having only a "neutral" background? Could such a neutral background involve truth to "instinct," what Proust labels "authenticity"? Or must authenticity in some sense be sacrificed in order to achieve justice and unity? Must the individual become no more than an individual in order to achieve objectivity, or is it possible, from the subjective sphere of the individual, to rise to an objective sphere that allows respect for particular identities in the context of a universal justice? If, as Proust's changing representations of the Dreyfus affair suggest, truthfulness to the intimate sphere demands impartiality towards the events of the political sphere, then can such an impartiality be squared with the demand for justice? Or does Proust suggest that the loyalty to the intimate sphere demanded by the ethical process and by the work of art implies a turning away from the cause of justice? If so, then Proust, like Plato, would be suggesting a tragic conception of the state in which justice depends on a lie; for Proust, the lie of the homogenous personality and the homogeneous population.

The alternative to such a tragedy would be that the individual, instead of being simply a Frenchman, a page in an account-book or the record of a will, could be understood as a complex site where a series of competing identities and allegiances could be negotiated. That Proust envisioned a way of being French that would not level all Frenchmen to a form of social homogeneity is clear. In a letter of July 29, 1903 to his friend Georges de Lauris, Proust reacts against the anti-clerical laws currently being passed by the radical government and cites Renan in support of some of his views. He questions Lauris's reasons for supporting these laws:

I simply fail to see what you want. To make *one* France . . . I do not think you want all Frenchmen to be alike, a dream that is fortunately stupid, because it is unrealizable. But I trust that you do want all Frenchmen to be friends, or at least, setting aside the special and individual reasons they may have for hating one another, capable of being so, and accordingly that you hope that no *a priori* enmity will ever, in any situation, pervert the course of justice, as happened some years ago.[51]

The letter goes on to mention the clerical supporters of anti-semitism. While opposing their excesses, Proust also proposes to allow their schools to remain independent. Proust hoped, it seems, for a form of equality that would allow for justice and the moral unity of the nation without requiring all Frenchmen to be alike. His conception of the self as fragmentary and made up of competing roles could serve as the basis of a vision of such a liberal nationalism that would make it possible for all Frenchmen to be friends or at least not to have *a priori* enmities. The nation-state, however, in the era of the crisis of liberal nationalism, seemed to demand not just capacity for friendship but in fact that each individual form a cell of the body of the nation. The differences among Frenchmen made such a moral unity impossible, except if the potential "*a priori*" enmities were put aside, and this prospect demanded the suppression of the very differences among Frenchmen that Proust wished to protect. Friendship, not fraternity, would be the basis of a Proustian Frenchness.

Yet the nation-state demanded a different type of allegiance, and the search for friendship in Proust's own life demanded certain compromises. The history of Proust's personal relations with Barrès shows some of the difficulties Proust associated with his Jewish heritage. Although they were on opposite sides of the Dreyfus affair, Proust and Barrès maintained mostly cordial relations with one another, and Barrès was eventually to support Proust's abortive bid to be elected to the Académie française. On one occasion during the affair, Proust was listed in the anti-semitic newspaper *La Libre Parole* as being among a group of Jewish intellectuals who "abominated" Barrès. At the time, Proust wrote to a friend that he could not correct this impression without announcing that he was not, in fact, a Jew, an announcement he refused to make because, "although true, [it] would have hurt my mother."[52] Later, in 1903, Barrès found this excuse unconvincing, but it seems to point to a crucial ambivalence of Proust's with regard to the question of "Jewishness." Although he is not a Jew, he cannot say so because of loyalty to his mother. Jewish origin appears as a function of the intimate sphere of private allegiances that one must not betray, but it is also a marker in the public sphere that one cannot control without betraying precisely that intimate sphere. Proust prefers the truthfulness to his mother which requires a break with Barrès to participation in the public sphere of debate on terms that would require him to accept and proclaim his assimilation.

However, by 1905 – the year of the law on the separation of church and state – the process of reconciliation affecting the country as a whole had started to touch Proust himself. In a letter to his friend Robert Dreyfus, the author of a critical work on Gobineau, an antagonist of Barrès, and himself a Jew but no relation of the accused colonel, Proust expresses his regret that he can invite neither Dreyfus nor Reynaldo Hahn to join a party at his house at which Robert de Montesquiou, one of the models of the Baron de Charlus, is to read his poetry. Montesquiou has vetoed their presence on the grounds that "it would change the character of his reading." Proust does not explicitly state that Montesquiou's virulent anti-semitism is the reason for his refusal to allow Dreyfus and Hahn to attend. In the next paragraph of the letter, Proust recommends to Dreyfus that he resolve his quarrel with Barrès by publicly announcing that he did not intend (as rumor had it) to accuse Barrès of plagiarizing Gobineau:

I feel that there's no substitute for a public rectification. For I remember a similar case several years ago. *La Libre Parole* had said that a certain number of young Jews, among them M. Marcel Proust, etc., reviled Barrès. To rectify the situation I should have had to say that I wasn't a Jew and I didn't want to do that. So I allowed it to be said as well that I had demonstrated against Barrès, which was untrue. Having met him, I told him that I'd felt it was useless to issue a denial. But I sensed that he didn't agree that it would have been useless.[53]

The path he counsels for his Jewish friend is precisely that of public reconciliation, which during the Dreyfus affair Proust himself had rejected. The friendship among Frenchmen comes to override their political differences in Proust's own life, even though such friendship demands compromises in social life. It seems that by the time of the triumph of the secular republic, Proust himself had come to accept a certain level of injustice and even untruthfulness to his own intimate sphere as the price of social acceptance and full participation in the public sphere. It does seem unfair to criticize Proust for failing to be more heroic, when in fact his public support of Dreyfus was a heroic stance in itself. Yet, the urge to be accepted as a full member of a society and public sphere from which his origins threatened to exclude him seems to have taken its toll on Proust's truthfulness to his own intimate sphere, and to have forced him, at least on occasion, to choose between truthfulness to his mother and acceptance at the bar of the nation-state's form of justice. It is part of the tragedy of the nation-state that Proust found these two options irreconcilable.

CHAPTER FIVE

"Il vate nazionale": *D'Annunzio and the discourse of embodiment*

Gabriele d'Annunzio's political opinions and activities seem the polar opposites of Proust's. Where Proust took the Dreyfusard, anti-nationalist side in the Dreyfus affair and deconstructed the idea of the moral unity of the nation in his novel, d'Annunzio, a hero of the Italian nationalists, proclaimed himself the "vate nazionale," national poet-prophet. When he first came to play an important part in Italian politics, during the First World War, d'Annunzio had already been a famous poet and novelist since his youth in the 1880s, and had been a member of the Italian parliament, where his erratic voting record enacted his political slogan (adapted from Nietzsche), "beyond right and left."[1] After a stay in Paris, where he managed to avoid his Italian creditors while at the same time learning the art of French nationalist propaganda, he returned to Italy as a hero of the movement in favor of intervening in the First World War. When Italy did intervene, in May, 1915, d'Annunzio, who was fifty-two years old, joined the Italian armed forces as a freelance thrill-seeker, participating in a number of dangerous missions as both soldier and propagandist. His favorite task was accompanying aviators on dangerous flights over Austrian territory. During a crash-landing after a reconnaissance mission over Trieste in 1916, d'Annunzio lost the sight in one eye and badly damaged the other. Forced to remain immobile for two months, with his eyes bandaged, he stayed in a dark room of the Casetta Rossa of his friend Fritz von Hohenlohe on the Grand Canal in Venice. There, he wrote the first draft of a poem-novel, *Il Notturno* (*The Nocturne*), full of patriotic rapture and self-praise. Since he could not see, he wrote the *Notturno* one line at a time on thin strips of paper that (echoing Dante) he compared to the leaves on which the sibyls wrote their prophecies before scattering them to the wind.[2] Although his daughter Renata transcribed these strips of paper and they were even set in type during 1917, they remained unpublished. After the war, d'Annunzio led a group of demobilized soldiers, against the wishes of the liberal Italian government, to conquer Fiume, a town in Croatia with a large Italian population whose future was in dispute at the Paris Peace Conference. D'Annunzio's constitution for Fiume and his oratory served as models for the growing Fascist movement, with which d'Annunzio sympathized, and whose rise to power he later facilitated. After sixteen months of bold experimentation in modern symbolist politics, d'Annunzio was forced by the Italian government to leave Fiume. Upon his retirement from active politics, he completed *Il Notturno*, which was finally published in 1921. During the remaining seventeen years of his life, which were largely devoted to sexual pleasure, d'Annunzio became a sort of elder statesman of the Fascist regime. He occasionally lent Mussolini much-needed political support, and received in exchange the title Prince of Monte Nevoso and generous subsidies for his lavish private life. D'Annunzio and Proust had a few friends in common, notably Robert de Montesquiou. D'Annunzio even makes a brief appearance in *A la recherche* as an admirer of the Duchesse de Guermantes. He shared with Proust a milieu and a streak of self-indulgence. Otherwise, no life seems more different from Proust's.[3]

Yet, the *Notturno*, d'Annunzio's last major prose work, takes up many of the themes dear to d'Annunzio's "high" modernist contemporaries, Proust and Joyce. Not only does the interruption of the process of composition for the demands of war recall the fate of Proust's *A la recherche*, but, as Paolo Valesio has noted, the *Notturno* is, like Proust's novel, "the culmination of . . . experiments in the semifictional prose of remembrance, description, and reflection."[4] In particular, d'Annunzio concerns himself with the shaping of the present by the past and the quest for a moment of pure authenticity in which the present-day self can achieve unity with the self as it has been formed through a lifetime of personal experiences and a long history of national conflicts. As it is for Proust, the moment between sleep and wakefulness, the period of twilight, is central to d'Annunzio's most experimental prose. Like Proust, d'Annunzio explores the theme of the multiplicity of selves. The "I" who is trapped in an injured, sightless body seeks a unity with the remembered "I" of d'Annunzio's childhood and the first days of the war. This unity is to be attained only through d'Annunzio's complete identification with his dead comrades and the total submission of his will to his fate as a member of the Italian nation. Like Proust's *A la recherche*, d'Annunzio's *Notturno* begins with the narrator's complete isolation from the world and contemplation of his own subjectivity in a darkened bedroom. Just as it did for Proust, this withdrawal from the world reveals to d'Annunzio the presence of an inner book of unknown signs, engraved upon him by his nation's history and by his activity in the outside world. The task of deciphering this inner book demands a complete withdrawal of the novelist into himself and a submission to instinct. D'Annunzio's enforced immobility and the bandaging of his eyes makes this withdrawal from the world a physical reality. Whereas Proust defended his private space, however, as a realm of autonomy in which truthfulness to the author's own interpretation of his experience took precedence over the demands of justice and moral unity, d'Annunzio has no doubt that these three aspects of experience can and will be reconciled, quite literally, in his own person. Proust treated the retreat from the world as the basis for the act of individual autonomy that reinstated a radical dualism between the remembering and remembered selves, the ethical and the sociological persons. D'Annunzio's intimate experience of himself, on the other hand, serves to eliminate any distance between remembered and remembering, sociology and ethics. Thus, although they appear to have so little in common, Proust and d'Annunzio shared at least in part a conception of the novelist's task, inspired by Nietzsche, as a submission to fate and instinct. This submission led Proust to attempt to serve his nation by ignoring it and delving ever deeper into his own autonomous realm of intimate experience. It led d'Annunzio relentlessly to reveal the potential of a transformative, communal politics that would raise intimate experience to the prominence of a symbol for national redemption.

Whereas each of the works examined so far has been a form of fictionalized autobiography – and both Joyce's and Proust's works have announced themselves as such – d'Annunzio's *Notturno* does not present itself as fiction. The "I" who is the focus of d'Annunzio's investigation of the vagaries of memory and the fragmentation of personality is always the same "I" – and the narrating "I" never acknowledges a radical distance between itself and the narrated "I" that is the subject of its stories. The thematic content of the novel-memoir displays this underlying unity of the dannunzian self in so far as d'Annunzio never departs much from the known facts of his very public life. More importantly, however, the formal structure of the *Notturno* enacts the underlying unity of d'Annunzio's various selves by its insistence on a lyrical present tense in which the reintegration of personality figured by d'Annunzio's convalescence can take place. This lyrical present tense, in which the novel both begins and ends, and which is the predominant tense throughout the novel, recalls d'Annunzio's nationalist oratory and gives his prose the quality of an incantation. The *Notturno* reveals, through its celebration of the unity between the recovering body and the reintegrated will, the transfiguration of even the most private, intimate space by the myth of the nation-state and the nationalist ideal of a total fusion of state and society, public and private, through the redemptive power of war and the heroic figure of the leader whose most private act is a mystical rite for the community of the nation.

The incantatory lyricism of the *Notturno* gestures toward the body of the novelist-poet-hero, which it presents as the site upon which the history of Italy's subjection can be redeemed. Like Joyce, d'Annunzio draws on the symbolism of the incarnation and resurrection to describe the narrator's role in embodying the national will. D'Annunzio however makes this analogy almost gruesomely physical by staging his own injured body as the site of the rebirth of the Italian nation. Michael Tratner has recently shown the extent of the influence of d'Annunzio's early, decadent novels on the young Joyce.[5] The remarkable similarities between d'Annunzio's most "modernist" of works, the *Notturno*, and Joyce's *Portrait*, suggest that both Joyce and d'Annunzio had come to imagine the possibility of restructuring narrative as a means of redemption that would reconcile the first- and third-person perspectives on human action in the person of the Christ-like narrator-hero. Where Joyce enacted this vision through a heightening of unstable modernist irony, however, d'Annunzio removed irony altogether from the traditional novel form. The *Notturno* belongs to the history of the modernist novel because it shows a novelist who has turned himself into a character and in so doing has broken down the traditional boundaries between genres. The *Notturno*'s hybrid form – novel, collection of poems, memoir – undermines the conventions of novelistic voice and enacts the fantasy of the narrator-hero. In d'Annunzio's work, the narrator and hero become one in lyrical moments in which the hero's intimate experience serves the nation as a whole. This absolute collapsing of external and internal perspectives on the self makes possible not only a transfiguration of the novel form achieved through the complex intermingling of lyrical and narrative elements, but also the birth of a particularly modern form of hero-worship that would be d'Annunzio's major contribution to the Fascist movement.

FIUMANISM AND FASCISM

D'Annunzio scholars have debated the importance of d'Annunzio's writings and political activities to the rise of Fascism and have even questioned whether d'Annunzio himself supported the Fascist cause. The conventional view, summarized by Christopher Seton-Watson, is that d'Annunzio, although lacking political acuity, was a great propagandist, and invented at Fiume many of the most important symbols of the Fascist regime:

The uniforms and the black shirts, the "Roman salute," the "oceanic" rallies, the party hymn, *Giovinezza*; the organization of the militia into cohorts and legions, commanded by consuls; the weird cries of Eia Eia Alalà!, the demagogic technique of "dialogue" between orators and massed audiences; all the symbolism, mystique and "style" with which the world was later to grow so familiar, were plagiarized from D'Annunzio.[6]

Indeed, d'Annunzio later asserted that he had been "the definite precursor of everything that is good in Fascism."[7] Scholars in recent decades have attempted to distinguish d'Annunzio's politics from those of Mussolini's Fascists and to rehabilitate d'Annunzio. On the extreme revisionist end of the spectrum, Alfredo Bonadeo claims that, if the Italians had accepted d'Annunzio as their leader and he himself had overcome certain flaws in his personality, "D'Annunzio's genius could have been a model and a force in bringing Italian culture and politics to the European forefront and in leading twentieth-century Italy into a future free from tyranny and war."[8] More convincing as critics of the view that d'Annunzio was a proto-fascist are Renzo de Felice and Michael Ledeen, who have emphasized the "leftist" elements at Fiume, including the participation of syndicalists, the establishment of a corporatist constitution, and the project for a "League of Fiume" that would represent the oppressed nationalities whose interests were ignored by the League of Nations.[9] D'Annunzio's most consistent political conviction was a mystical nationalism in which he cast himself in the role of Italy's savior. Even if d'Annunzio's own ideology was idiosyncratic, it is certainly the case that Fiume marked the coalescence of elements of the syndicalist, anti-statist left with the nationalist right. As Alatri has argued, this very combination was not so much proof of the sincerity of d'Annunzio's "leftism" as a sign of things to come in Fascist Italy.[10] Fiume marked the first real emergence of the anti-liberal forces that were to bring down the government after Mussolini's March on Rome in 1922: disgruntled veterans, nationalist-minded syndicalists, and intellectuals who throve on anti-bourgeois rhetoric, including not only d'Annunzio but also the futurists.

D'Annunzio's "regency" in Fiume ended ignominiously after the Italian government signed the Treaty of Rapallo with Yugoslavia, which secured independence from Yugoslavia for Fiume, guaranteed rights of Italian speakers in the town, and gave Italy sovereignty over much of the surrounding Istrian coast. Against the wishes of most of Fiume's population, d'Annunzio refused at first to accept the treaty, demanding full incorporation of the city into Italy. The city was retaken from d'Annunzio's legionnaires by Italian forces during the Christmas season of 1920 (the "Natale di sangue" or "Christmas of blood"). After this debacle, d'Annunzio's star waned and Mussolini's rose. The Fascist party gradually absorbed the nationalists who had supported d'Annunzio. D'Annunzio himself appeared to some sectors of liberal Italian public opinion to be a possible alternative to Mussolini between 1922 and 1925, when d'Annunzio's support on the nationalist right might have helped him to prevent Mussolini from undermining the constitution. However, the soldier-poet remained passive at the decisive moments, such as the March on Rome. He did challenge Mussolini openly on a few occasions, notably in defending from Fascist attacks some syndicalist unions that had supported him at Fiume, but he eventually made a deal to support Mussolini in exchange for recognition of his union allies, and apart from the occasional negative remark about Fascism as "agrarian slavery" or the "fetid ruin" of Italy in the wake of Matteoti's assassination, d'Annunzio never seriously protested against Fascism. Indeed, he apparently enjoyed the tributes he received from Mussolini, although he never again became active in politics, perhaps not liking to play a supporting role.[11]

Although d'Annunzio seems to have been jealous of Mussolini's success, there can be little doubt that, as both Jared Backer and Hans Ulrich Gumbrecht have recently argued, d'Annunzio himself subscribed to, and indeed invented, a number of major factors in Fascist mythology. Apart from the various rituals themselves, there was a pervading quasi-religious ethos at Fiume that contributed to the downfall of the liberal state. Symbolic of this ethos was what Gumbrecht calls the "interplay between the hope for redemption, the act of redemption, and the postponement of its attendant reward," that structured so much of Fascist rhetoric.[12] D'Annunzio made the individual hero-leader (himself) the focus of a drama of redemption modeled on Christ's sacrifice. His innovation was to make the hero-leader capable of redeeming the nation without himself dying. He did so by presenting himself as the embodiment of the national will, a role that, while it had precedents in the nineteenth century, became much more effective once it was united with the experience of death and dismemberment on a massive scale in the trenches of the First World War. As Emilio Gentile has noted, the war played an important part in welding together the disparate populations of the Italian kingdom, and thus helped to accomplish the task outlined by Massimo d'Azeglio at the time of Italian unification in 1860: "We have made Italy; now we must make Italians."[13] Part of the purpose of the Fiume expedition was to maintain this unity. After the war, the hero-leader, whether d'Annunzio, Mussolini, or Hitler, could claim, along with the other surviving veterans, who had indeed in some cases suffered greatly, to have undergone the sacrifice demanded of the Christ-figure in earlier forms of the redemption myth. This representation of the leader's body as the focus of a narrative of redemption was one of the central tropes of what Gentile has called the "sacralization of politics in Fascist Italy."[14] By proposing to speak for the dead soldiers, these leaders made their own claim to embody the genius of the nation or race more convincing. They could also use the myth of redemption to draw on the large mass of demobilized soldiers who were the main support of fascist movements in their first phases. Although d'Annunzio's vision of a renewed Italy had little in common with the reality of Mussolini's Fascist state, his skill at myth-making played a vital role in Mussolini's rise to power.

A major concern of Italian nationalists, and a central reason for the decision to break with Austria and intervene on the side of the Allies in 1915, was the cause of irredentism. The "unredeemed" (irredenti) lands of Italian speakers within the Austro-Hungarian empire were a thorn in the side of the united Italy throughout its first half-century. D'Annunzio's military actions during the war mainly took place on the north-eastern frontier, and the motive for the invasion of Fiume in 1919 was to force the Allies to cede to Italy all the Dalmatian lands in which there were significant numbers of Italian speakers. A number of themes of d'Annunzio's later Fiuman propaganda are already present in his interventionist writings of 1915, notably the claims that "the nation is a fact of a spiritual nature and that the idea of sacrifice is at the root of its spirituality" and the claim that the Italian people "knows that, beyond territorial integration, it will arrive finally at the true unity of its conscience and its virtue."[15] D'Annunzio also presented the cause of irredentism as the continuation of the Risorgimento ideals of Mazzini and Garibaldi. At the same time, however, he attacked the institutions of liberal democracy, and especially the "enemy within," the Liberals under Giovanni Giolitti and the center-right Prime Minister Antonio Salandra. The culmination of d'Annunzio's campaign in favor of intervention came on May 6, 1915, at Quarto, where he gave a speech in remembrance of Garibaldi's Thousand, the volunteer soldiers who had, in 1860, sailed from Quarto to Sicily to participate in the battle to unify Italy. In his speech at Quarto, d'Annunzio made one of his most public uses of christological imagery by rewriting the Sermon on the Mount:

> O blessed be those who have more, for more will they be able to
> give, more ardent shall they be.
> Blessed be those who are twenty, chaste of mind, temperate of
> body, whose mothers are brave.
> Blessed be those who, waiting and trusting, waste not their
> strength but preserve it with a warrior's discipline. . . .
> Blessed be the young who hunger and thirst for glory, for they will
> be sated. . . .
> Blessed be the pure of heart, blessed be those victorious
> returning, for they will see the youthful face of Rome, the brow
> recrowned by Dante, Italy's triumphal beauty.[16]

Apart from the obvious hubris of d'Annunzio's self-presentation as a new Jesus, the most remarkable element of the speech is its revision of the very terms of the Sermon on the Mount itself. For whereas Jesus promised the meek that they would receive their reward in the hereafter, d'Annunzio promises the ardent an earthly Paradise right now.

D'Annunzio's fantasies at Fiume of himself as a "redeemer of the victory" in the First World War, which Gumbrecht has analyzed extensively, drew on his lifelong penchant for using religious imagery to describe his own task on this earth. His very name, d'Annunzio, led him into this tendency. As d'Annunzio's biographer, Paolo Alatri, records, Gabriele's paternal grandfather's name was Rapagnetta, but his father, who had been adopted by an uncle named d'Annunzio, was known as Rapagnetta-D'Annunzio (Alatri, p. 1–2). It seems to have been Gabriele's parents, Francesco and Luisa, who decided to drop the distinctly less noble Rapagnetta altogether. "D'Annunzio" was not only more noble than the grandfather's name, but also echoed the Biblical annunciation. The first name, Gabriele, which was indeed given to him by his parents, was of course also the name of the archangel who foretold the birth of Jesus. Mostly, d'Annunzio liked to present himself as the bearer of an annunciation, with the new Italy or the glory of war in the role of the messiah to be announced. In the *Notturno*, however, he seems to indulge the temptation to think of himself not only as the one doing the announcing but also as the one announced.

D'Annunzio managed to make himself into a particularly convincing

Christ-figure only after February 1916, when he himself lost an eye in the war. This "sacrifice" became a crucial element of d'Annunzio's fantasy of himself as redeemer of the Italian nation, which he managed to convince a large number of demobilized soldiers to share and which in turn inspired similar and more successful mass fantasies under Mussolini and Hitler. The story of this injury, and d'Annunzio's recuperation or rebirth after the accident, is the focus of the *Notturno*, which for this reason – although far from being a political manifesto – is a crucial text in the history of Fascist mythology. By 1915, d'Annunzio was ready to make his most original contribution to modern nationalist mythology, but he needed the air accident of February 1916 to complete what, in the *Notturno*, he would call his "new myth" of the "sacrificed poet."[17] It is hard to believe that d'Annunzio would have been satisfied, after all his daring adventures during the war, if he had not managed to achieve a significant mutilation that, like the stigmata of Catholic saints, could confirm the reality of his auto-hagiography. It is in the *Notturno*, written between 1916 and 1921, that d'Annunzio developed much of the rhetoric and ideology that would serve him so well at Fiume. Gentile and Gumbrecht have both emphasized the role of the incident at Fiume (which took place in 1919–20, between the penultimate and final drafts of the *Notturno*) in the later history of Fascism. The *Notturno* bears witness to the close relationship between modernist experiments in the form of the novel and the search for a new conception of the nation-state that would overcome the perceived deficiencies of liberalism.

A number of critics have noted the surprising fact that at the height of d'Annunzio's political activity, he wrote his most intimate novel, in which, as Charles Klopp puts it, "the dreams of domination that have always been essential to his political and sexual ideology have been temporarily set aside."[18] D'Annunzio's eagerness to show that he has submitted himself to his fate is in part a technique for portraying his political activities as emanating from a higher force beyond his control. He was a very skillful master of this sort of nationalist rhetoric, which cloaks the actions that serve the leader's own personal interests in the mantle of obedience to the national will. He was an enthusiastic participant in the rites of the new religion. In establishing himself as its "prophet, bard, and high priest," he seems truly to have thought that he was submitting to the will of the nation and to historical necessity.[19] Self-absorbed but unselfconscious, d'Annunzio believed fervently in the new role he played. Partly because of the difficulty of distinguishing the "real" d'Annunzio from the role of "vate nazionale," those critics concerned with the development of d'Annunzio's literary style have had their sharpest disagreements over whether or not the *Notturno* represents a genuine act of submission to fate or merely a pose. Thus, Alfredo Bonadeo finds in the *Notturno* the summit of d'Annunzio's achievement, which "lies in the shaping of his heroic myth founded on the role of death in the enhancement of his spiritual self."[20] Paolo Alatri, on the other hand, argues that "On the whole, despite variations in tone, the *Notturno* is an uninterrupted self-glorification, in which political discourse, when it is or is meant to be political, is entirely identified with autobiographical discourse and dominated by the most impulsive egotism" (p. 373). Both judgments are accurate.

Surprisingly few critics have considered the *Notturno* in relation to d'Annunzio's political activities between 1916 and 1921. Many seem to take the poem-novel at its word as an immediate account of the events of 1916, and thus ignore the interpenetration of d'Annunzio's experiments in prose form with his experiments in political symbolism. The *Notturno* is, however, a key text in understanding the transformation of d'Annunzio's personal image from the decadent, weak-willed lover of the early novels to the heroic leader of Fiumanism. Jeffrey Schnapp has argued that in d'Annunzio's appropriation of Nietzsche, what might be called the "feminine" elements of d'Annunzio's style produce a distinctively Italian Nietzsche that emphasizes a poetic, aesthetic, and erotic revision of Nietzsche's myth of the *Übermensch*.[21] The *Notturno* seems to represent an important phase in the adaptation of the myth of the *super-uomo* to politics. For here, the submissiveness of the hero's will transforms itself into a new style of leadership. The hero is no longer, as in *Il Fuoco*, the powerful and spiteful seducer of the crowd that worships him. Instead, he has learned to suffer, and it is in his ability to suffer and to submit himself to the will of the nation that d'Annunzio produces a virile sort of femininity. He has combined what Schnapp has called the roles of dictator and dandy and become "the hypertrophic individual who is at once man of the crowd and master of the crowd."[22] The hero of the *Notturno*, who lies supine on his bed as his past and Italy's history flow through him, is the model of such a new man of the nation, a man who can convert submission into leadership. Like later Fascist cultural heroes, inspired largely by the Futurists, his body is the focus of all history and spectacle, and it is also intimately linked to a machine: the airplane, which d'Annunzio represents as the modern crucifix. Strangely, it is in the intimate genre of the prose-poem that d'Annunzio made some of his most far-reaching experiments with the politics of spectacle. I propose here to show the role that the *Notturno* itself played in the development of d'Annunzio's conception of himself as redeeming hero-leader, and to suggest some of the ways in which this important ideological development related to the broader experiments in the novel that I have examined in earlier chapters of this study.

D'ANNUNZIO'S INFERNO: THE LYRICS OF SUFFERING

The structure of d'Annunzio's poem-novel recalls that of Dante's *Divine Comedy*, and in doing so it calls attention to the persistent theme of d'Annunzio's redemption of his nation through the suffering inflicted upon him by his wartime accident. The *Notturno* consists of three "offerings" ["*offerte*"], each of which in turn consists of between eighteen and sixty-six shorter passages. These short passages resemble the cantos of the *Divine Comedy*, in that they present themselves as self-contained units, while sometimes continuing longer narrative sections of the novel as a whole. They range in length from one line to several pages, and in the first editions of the novel each began on a new page. In many of the cantos, d'Annunzio visits with ghosts from his own past, who resemble the souls that Dante encounters on his journey. Unlike Dante, however, d'Annunzio also spends much of the novel simply contemplating his present state – namely, his enforced immobility in the darkness of his bedroom at the Casetta Rossa. Paolo Valesio has noted what he calls the "sibylline presence" of Dante in the text, but has not commented on the structuring role that the analogy with the *Commedia* plays in d'Annunzio's novel.[23] The tripartite structure of the novel seems to refer both to Dante and to the resurrection. It thus helps d'Annunzio to unify his vision of his own suffering as a new enactment of the incarnation. The *Divine Comedy* itself presents Dante's journey as an allegory of Christ's death and resurrection. After a prologue set on Maundy Thursday, Dante descends into hell on Good Friday, spends Saturday in Purgatory, and emerges into Paradise on Easter Sunday, all apparently in the year 1300 AD. A similar play with dates structures d'Annunzio's *Notturno*, which ends on Easter Sunday 1916. (It is a strange coincidence that d'Annunzio centers his own vision of sacrificial politics on a date that was also to play a major role in Irish nationalist mythology). Although the first passages of the novel appear to take place in February or March, 1916, most of the first "offering" describes events from Christmas week, 1915. The general temporal structure of the novel, then, runs from Christmas in the first offering, through Lent in the second offering, to the Holy Week in the final offering. The dramatic movement of the novel re-enacts more precisely the events of the resurrection, beginning with the symbolic death of d'Annunzio's blinding, continuing with his encounters with the dead and a rather weak form of penitence, and ending with his rebirth. A number of direct references to Dante throughout the text suggest that d'Annunzio had this conception of the structure of the *Notturno*, although he probably decided on it late in the composition, presumably after Fiume, since the novel did go to the printer's in 1917 in a form that lacked this tripartite structure.[24]

If the overall structure, then, resembles that of the *Divine Comedy*, d'Annunzio's project is nonetheless considerably riskier from a theological point of view than Dante's. Dante's allegorical mode of representation allowed him to present himself as re-enacting the events of Christ's passion without claiming to replace Christ. Indeed, as Erich Auerbach and other students of the Middle Ages have shown, it was in the nature of every life to mirror in certain respects that of Christ. As Dante's letter to Can Grande shows, the allegorical form of the *Commedia* allowed for "polysemy."[25] The narrative could both describe events in the life of Dante at the literal level and describe the spiritual events of the incarnation, passion, and resurrection at the allegorical level. D'Annunzio presents himself, however, not simply as re-enacting the general pattern of Christ's life but as taking on the role appointed to Christ. D'Annunzio's own spiritual rebirth also redeems the Italian nation. There is no distinction between a literal and an allegorical level. D'Annunzio is not content with mirroring the incarnation but wants to make his own physical suffering the grounds for a literal rebirth of the Italian nation. This conception of his own life as not merely following the pattern of Christ's but in a sense replacing it belongs of course to an entirely different universe from Dante's. His own incarnation and resurrection serve a new god, the Italian nation, and d'Annunzio, like Joyce, seems quite aware of the idolatrous and blasphemous nature of this new worship.

Each of the novel's offerings begins with d'Annunzio in bed, describing in the present tense his wounds and his gradual convalescence. From there, he continually reverts to incidents in his past that appear to haunt him. The act of writing is itself the most important scene in the novel. It is the bed on which d'Annunzio lies as he writes that forms the center of the narrative, much more consistently in fact than the persistent scenes of going to sleep and awakening in Proust's *A la recherche*. The novel begins in a present tense in which the time of writing and the time of the events being narrated appear identical. This present tense creates a sense of immediacy that emphasizes the physical reality of d'Annunzio's situation:

> Ho gli occhi bendati.
> Sto supino nel letto, col torso immobile, col capo riverso, un poco
>   più basso dei piedi.
> Sollevo leggermente le ginocchia per dare inclinazione alla
>   tavoletta che v'è posata.
> Scrivo sopra una stretta lista di carta che contiene una riga.
>
> [I have bandaged eyes.
> I lie in bed on my back, my torso immobile, my head thrown
>   back, a little lower than my feet.
> I raise my knees slightly to tilt the tablet resting against them.
> I write on a strip of paper wide enough for only one line.][26]

This opening passage illustrates the difference between d'Annunzio's and Proust's searches for time lost. Both searches begin in bed. Yet, whereas Proust begins his text in the past tense ("Longtemps, je me suis couché de bonne heure"), and seldom uses the present tense at all, d'Annunzio begins in the present tense and continually returns to it. He thus emphasizes the action of writing which in a sense freezes time at the moment of the pen's inscription on the paper. His "sto supino nel letto" resembles Descartes's "je suis, j'existe" more than anything in Proust. The repeated present tense creates a moment of insistence on the correspondence between the willing, thinking "I" and the body, and emphasizes both the spatial and temporal senses of the word "presence." The first sentence, in fact, describes the body as something possessed by an ego that may seem separable from it: "I have bandaged eyes." In the second and succeeding sentences, however, the correspondence between the thinking thing and the extended thing (to borrow Descartes's terminology) is more strongly emphasized: the "I" who lies in bed is both the poet's physical body and his mind. The verb "sto" ("I am" or, here, "I lie") emphasizes the bodily presence of the poet in his bed. Related etymologically to the Greek "stasis" and "ecstasy," the Italian "stare" is "the fundamental verb of immobility, either relaxed and passive or vigilant and resisting."[27] Unlike the English "to be," it generally indicates a physical location, rather than an abstract state, for which Italian uses the verb "essere." The narrative of *Il Notturno* will transform the poet's immobile stasis into a vital ecstasy. It will do so by highlighting and conferring magical powers on the very moment of the poet's writing, in which the mental and bodily "I" are both equally present. A large proportion of d'Annunzio's sentences is in the first-person singular (and must therefore be translated into English with the pronoun "I"). The almost incantatory repetition of short sentences in the present tense, encouraged by d'Annunzio's method of composing the work one line at a time, contrasts sharply with Proust's long sentences full of subordinate clauses.

The *Notturno* presents a series of "nows," moments at which the events of the narrative are presented as being transcribed as they occur. These moments of correspondence between the narrated events and the act of narration or transcription create a lyrical present tense, akin to the convention of lyric poetry according to which the poet is the speaker of the poem. Adverbs of time, especially "oggi" ("today") and "ora" ("now"), frequently repeated throughout the novel, serve to emphasize this correspondence. The lyrical moments of "self-presence" occur not only when d'Annunzio organizes certain cantos of the *Notturno* as verse, but also in a number of other instances where the text presents itself as an immediate transcription of the consciousness of the poet-novelist. These are moments of what Giorgio Bárberi Squarotti has called the *Notturno*'s "double immediacy": "the immediacy of the [poet's] vision and the immediacy of the writing that records it."[28] Bárberi Squarotti has argued that the writing of the *Notturno* is "without time and without space," and that this lack of "spatio-temporal density" creates for d'Annunzio a "tragedy without catharsis" (pp. 316, 318). What Bárberi Squarotti thus ignores, along with many other readers of the *Notturno*, is the alternation of such lyrical stasis with a narrative that subordinates this lyricism to itself. The present tense alternates throughout the novel with a series of scenes in the past tense. The sentences in the past tense, however, unlike so many of Proust's, generally take place in a simple past rather than an imperfect. The past-tense passages describe the fate that brought d'Annunzio to his current moment of potential transfiguration. The moments of the *Notturno* that present themselves as outside time and space serve to confirm the novel's narrative of redemption, in as much as they proclaim the capacity of the immobile body for an ecstatic relationship to secular time that permits it to resurrect itself from its moral and physical stasis. By its very immobility and passivity in the face of the forces of history and violence, the recovering body of the poet becomes the location for a national catharsis that converts the tragedy of war into a divine comedy. D'Annunzio's alternation of lyric and narrative moments, then, serves to reinforce his myth of his own body as the passive instrument by which the suffering of history can be transformed into the ecstasy of redemption in a moment of ideal self-presence that unites the individual body and the collective will.

The goal of the *Notturno* will be, d'Annunzio announces early on, to sculpt fire into stone, and to make something permanent out of his intimate, nocturnal experience of convalescence: "I scratch my signs in the night which presses solid against either thigh like a nailed board" (*Nocturne*, p. 217). This permanence is to be achieved as a form of incarnation and resurrection:

When the doctor's harsh sentence plunged me in darkness and in the darkness assigned me the narrow space my body will occupy in the grave, when the wind of action grew cold on my face, almost erasing it, and the ghosts of battle were suddenly excluded from this black threshold, when silence reigned in me and around me, when I had relinquished my flesh and recovered my spirit, from my first confused anxiety arose once more the need to express, to signify. (*Nocturne*, pp. 217–218; *Notturno*, pp. 49–50)

The metaphors of sculpting, fire, and wax recur throughout the *Notturno*. Visions appear in "the inferno" of d'Annunzio's blinded eye like sculptures on a wall of molten rock (*Notturno*, p. 53). He needs to be able to write in order to sculpt these images before they burn away, and his "new art," of writing while blindfolded, is the act of such a sculpting, such a transfiguration of the moment of inspiration into the permanence of rock (*Notturno*, p. 50). D'Annunzio feels himself to be an Egyptian scribe, sculpted out of basalt, as he lies still and moves nothing but the thumb and index finger that hold his pencil and paper. He is haunted throughout the novel by his terror at the idea that his fingers may be shaping wax instead of moving a pencil: "I have for a moment the confused sensation of holding not a wooden pencil but a piece of warm, red wax. It is a moment of indefinite horror" (*Notturno*, p. 54). The possibility that his words will melt is comparable to the risk that the wind will erase his face, for it is only through the physical trace of a written inscription that his inspiration can be made permanent.

The act of making permanent his own inspiration parallels, or perhaps embodies, the "new myth" of the sacrificed poet-hero that d'Annunzio invents in the course of meditating on his injury. The adaptation of Christian images to a nationalist mythology begins on the first page of the novel. As d'Annunzio recalls the scene of his wounding, he intones:

It is no longer fire, but blood that spurts. No longer sparks but
  drops. The hero-pilot brings back to the fatherland the
  sacrificed poet.
Oh, immense glory!

> What divine or human fist threw to the furrows of the earth a
>   more august seed?. . . .
> I see my face transfigured in future centuries of greatness.
>
> *(Notturno*, p. 55)

The "new myth" of the poet sacrificed for his country is more beautiful,
d'Annunzio claims, than the old myth of Orpheus destroyed for his
music. That the act of writing about his suffering recalls and in a sense
re-enacts the incarnation is a subtext of the entire novel. The writing is
itself a mystical rite comparable to the creation of the universe in the
Gospel of St. John:

> There is something religious in my hands that hold it [the paper].
>   A virginal feeling renews in me the mystery of writing, of the
>   written sign.
> And I tremble before this first line that I am about to trace in the
>   darkness.
> O, art, art pursued with so much passion and glimpsed with such
>   desire!
> Desperate love of the word engraved through the centuries.
> Mystical intoxication that sometimes made a word of my very
>   flesh and my very blood!
> Flame of inspiration that suddenly melted the ancient and the
>   new in an unknown alloy!   *(Notturno*, p. 52)

The physical process of writing takes on great significance throughout
the novel because it is the bodily presence of the poet-novelist, and in
particular the wounds that he has suffered in the service of his country,
that allows the resurrection of the nation's fortunes that d'Annunzio
hopes to achieve. For this reason, d'Annunzio refuses to dictate and
"rejects intermediaries and witnesses" (*Nocturne*, p. 218). His voice is not
corporeal enough for the form of embodiment he seeks in his writing,
which he continually describes with metaphors such as "sculpting." The
injury itself seems to have a similar effect on d'Annunzio's body, which
becomes fixed and immobile but also seems to give his flesh perma-
nency: "My head remains immobile, constrained in its bandages. From
my hips to the nape of my neck, a will for inertia leaves me fixed as if
the embalmer had performed his work on me." The task of the *Notturno*
will be to transform this frozen flesh into living spirit, by reenacting not
only the incarnation itself but also the passion and the resurrection.

After an introductory series of cantos devoted mainly to the first
stages of d'Annunzio's recovery and to his memory of his accident, the
first offering continues with d'Annunzio's recollection of the week of his

friend Giuseppe Miraglia's death. In the various "cantos" within each "offering," d'Annunzio describes either his emotions on a given day in 1916 or his memories of earlier experiences. At times, a series of such short passages creates a miniature narrative. As a result, there is an intertwining of a variety of narrative strands in each offering. Although there is a complex layering of events and times, there are in fact two main narrative strands running through the first offering. One describes d'Annunzio's gradual mastery of the "new art" of writing while blindfolded and his turbulent emotions during his convalescence. The other describes the week of Miraglia's death. D'Annunzio often uses the present tense to describe his memories of events in the narrative past. Thus, at one moment, d'Annunzio will be describing his current sensations in his hospital bed, and at the next, he will be describing a funeral he attended months earlier. There are, however, usually clear indications that a change in narrative time has taken place. Nonetheless, the sensation that the past and present are intermingled is strong. D'Annunzio describes at length his vigil over the body of Miraglia, during the week after Miraglia's death on December 21, 1915. The use of the present tense to describe both the "current" events of the convalescence in March and April, 1916 and the "remembered" events surrounding Miraglia's death in December, 1915, allows the two narrative sequences to intertwine with one another. Thus the "agitated night" spent on December 20, 1915, resembles the agitated moments of inspiration in the hospital bed in March, 1916. When he awakens, it is not immediately apparent whether it is the d'Annunzio of March, 1916 who has recovered his sight or the d'Annunzio of December, 1915 whose vision is being recalled: "With the windows open, I see the sun that strikes me on my pillow" (*Notturno*, p. 68). In the various narrative sections of the middle part of the novel, the recovering d'Annunzio's "past" is quite literally "present" to him.

A short ode in prose to male companionship leads into one of the longest narrative sequences in the novel, the "giorni funebri," which makes up about two-thirds of the first offering. Throughout the first offering, the airplane becomes the symbol of the modern sacrifice, partly because the wings of the airplane form the shape of a cross. D'Annunzio also glorifies the companionship encouraged by the fact that the aviators of the First World War fly in pairs. He praises "the virile couple, the couple of battle, reborn in the creation of the human wing, driving and wounding, noble weapon, celestial weapon, ruled by a single will, like the double lance of the Greek youth. The comrade *is* a comrade" (*Notturno*,

p. 61). Like the heroes Ulysses and Diomedes in Dante's *Inferno*, the two aviators who die in the same accident burn together, "in one flame" ["dentro ad un fuoco"], with their bodies intertwined. As Alfredo Bonadeo has documented, Miraglia was d'Annunzio's favorite pilot.[29] With a certain gusto for morbid details, d'Annunzio describes his friend's rotting corpse and the elaborate ritual of soldering his casket shut, necessitated by the risk of flooding in Venetian graveyards. The entire passage, known as the "giorni funebri" ("funereal days") marks the narrator's first confrontation with the physical effects of death. He pays special attention to the stigmata that seem to suggest a parallel between the injuries Miraglia received and d'Annunzio's later injuries. The first recollection of the body of the dead friend makes the parallel explicit:

> My companion is dead, is buried, is dissolved.
> I am alive, but laid precisely in my darkness as he is in his.
> I breathe but I feel that my breath passes through violet lips such
>   as his were in the first hours, a mouth that has become almost
>   insensible opens, hardened by the metallic flavor of the iodine
>   that circulates in my body.
> I resemble him also in my wound: again I see the strip of cotton
>   that covered his right eyesocket, destroyed by the crash.
> So his death and my life are one and the same thing.

By imaginatively associating his own accident with Miraglia's, d'Annunzio establishes his claim to have undergone the equivalent of death. In another typical example, d'Annunzio enumerates Miraglia's injuries, which happen to resemble his own: "The bandaged head. / The clenched teeth. / The right eye injured, bruised. / The jaw broken on the right: the swelling is beginning" (*Notturno*, p. 70). One of the most vivid examples of this technique is his remark that "sometimes I see myself as he [Miraglia] might have seen me from his coffin. I am sometimes the corpse and sometimes the one who contemplates it" (*Notturno* p. 63). Echoes of Dante haunt the entire passage, as when d'Annunzio compares the gaze of the ghost of Miraglia to that of the heretics in the sixth circle of Hell.

At the end of the first offering, the scene returns to d'Annunzio's bedroom, where he echoes the many moments in Dante's *Inferno* when words fail the poet: his hand refuses to move and he lies "immobile, with my whole body rigid, not daring to trace another single sign in the darkness" (*Notturno*, p. 91). The scene seems to echo Dante's position in the final canto of the *Inferno* when, he explains, confronted with the massive body of Dis (Lucifer), "O reader, do not ask of me how I / grew faint and frozen then – I cannot write it: / all words would fall far short of what it was. / I did not die, and I was not alive."[30] Like Dante, d'Annunzio seems reduced to silence, and to an inability to write, by his confrontation with the depths of the underworld. This silence also prepares him, however, to undertake a healing process in the second offering, d'Annunzio's purgatory.

d'annunzio's purgatory: the narrative of redemption

The lyrical passages of the first offering, in which the poet describes his suffering, have received far more critical attention than most of the later passages. In the "annotation" to the *Notturno*, a sort of epilogue dated November 4, 1921 (the third anniversary of the armistice with Austria), d'Annunzio explains that in the spring of 1916 he wrote his "commentary on the darkness" on "more than ten thousand" strips of paper, while blindfolded, and then had his daughter Renata copy them out before sending them to the printers in the autumn of 1916 *(Notturno*, p. 243). D'Annunzio also claims that the additions he made after 1916 were based on transcriptions he personally made of other strips of paper that Renata was unable to decipher. While writing on the strips of paper, d'Annunzio claims, "I had inside my injured eye a smithy of dreams that my will could neither direct nor interrupt. My optic nerve drew on all the levels of my culture and my previous life, projecting into my vision innumerable figures with a rapidity of transition unknown to my most ardent lyricism. The past became present" *(Notturno*, p. 244). D'Annunzio then reviews his various feats of the five years since 1916, including a number of battles during the war and of course the invasion of Fiume. He explains that he has overcome his reluctance to publish his "sibylline leaves" in the hope that "courage arises from thought" and that his "will for sacrifice" will be remembered in future generations, because the drama of Fiume has been "the drama of the whole fatherland" *(Notturno*, p. 249).

Carla Riccardi has made a study of the manuscripts in preparation for a critical edition, and I have had an opportunity to study the early drafts of the manuscript, which are in the archive of the Vittoriale degli italiani, the villa on Lake Garda to which d'Annunzio retired in the 1920s. The manuscripts include a good number of the original strips of paper, collected in bundles, Renata's copy of the first draft, the galley proofs which were prepared in 1917 (not, as d'Annunzio claimed, the autumn of 1916),[31] and the corrections and additions to those proofs made probably (judging from references in d'Annunzio's correspondence) in two phases, in 1917 and 1921.[32] Riccardi's research has brought to light two crucial facts about the composition of the work: that only about one quarter of the novel actually originated on d'Annunzio's "more than ten thousand" (actually fewer than three thousand) strips of paper; and that d'Annunzio interpolated long narrative passages into the text after the initial composition in 1916, some of which had been written *before* his accident. The longest of these interpolations was the *giorni funebri* (the passage describing Miraglia's death in the first offering), which was actually written in January, 1916. A number of other, shorter passages also originated in notebooks, rather than on the strips of paper. Given that none of the strips of paper corresponding to the additions made after the autumn of 1916 survives, it seems reasonable to assume, as Riccardi does, that many of these revisions were in fact added later in the process, whether from existing notebooks or, as is clearly the case with a number of passages preserved at the Vittoriale, as additions written on the 1917 galley proofs probably during the final revisions in 1921.[33] An examination of the proofs shows that, like Proust, d'Annunzio often added several layers of new material during the process of revision.

It appears, from the state of the manuscripts at the Vittoriale, that what d'Annunzio actually wrote on the strips of paper was the first 11 "cantos," about one-third of the first offering, and approximately 23 of the 104 later cantos, all written in the present tense and focused on d'Annunzio's physical suffering and recovery. As it has been reconstructed by Riccardi, the first complete draft of the *Notturno* included only one major narrative section, the *giorni funebri*. Apart from this long narrative, the remaining two-thirds of this draft consists almost entirely of lyrical passages in the first-person singular. All of them originated on the strips of paper on which d'Annunzio wrote during his months of recuperation. The first draft, like the eventual published version, begins in February, 1916, "flashes back" to December, 1915, and then proceeds through March and April, 1916, to the Holy Week. The narrative structure, however, is much more straightforward than that of the final version. It resembles more closely a conventional diary or journal. Although the idea of the new myth of the sacrificed poet is present, the novel is almost entirely a chronicle of the war and the healing process and includes few references to the more distant past. D'Annunzio seems to have arrived at the overall narrative structure only gradually. Riccardi, who has published extensive descriptions of the various phases of composition, has said little about the relationship of d'Annunzio's evolving plan for the work to his contemporaneous political activities. Read against the background of the Fiuman enterprise, the first and final drafts make it clear that the revisions that d'Annunzio eventually undertook, mainly in October and November of 1921, had three main effects: to increase the density of references to the narrator's past; to heighten the sense of narrative progression; and to emphasize the significance of the *Notturno* as a "national" story, in which the sacrificed poet becomes a hero for the Italian "race."

In the portions of the second and third offerings written in 1921, d'Annunzio develops more consistently the technique of alternating between lyrical and narrative passages. The period of convalescence described in the second offering of the novel corresponds to the first part of Lent in 1916. Near the beginning of the offering, d'Annunzio remarks: "It rains wildly on the evening of Ash Wednesday. A cloud burst in March" (*Nocturne*, p. 231; *Notturno*, p. 104) (Ash Wednesday is the first day of Lent; the final offering will begin on the first of April). Lent, traditionally the period of repentance, corresponds well to Dante's purgatory. The narrative passages of the offering generally involve the poet's confrontation with his past and his upbringing, and these encounters with the ghosts of his own past help him to examine his own conscience and arrive at the conviction that his destiny is to sacrifice himself for his nation.

Like the novel as a whole, the second offering begins with d'Annunzio undergoing agony as he lies in bed and thinking of the flight on which he was wounded. The identification between the wounded poet and Christ becomes stronger as d'Annunzio imagines himself half-dead and half-alive, and contemplates the Passion:

I seem to be half-alive. Half of my spirit has crossed over; the other half is on the way, is inquisitive about the matter of this world, observes the machinery of its own tragedy.

I think of the instruments of the Passion hung on the beam that no longer carries the burden of the tormented body. I think of the great crosses upright at the hesitating crossroads, the crosses without a crucified, at whose summit is the watchful cock that has not crowed the third time.

Four species of wood composed the cross of the sacrifice: cedar, cypress, palm, and olive. In our West, for the palm and the cedar do we not wish to substitute the ash and poplar of the heroic wing? (*Notturno*, p. 96).

The materials from which the airplane is made replace the materials of the cross. The task is not to replay but to substitute for the crucifixion.

D'Annunzio then begins to remember a series of events prior to the death of Giuseppe Miraglia, notably his own speech in favor of intervention in the war made on the Capitoline Hill in 1915. The current moment of his passion on his sickbed seems to him to mingle inextricably with the remembered moment of his great speech: "I feel my pallor burn like a white flame. There is no longer anything of me in me. It is as if I were the demon of this tumult, the genius of the free people . . . I am no longer intoxicated with myself, but with all of my race." In an image that resembles Stephen Dedalus's conception of himself as "forg[ing] in the smithy of [his] soul the uncreated conscience of [his] race," d'Annunzio describes his own words to the crowd on the Capitoline as "like those blows of the founder's mallet struck to open the tap out of which the molten metal flows into the mold. The crowd is like an incandescent pouring of metal." He proclaims a sort of dialectical relationship between himself and the people: "I lead and am led. I ascend to crown and I ascend to crown myself." When, at the end of this passage, d'Annunzio refers to the people as "once again possessed by its true god," it seems a fair question whether this true god is Mars (the god of war) or d'Annunzio himself (*Nocturne*, pp. 228–231; *Notturno*, pp. 97–100).

Throughout the "second offering," d'Annunzio's identification with Christ grows ever stronger. In memory, he recalls a visit he made before the war to his mother, who had become senile, and their home-town of Pescara, "la piccola patria" ["the little fatherland"].[34] His mother's uncomprehending face reminds him of the savior's: "Was not the face of the savior so when he had taken on himself all the sins of the world?" (*Notturno*, p. 123). He thinks of how he "bore" his mother inside himself into battle, just as she once bore him. The war represents a sort of rebirth: "it was a love so dense that it did not let me perceive whether I was her creature or she was my creature. / It was a flame so blinding that it did not allow me to distinguish if I burned imperfectly for her or she burned completely for me. / It was a sacrifice so vehement that, suspended between the cradle and the tomb, I did not know whether she was my mother or my Fatherland" (*Notturno*, p. 113). In this image of the mother as Fatherland who is both creator and creature of the poet, d'Annunzio gives full rein to the fantasy of male autogenesis that is one factor in the story of the virgin birth. The passage of memories of his mother ends with another of d'Annunzio's dated entries, for March 12, 1916: "Today is the day of my birth" (*Notturno*, p. 124).

The remainder of the second offering describes the disintegration of d'Annunzio's self and its reintegration or rebirth through his embracing of the myth of the holocaust, the sacrifice that is entirely burnt. As Francesco Spera has noted, the text becomes ever more fragmented even as d'Annunzio's body begins to recover from its wounds.[35] It seems that d'Annunzio must reach a moment of absolute disintegration before he can embrace the spiritual rebirth necessary to his task. The holocaust serves as d'Annunzio's model of the sacrifice made by the nation in war. It would later be one of his epithets for Fiume, "the city of the holocaust." The image originates in late Hellenistic Greek and, before the 1940s, was associated mainly with classical Greek religious practices and with the New Testament.[36] It is successful for d'Annunzio's own propagandistic purposes only in so far as he is able to present himself as having been entirely destroyed by the war and then born again, risen from his own ashes. Through an act of imaginative identification with his dead aviator-colleagues, he is thus able to present himself as a new Icarus, a hero who flies too close to the sun, is burnt, and falls to earth, but (unlike the original Icarus) still manages to be reborn. As it did for Joyce's Stephen Dedalus, the myth of Daedalus the inventor (Icarus's father) plays a role in d'Annunzio's fantasy. In one of the passages in verse, d'Annunzio describes the Italian pilots, including himself, as "the sons of Icarus and the Sirens, / the grandsons of Daedalus of the Labyrinth" (*Notturno*, p. 143). The apparent depths of d'Annunzio's disintegration come at about the mid-point of the novel: "Here I am, as if at the beginning of dissolution. I am full of substances that disintegrate and of juices that ferment. I hear in myself the gurgling that I have heard once before in the depths of night as I watched over the corpses between the funerary wreaths" (*Notturno*, p. 130). Like the corpses of his friends, d'Annunzio's body is beginning to rot. He confronts death, and in this encounter he gains poetic inspiration that facilitates his rebirth. Along with visits to his past, this section of the novel is interrupted by a series of lyrical moments, including a number of passages in verse. As d'Annunzio writes, "at the height of lyrical power is the heroic poet" (*Notturno*, p. 131). It is the threat of death that brings him to this height.

In the final cantos of the second offering, d'Annunzio's passage from Purgatory to Paradise, which are typeset as verse, the image of Icarus falling from the sky is transformed into that of the phoenix that rises from its own ashes. In each of the first five stanzas of the last poem, d'Annunzio feels (or hears) his god in himself: "sento in me il mio dio." At the end of the poem, this refrain is transformed so that d'Annunzio claims to serve his god in himself:

I hear the phoenixes sing . . .

All the ash is seed,
All the twigs are sprouts,
All the desert is springtime,
In myself, I feel my god.

O Phoenixes of the Holocausts,
I will not reveal the sacred word
that opens and closes each round of the hymn.
In myself, I serve my god.   (*Notturno*, p. 180)

The elevated tone emphasizes the transfiguration of the creature
(d'Annunzio) from mere admirer of the god to servant, and the intimate
experience of communion with the god as the source of a rebirth. The
potentially humbling experience of finding one's god everywhere
becomes a dannunzian exercise in self-glorification. When d'Annunzio
feels or hears his god inside himself, he may be suggesting that he is
merely the passive organ of greater forces. When he claims in the final
stanza, however, "in myself, I serve my god" ["servo in me il mio dio"],
he suggests literally that even the most self-serving and egotistical activities are, on his part, only manifestations of his love of god. Placed at the
end of the second offering, this poem recalls the purifying flame through
which Dante passes at the end of the *Purgatorio*.

D'ANNUNZIO'S PARADISE: THE RETURN TO BATTLE

In the final section of the novel, now that d'Annunzio has clearly
become the hero-poet-messiah, it is no longer a question of further dis-
coveries, but primarily of waiting for the ultimate moment of transfiguration. In another of the passages apparently added in 1921, as he
listens to church bells, unable to raise himself from his bed, d'Annunzio
asks rhetorically: "How many days until Maundy Thursday?" The bells
will not allow him to raise himself just yet. "If I cannot live," d'Annunzio
tells the bells "then I want to die." "Living, you will die," respond the
bells. D'Annunzio accepts their message. He seems to lose all substantiality, his body is on the verge of being transformed into spirit. He is all
surface and present tense: "Now I am flattened, in this bed, soul and
body. I have no more profundity. I have no more depth. I am without
yesterdays and without tomorrows. Living, I die" (*Notturno*, p. 191). His
will becomes a force outside himself to which he must submit: "I feel my
will not in me but over me, almost a sharpened blade, exactly as long as

my subdued body" (*Notturno*, p. 198). The wounds of his body, like the scars in the earth made by trench warfare, become throughout this final section a symbol of the submission of the body to the will and the capacity for the free-floating will to control the body entirely, if it is only capable of achieving power over the body by enduring sufficient pain and renouncing the desire for wholeness. The very renunciation will, in d'Annunzio's rhetoric, lead to the achievement of wholeness.

Alfredo Bonadeo has argued that in the *Notturno* d'Annunzio confronts his guilt at the sacrifice of so many soldiers and friends to the gods of war: "By identifying himself with Miraglia in death, D'Annunzio plumbs the depth of the grief and horror that death inflicts on the living, he strips death of its mystery and terror, and he dispels its power." The morality of self-sacrifice that d'Annunzio developed, Bonadeo argues, "freed [d'Annunzio] from the greatest of the bodily constraints, the fear of mortality, conferring on the warrior-poet a power that his spirit had never tapped."[37] Apparently with no more irony than d'Annunzio himself could muster, Bonadeo accepts d'Annunzio's equation of his own sacrifice of an eye with the sacrifices of his friends who actually did die in the war. It seems obvious enough, but perhaps needs restating, that this equation is a means by which d'Annunzio justifies his own support of the war in the face of so much carnage. It is only if the sacrifice of a number of individual Italians can be refigured as a sacrifice on the part of Italy as a whole that the logic of organic, proto-fascist nationalism can justify so many deaths. D'Annunzio's giving up a part of his own body is a tremendous refinement on this very conventional militaristic myth. As Gumbrecht has noted, d'Annunzio was to continue to refer to his loss of an eye as a justification of his own redemptive nationalism throughout the post-war period.[38] By actually losing a part of himself, d'Annunzio can figure himself as having participated in the sacrifice. If, then, d'Annunzio claims to identify himself with the dead soldiers, he only does so in the service of an ideology that will lead to further deaths. His actions in putting himself in physical danger may indeed have been heroic, and his belief that he was the embodiment of the genius of the Italian nation perfectly sincere, but his work nonetheless glorified sacrifice, death, and war and presented a justification for the deaths incurred in war. It was in no respect a protest against war or a retraction of d'Annunzio's militaristic views, as Bonadeo sometimes seems to suggest. The soldiers died in the trenches, and d'Annunzio lost an eye, not to usher in an era of peace but to glorify the god of war. This form of the Christian mythology of redemption is clearly heretical.

The title "Notturno" seems to have fit the first draft of the novel more adequately than it does the final, published version. The "effusive lyricism" of the nocturne, "usually quiet and meditative in character" has sometimes in the twentieth century, according to the *New Grove Dictionary of Music*, been "replaced by an attempt to capture the fevered visions and dreams of the night."[39] While revising the *Notturno*, d'Annunzio transformed it from a lyrical meditation on his suffering into a narrative of redemption that embraced the entire Italian people. He did so by placing his own lyrical musings in the context of the heroic role he had established for himself in Italy's interventionist movement, and by linking this role to his conception of his own life as entirely dedicated to the Italian nation. The narrative elements that d'Annunzio added, mainly in 1921, generally serve the purpose of transforming the solitary brooding of the original *Notturno* into an ecstatic phase of fulfillment of a redemptive schema. The conclusion of the text exemplifies this transition. Despite d'Annunzio's claim that he wrote the entire final section of the novel, the "settimana santa" or "Holy Week" while blindfolded in bed, the manuscripts at the Vittoriale show that the first version of the novel ended on the evening before Easter, with d'Annunzio listening to the church bells of Venice and the "silent music" of his heart as the sun sets (p. 237 in Ferrata's edition). D'Annunzio seems prepared to die, as the presence of a black gondola suggests the barges on the river Styx. The original draft thus ends on an elegiacal and nocturnal note, with the poet's rebirth and redemption very much in doubt.

As revised in 1921, the novel's ending fulfills the demands of the narrative of redemption. On Easter Sunday, April 23, 1916, as expected, d'Annunzio achieves his own personal resurrection in tones that recollect the last judgment. The passage begins with self-doubt:

The titanic Christ, having forced the heavy cover of the sepulchre, still keeps one foot in the hollow stone. But with his head raised, with his arms raised, with the impulse and violence of his whole passion, hurls himself toward heaven.

Was my heart then not mad enough? Was my pulse not hurried enough?

Was this impassioned image of power needed so that I could feel more miserably my own shabbiness? (*Notturno*, p. 238)

D'Annunzio presents Christ's resurrection as an act of great forcefulness that he would like to imitate but cannot. Two reversals of the Christian tradition are involved here. In the first place, Christ becomes "titanic," a figure of strength and almost rebellion against death, rather than the meek lamb of the more common Easter iconography. The idea that Christ would scale heaven with "rapina" [force, violence] turns Christ

Himself into an almost Satanic figure. The second reversal consists, as has already been noted, in the fact that while presenting himself as a weak and pitiable figure by comparison with Christ, d'Annunzio is preparing his own resurrection which will in fact assert a power he has derived from a new god. D'Annunzio intends to resurrect himself not so much by devotion to Christ as by virtue of his own power, or perhaps of the power he inherits from his dead comrades.

The author realizes the danger of the almost blasphemous imitation of Christ he is attempting: "Non sorgo." ["I do not arise."] His body becomes no more than a conduit for forces that flow through him, almost literally: "Ho sete. Sono tutto sete e orgasmo. L'imagine del fiume mi supera, mi sommerge, mi corre sopra" ["I am thirsty. I am all thirst and excitement (or orgasm). The image of the river conquers me, submerges me, runs over me"].[40] Haunted by the memory of his dead comrades, unable to distinguish the living from the dead, he speaks with his friend Oreste Salomone, who, though living, seems to d'Annunzio to have returned from the grave. D'Annunzio demands of this fellow refugee from death: "You tell me if we can live anymore without a heroic reason to live. You tell me if we can continue to be men without the certainty that the hour for becoming superhuman will return, Oreste" (*Notturno*, p. 240). Oreste (or, d'Annunzio wonders, the ghost of Oreste?) asks him to write, and d'Annunzio heroically takes up his pen. In a final act of inscription and decipherment in which the two spirits meet, d'Annunzio (with his eyes still bandaged), writes on one of his strips of paper, and Oreste reads, the following question: "Ma se ci fosse una morte anche più bella?" ("But if there were a still more beautiful death?"). What is this more beautiful death? Is it to be more beautiful than the death that awaits d'Annunzio in 1916, or more beautiful even than the death of Christ? The two heroes share the ideal of writing as a death that also allows a resurrection, and it seems that d'Annunzio himself decides to recover so that he may continue to write and to serve his country. His ultimate resurrection is in the name of further battles. The final paragraphs, set on Easter, 1916, seem not to have been written before 1921, so that the future to which d'Annunzio appeals may indeed be his leadership of the invasion of Fiume in 1919–20. In the novel's final ecstatic moments, he calls out to liberation to come and return him to battle:

> Oh, liberation, liberation,
> take me away from the pity of those who love me and the love of
>   those who pity me, and this music, and this raving, and all this
>   softness that is unworthy of my straw bed.

O liberation, liberation,
come and release me; come and strengthen my kneecaps and
elbows and wrists; come and infuse my blood with salt and iron
again; come and remake me alone with my parched guts; and
hurl me again into battle.

Vide cor meum.

As he knew well by the time he wrote these words in 1921, d'Annunzio
was indeed to arise from his hospital bed and enter into battle once
again, in the role of savior of his country at Fiume.

GABRIELE'S "VITA NUOVA": THE "NOTTURNO" AND THE ART OF THE NOVEL

D'Annunzio's most interesting formal experiments in the *Notturno* contribute to the transformation of the lyrical meditation on solitude into a
narrative of redemption. Along with the *Divine Comedy*, Dante's *Vita nuova*
(*The New Life*) serves as a model for d'Annunzio's alternation of lyric and
narrative in the *Notturno*. D'Annunzio had always been fascinated by the
myth of rebirth in the *Vita nuova*, and had referred to it in a number of
his novels, beginning with the first, *Il Piacere*. D'Annunzio's process of
revising the *Notturno* in fact resembles Dante's composition of the *Vita
Nuova*, in which he took the poems he had written earlier in his life and
inserted them into a narrative structure. Dante's prose narrative explains
the occasions and context of the lyrical poems it presents and then offers
a brief interpretation of each poem. Although the allusions to the *Vita
Nuova* appear mainly in the cantos that d'Annunzio wrote in the spring
of 1916 on the strips of paper, it seems that he must have developed the
parallel between his own text and Dante's over the course of the following five years, for the final draft resembles the *Vita Nuova* more clearly
than the 1916 version. Narrative passages focused on revealing
d'Annunzio's present state of mind to be a product of his lifetime of
service to the genius of Italy here alternate with the persistent present
tense of the lyrical cantos. Apart from adding most of the narrative
material written in the past tense that appears in the second and third
offerings, d'Annunzio emphasized the alternation of lyric and narrative
by adding a number of passages in verse. D'Annunzio thus deepens his
presentation of his ecstatic experiences by placing them in a historical
context. The eschatological horizon of the *Notturno* – the implied narrative which surrounds and makes sense of the actual present tense of the
lyrical texts – runs from d'Annunzio's childhood in the "little fatherland"

of Pescara, through his assumption of the role of leader of the interventionist movement in 1915, to his injury, recuperation, and rebirth and to a glimpsed future in which he will lead the Fiuman enterprise. With this narrative context, d'Annunzio strengthens the claims of the lyrical moments to embody a transformation and rebirth. D'Annunzio juxtaposes the moments of the lyrical present with the narratives of his biographical past without any mediation or explanation, so that, as he repeatedly states, the "past" and the "future" are always "present."

The most significant allusion to the *Vita Nuova* in the *Notturno* comes when d'Annunzio listens to his daughter Renata reading to him from Dante's own experiment with the intermingling of narrative and lyric: "Through her mouth, the sonnets of the *Vita nuova* touch me deep inside as they did when I read them at sixteen . . . And, myself remaining [*stando io*] with my most bitter pain, 'like those who cannot move themselves,' there appeared to me also certain faces of dishevelled women who said to me, 'Your youth is dead'" (*Notturno* 125). This passage alludes to the moment in the *Vita nuova* in which women appear to Dante to tell him of the possibility that Beatrice will die and that he himself will die. The *Vita nuova* records Dante's encounters with Beatrice, who appears to him on a number of occasions throughout the book both before and after her death. The narrative of Dante's relationship with Beatrice alternates in the text with the lyric poems he has written for her. As Robert Pogue Harrison has argued in his *The Body of Beatrice*, the alternation of lyric and narrative in that text serves to emphasize the mystical quality of the poet's encounters with his dead beloved. Drawing on the work of Paul Ricoeur, Harrison argues that the narrative aspects of the *Vita nuova* undermine the poet's attempt to fuse "memory and anticipation in one sublime instant of lyric self-presence." Deprived by Beatrice's death of the "epiphanic plenitude" of lyric time, Dante must move beyond lyric holism into a narrative "pervaded by futurity."[41] The task of the narrative in the *Vita nuova*, according to Harrison, is precisely to overcome the fantasy of self-presence. Harrison's interpretation of Dante's work can help shed light on d'Annunzio's use of the same text. D'Annunzio's rewriting of the *Vita nuova*, rather than emphasizing a dialogue between a self and another, continually returns to a myth of "epiphanic plenitude," which consists in the self's dialogue with itself. If Dante, then, attempted to escape from the solipsism of lyric into the futurity of narrative, d'Annunzio attempts to focus the past and future of narrative on the lyrical present in which the poet performs his "magical" transformation of the past into the fulfillment of a redemptive narrative of history.

The lyrical ecstasies of the *Notturno* induce a trance-like state in which, in d'Annunzio's words, poetry and illness become a form of magic: "Is this my magic? Truly, then, is illness essentially magical? Everything is present. The past is present. The future is present. This is my magic. In pain and in the darkness, instead of becoming older, I become ever younger" (*Notturno*, p. 136). In addition to the present-tense verb, d'Annunzio frequently relies on adverbs of time, such as "now" or "tonight," to emphasize the magical self-presence he expects to achieve in his moments of absolute lyricism.

The nature of d'Annunzio's reinterpretation of Dante's work becomes more apparent in his adaptation of a motto from the *Vita nuova*. The allusion comes as d'Annunzio, in the second offering, faces the prospect of remaining permanently in his current state of physical and spiritual stasis: "My spirit is struck by the same immobility that grasps my bones" (*Notturno*, p. 109). After lamenting his spiritual weakness, d'Annunzio writes, in italics, *"Vide cor meum"* ("Behold my heart," in Latin). The expression appears again at the very end of the novel, at the bottom of the last page, immediately below the invocation of "liberation" (*Notturno*, pp. 109, 242). It is an allusion to a vision of Dante's in the *Vita nuova*, in which an allegorical figure of Love holds up a burning heart and tells Dante, "Vide cor tuum" ("Behold your heart"). The figure of Love then forces a young woman, associated with Beatrice, to eat the heart. Dante's own text seems to allude to Christ's institution of the Mass.[42] Although the overall meaning of the original passage in Dante is highly ambiguous, it seems that d'Annunzio is using the allusion once again to reinforce his own re-enactment of Christ's passion. Instead of having a god-like figure appear to him and present him with his burning heart, d'Annunzio presents his heart to himself, or to his reader, and thus once again a figure of submission to God's will becomes a trope of self-assertion. In place of the self-abasement demanded by a loving relationship to the other, d'Annunzio presents what Renato Barilli has called a narrative "short-circuit," whereby "action, war, the external world intervene [in the text] only as recorded in the 'black box' of the brain."[43] This short-circuit, the demand for absolute self-presence, again resembles the phenomenological attitude of Proust. Yet, whereas Proust always emphasizes the fleetingness of the self's presence to itself and the impossibility of ever completing the search through the "obscure country" of the self, d'Annunzio attempts to throw light on every part of his interior landscape and continually announces his successful achievement of self-presence. D'Annunzio's is a model of authenticity that has, as Barilli has also noted, much in common with Heidegger's notion of being-toward-death (p. 242).

The *Notturno* is perhaps the extreme case in d'Annunzio's prose of a process described by Niva Lorenzini in her essay on d'Annunzio, *Il Segno del corpo*: "This physical contact with things . . . is the extension of the ego in a gesture (writing) which makes them one's own before inquiring about them, so that their revelation is identified with the immediate, thunderous revelation of states of consciousness from which are absent both the differentiation 'subject/object' and the ordered process of a logic that distinguishes and classifies."[44] D'Annunzio abandons both the spatial and temporal modes of distantiation typical of the realist novel. Like Joyce's Stephen Dedalus, Conrad's Marlow, and Proust's narrator, the d'Annunzio of the *Notturno* is in important respects a descendant of Lucien de Rubempré and the other heroes of the novel of disillusionment. Yet, whereas so many other heroes of the nineteenth-century novel find that the material world is unable to match the greatness of their own spirits, d'Annunzio takes it upon himself to transform the world in the image of his soul.

Most of d'Annunzio's early novels belong to the first phase of the transformation of the disillusionment plot structure associated with symbolism and decadence. Like Proust's narrator, d'Annunzio's heroes see their task as demanding a transformation of life into art. For d'Annunzio, however, this theme always involves an element of the ritual conception of art as a sacrifice that serves to bind together the community. To make one's life into a work of art is not to withdraw from life and dedicate oneself to an otherworldly undertaking but to live thoroughly in this world. In d'Annunzio's first novel, *Il Piacere (The Child of Pleasure)*, published in 1889, the protagonist, Andrea Sperelli, is the "last descendant of an intellectual race," the Sperellis, an old aristocratic family.[45] He is both hero and victim of his passionate love affairs with two women, and he sets out to follow his father's advice: "You must *make* your own life as you would any other work of art. The life of a man of intellect must be a work of his own creation" (p. 36). Like many products of the decadent generation (including Proust's narrator), Sperelli seems to lack the will-power to act on this advice. However, like d'Annunzio himself in the *Notturno*, he suffers a serious wound (in a duel) and undergoes a rebirth during his convalescence. From this point on, he sees his art as a sacrifice like Christ's, although it is to love rather than to the nation that he applies his analogies between art and the resurrection.[46]

In the *Piacere*, as in d'Annunzio's later novels, there is little ironic distance between the narrator and the protagonist. Apart from the occasional moralizing comment on the protagonist Sperelli's lack of will-power, the narrator for the most part simply records Sperelli's experiences with an aura of reverence. On the few occasions when he presents another perspective than Sperelli's own, it is that of an adoring woman who finds herself entirely in Sperelli's power, as in the transcription of the diary of his beloved, Maria de Ferrès. Indeed, the novel resembles Huysmans's *A Rebours* and the other examples of the "unipersonal subjectivist" approach, which Erich Auerbach condemned in the following terms: "[E]arlier writers, especially from the end of the nineteenth century on, had produced narrative works which on the whole undertook to give us an extremely subjective, individualistic, and often eccentrically aberrant impression of reality, and which neither sought nor were able to ascertain anything objective or generally valid in regard to it."[47] Auerbach differentiated Proust and the other modernists from earlier unreliable narrators:

Now with Proust a narrating "I" is preserved throughout. It is not, to be sure, an author observing from without but a person involved in the action and pervading it with the distinctive flavor of his being, so that one might feel tempted to class Proust's novel among the products of the unipersonal subjectivism we discussed earlier. So to class it would not be wrong but it would be inadequate. It would fail to account completely for the structure of Proust's novel. After all, it does not display the same strictly unipersonal approach to reality as Huysmans's *A Rebours* or Knut Hamsen's *Pan* . . . Proust aims at objectivity, he wants to bring out the essence of events. (pp. 541–542)

Does the *Notturno* resemble the "unipersonal" approach or something closer to Proust? In d'Annunzio's novels before the *Notturno*, the world does not correspond to the image of it held by the protagonist, but the protagonist makes no attempt to understand the world and simply accepts that only highly subjective perceptions are possible. The most important of d'Annunzio's novels to have been written in the first-person singular, before the *Notturno*, was *L'Innocente*, in which the protagonist tells how he murdered the innocent baby born of his wife's adulterous liaison. The novel takes a fairly common form of realistic first-person novels, which is to locate the teller at a particular point in time after the events of the narration itself have been completed, and then to narrate the entire story in the past tense. The narrator in such cases takes on a role very similar to that of the omniscient narrator, capable of offering foreshadowing and ironic distance from the events of the plot. The main difference between such novels and those with a third-person narrator is that the first-person narrator generally describes only his or her own perceptions of events and seldom transcribes the thoughts of other characters. The form ultimately resembles that of the novel of disillusionment, in that the narrator normally tells the story from the position of an outsider, having already undergone the crisis of disillusionment, conversion, or self-knowledge that allows him to achieve a distanced perspective on his own past actions.

The realist and naturalist tradition, from which d'Annunzio derived the techniques of most of his earlier novels, presents events in a temporal perspective that treats each event as occurring at a single, discrete moment in a series of causes and effects. It does not generally allow for supernatural events or any other sort of event that lacks a cause. Part of the structure of novels of disillusionment involves the fact that at the end of the novel, the protagonist becomes capable of looking back over the sequence of events and discerning the patterns of cause and effect that his illusions prevented him from grasping while he was in the middle of the events. The temporal structure of the *Notturno*, on the other hand, demands that every event described in it be understood in a certain sense as depending on supernatural causes. There is a mystical significance even to the smallest event such as a childhood illness or the death of a beloved horse. The continual return to the present tense also demands that each remembered moment be understood not as a discrete event in a causal sequence but as intimately linked to the present moment through mystical connections that cannot be explained but only intuitively sensed. His memories resemble the effects of Proust's involuntary memory, but without the effort to translate them by way of voluntary memory that Proust considered crucial. This foreshortening of temporal perspective is one of many examples of the themes of d'Annunzio's early novels being transposed into a new key in the *Notturno*. In *Il Piacere*, Sperelli devotes himself to the now – the *nunc* – and accepts his fate of being without a will of his own in matters of love: "all of my efforts toward unity of purpose are for ever vain. I must resign myself to my fate. The law of my being is comprised in the one word – *nunc* – the will of the Law be done!" (p. 247). In the *Notturno*, the writing enacts this law of Sperelli/d'Annunzio's being.

This foreshortened temporal perspective corresponds to a collapsing of the usual visual metaphors of the realist novel. Visual metaphors also structured most of the modernists' experiments. The fact that the observer always must observe from somewhere underlay many of the notable experiments in technique and form among the modernists. The relationship to the world implied by techniques such as "impressionism" or "perspectivism" is that of the observer. The notion of a reconciliation of the ethical and sociological selves, which I have stressed throughout this study, amounts to a combination of the visual role of observer with the tactile role of participant. D'Annunzio's blindness allows him to draw on the trope of the blind seer, and he does so in a way that ultimately rejects any attempt to take the uninvolved position of the observer. His body becomes a war-ravaged landscape and he presents himself as capable of submitting himself to the forces that surge through him partly because he is no longer an observer in the classical sense. He occupies an entirely enclosed space, no bigger than that of a coffin, and yet this space is constantly traversed by impulses, history. "But only the past exists. Only the past is real like the bandage that binds me, is palpable like my body on the cross" (p. 57). The novel of disillusionment depends on the act of recognition whereby the protagonist comes to see the limitations of his own perspective and to judge matters in the light of the perspective offered by the omniscient, third-person narrator, but d'Annunzio deliberately rejects all analogies between vision and distantiation. All of his visions are intimate and entirely unique encounters with a reality vouchsafed only to the poet himself. Like the later surrealists, d'Annunzio embraces immediacy and attempts to transcribe dreams and waking life with equal vividness. He deliberately avoids all interpretation and instead presents the images that occur to his bandaged and wounded eyes with no hope of confirming them by an appeal to any other spectator. The model of his relations with other, living people is almost always tactile or aural rather than visual, and this alternative model of interpersonal relations seems once again to appeal to the possibility of an inspiration that will overcome any distinction among the various subjects and friends, uniting them all with the genius of Italy.

D'Annunzio's extensive revisions belonged to the first months of his retirement from political life. Yet, in a sense, the *Notturno*, for all its rhetoric of intimacy and privacy, was the very public expression of a powerful, new political myth. Alatri describes the advertising campaign that accompanied the publication of this "intimate" work in November 1921, eleven months after the "Natale di sangue" at Fiume and a year before Mussolini's March on Rome: "it is sufficient to recall the prospect of the Via del Corso in Rome, punctuated by banners carrying the title of the new dannunzian volume, which decorated the whole length of the

central artery of the city, hanging from the cords of electric lamps"
(Alatri, p. 380). That the nocturnal work of the twilight hours should be
advertised on electric lamps is a nice irony. The *Notturno*'s elimination of
the opposition "subject/object" corresponds to the demands of
d'Annunzio's brand of nationalism for an effacement of the barrier
between private and public. The injunction to "Render unto Caesar's
the things which are Caesar's; and unto God the things that are God's"
no longer makes any sense when the state has become the new church.[48]
D'Annunzio proudly mingles the demands of the kingdoms of earth and
heaven and embodies the intimate relation between the state and the
spirit in a narrative of the redemption to be gained by submitting even
the most intimate and obscure parts of the self to the service of the
nation.

Conclusion

Each of these four story-telling protagonists – Stephen Dedalus, Marlow, Proust's narrator, and d'Annunzio's nocturnal version of himself – finds an agonistic heroism in foregoing omniscience.[1] In a "world abandoned by God," these early modernist consciousnesses are aware of their distance from any God's-eye-view or indeed any form of objective knowledge that would be untainted by the cultural specificity and idiosyncrasy of their particular instincts, prejudices, and desires.[2] Yet, each struggles to make of this inevitable partiality the basis for a more universal type of knowledge. The attempt to tell their stories in a language comprehensible to others but true in its representation of their experiences encounters its limits in the very fact of language itself, and this is one reason why they can share their experiences best with those who share their own language. Language is not the only force that constrains their attempts to communicate. Stephen Dedalus speaks of the "nets" of "nationality, language, religion" that constrain the Irish soul at birth (*Portrait*, p. 203). The method by which the modernists achieve their attempts at universality is ultimately not to "fly by those nets," but to ponder the effects of those nets on their sympathies, their prejudices, and their very ability to speak. Their writings must embody the whole complex of national life. The novelist "can serve the glory of his country only by being an artist, that is, on condition that at the moment when he studies the laws, undertakes the experiments, and makes the conclusions [of art], as delicate as those of science, he thinks of nothing – not even his country – but the truth which is before him."[3] It is only in this way that novelists can redeem the experience of their own finitude. Walter Benjamin wrote that "what draws the reader to the novel is the hope of warming his shivering life with a death he reads about."[4] Each of these narrator-heroes obliquely dreams of his own death, but he dreams of it always as a sacrifice to the nation as a whole.

Although the actual political values of these novelists vary widely, each senses a crisis in the values of the nation-state. This crisis encourages the artist to abandon the posture of omniscient narrator and to bring the creator into his creation. Through this intervention, he hopes, at least symbolically, to overcome the conflicts created by his sense of the ways in which history has formed him. That humans are at once the subjects of history, its makers, and the objects of the processes of history, its artifacts, was the source of the nightmare from which the modernists hoped to awake. It was only in embracing a collective identity, what Lukács in another context called "the 'we' which is the subject of history," that the novelists imagined themselves capable of overcoming the antinomies that shape the modern individual and thus resolving the contradictions of their historical positions.[5] Recent interest in the relationship between Fascism and modernism has caused many critics to doubt the traditional connection between modernism and a cosmopolitan humanism. The political paradox of modernism was that literary experiment sometimes participated in the turn to authoritarian nationalism of a d'Annunzio, but just as often led to the cosmopolitan revaluation of national identity implicit in the multilingual punning of *Finnegans Wake*. What I hope to have shown is how these responses share the sense that the balance between the life of the individual and that of the nation, to which the realist novel was so well adapted, needed to change in the face of a collapse of the firm distinction between private and public spheres. The extreme disparity between the novelist's demand to "express [him]self in some mode of life or art as freely as [he] can" and the very immensity of the forces that seem to shape his consciousness creates the unwieldy structures and obscure language of modernist novels (*Portrait*, p. 247). At one level, the novelists described in this book may appear to have belonged to the end of a long tradition of European realism. All developed their techniques out of Flaubert's realism and in reaction to late nineteenth-century naturalism. In many respects, the multiple perspectives of "High Modernism" seem a relief from the musings of the engorged and doomed consciousnesses of these early modernists. Yet, much of twentieth-century literature seems to respond to the concerns of these early modernists, and Nabokov's Humbert Humbert, James Baldwin's John Grimes, Philip Roth's Alexander Portnoy, and the narrators of Margaret Atwood's *Surfacing* and Amitav Ghosh's *The Shadow Lines* all inherit the ambitions of Stephen Dedalus and Proust's narrator to speak for their cultures. The task at hand is greater than what the novelist can hope to achieve. As Hannah Arendt has written, "Although everybody started his life by inserting himself into the human world through action and speech, nobody is the author or producer of his own life story."[6] The modernists strain against the limits of narrative.

The two poles of modernism, its attempt to render the agonies of the individual alienated consciousness and its attraction to the phenomena of a rapidly changing society that is constantly transforming that consciousness, interact dynamically throughout modernist literature. It is not only Stephen Dedalus who at once wants to encounter the reality of experience and to speak for his God-forsaken race. The attempt to offer an authentic account of the "reality of experience" from the perspective of a single, isolated consciousness always needed to show how that consciousness was shaped by social forces, and indeed the very effort to explore the deepest recesses of the perceiving subject seems almost to have evolved from the attempt to show the most minute level of interpenetration between the subject and the apparently contingent reality against which it must fashion itself. The conflict between ethics and sociology, between the individual as human being and the individual as an actor responsible for fulfilling a certain social role, seems to belong uniquely to modern industrial society, although its roots may be as much in the religious beliefs of Christianity as in a given mode of production.[7] In philosophy, it was Kant who represented this conflict most thoroughly. Kant's "Copernican revolution" attempted to ground knowledge of the outside world in the cognitive faculties of the individual subject and moral judgment in the capacity of the individual's practical reason to legislate for itself in such a way that its moral laws could be made universal without contradiction.[8] The grounding of both pure and practical reason in the subject, however, only made more evident the conflict between the individual as subject of historical processes, as legislator for an imagined "kingdom of ends," and the individual as object of those processes, as a given person with particular needs and desires.[9] Throughout the nineteenth century, this conflict seemed integral to human experience, although a great number of "secular theodicies," as Stefan Collini has memorably called them, promised to overcome it.[10] At the turn of the century, a renewed interest in this conflict arose in part from the apparent failure of liberalism to achieve a "kingdom of ends," in which human beings would all regard each other as free and equal.

At the same time, the modernist novelists were involved in a sort of "Copernican revolution" of their own, a revolution in the form of the novel. The novel had always treated the conflict between the participant's and the observer's roles in social action as fundamental, and nineteenth-century realism had developed particularly sophisticated techniques for representing this conflict. These techniques relied on the conflict between an omniscient third-person narrator, who represented "what" the individual characters were, their sociological roles, and the first-person voices of characters themselves, who spoke from their own perspectives, about "who" they were. This conflict is the source of novelistic irony. The modernists developed a series of techniques that described this conflict between third- and first-person more vividly, and also sometimes seemed to promise to overcome it. By transforming the individual protagonist into the narrator (or, to look at it another way, by making the narrator into a character), the modernists at once show the extreme conflict between the sociological and ethical perspectives on action and attempt to reconcile this conflict. The narrator, instead of standing outside any human perspective at an Archimedean point, or even embodying the generalized perspective of society as a whole, borrows the perceptions and categories of a particular character. As Auerbach argued, however, this does not amount simply to the extreme subjectivism of some earlier "unreliable" first-person narrators.[11] Firstly, the modernists allow the possibility of "rising" from the position of character to that of narrator, of transforming purely subjective impressions into a sort of objective knowledge. Crucial to this process is the notion of self-consciousness, the individual's becoming aware of being both a subject and an object of historical processes. Secondly, the modernists do not begin with, or anywhere offer, an unproblematically "objective" account of human actions. This is not to suggest that earlier novelists took the objectivity of their accounts for granted. Balzac, for example, does not imagine it to be a simple matter to arrive at a truly impersonal or divine perspective from which a fully adequate account is possible; such an account, in Balzac, remains a product of convention and therefore highly problematic. The "objective" account, however, is presented as such, independently of the perspective of any characters, and the characters adapt themselves to it. The modernists, on the other hand, place a renewed emphasis on the difficulty of the process of arriving at such a shared account of reality, and the inevitable inadequacy of any such account to "things-in-themselves," that is to say, the inevitable and unbridgeable distance between words, or consciousness more generally, and things. It is in the development of new techniques for representing this difficulty that the modernists fundamentally changed the way novels were written.

The modernists tend to begin, like Descartes or Kant, with the perceiving subject, what Virginia Woolf called "the ordinary mind on an ordinary day," or in the case of the novelists I have studied here an extraordinary mind on an ordinary day.[12] The various formal techniques they use, however, involve attempted syntheses of what Ian Watt has called the "realism of presentation" and the "realism of assessment," that is the first- and third-person perspectives on events.[13] The modernists' "Copernican revolution" comes not in an outright rejection of the attempt to offer a neutral third-person account of human society that anyone can accept, but in the search for ways of developing such a third-person account out of a first-person account, a sort of phenomenological representation of consciousness according to which individual experience can be transformed into an intersubjective reality. Yet, the novelists all remain conscious of the impossibility of their task. The later modernists were to develop a variety of techniques for showing multiple consciousnesses focused on single series of events. The modernists I have examined here all start, in one way or another, with the consciousness of a single individual protagonist, and work from there towards the world and other human beings. It is this emphasis on the process of arriving from the first person to the third person, and the crucial role in it of consciousness and language, that contributes the distinctiveness of the techniques of modernism. It also accounts for the modernists' interest in translation and in the untranslatable. Because the shared language is the medium in which this development from purely subjective to "objective," or rather intersubjective, representations of reality must take place, the modernists emphasize the difficulty of moving from one language to another. This reinforces the sense, which some modernists shared with so many of their contemporaries, that the sharing of a language, and thus of a "culture," was a prerequisite for the rise of first to third person, that is, the achievement of a shared social vision.

Thus, the modernists' "Copernican revolution" brings them full circle to confront a "dialectic of Enlightenment."[14] For, whereas Kant believed that the critique of reason could lead to a reasonable faith in the existence of a shared external world and the autonomy and equality of all rational beings, the modernists seem for the most part to have doubted human rationality and autonomy. In particular, they became aware that any attempt to arrive at objective knowledge, by virtue of the fact that it had started from a given subjective position, would always remain "tainted" by subjectivity, always open to the skeptic's belief in an evil genius that has deceived the individual. In the realm of knowledge, this belief implies the possible claim that there is nothing really "out there" to correspond to the individual's consciousness. Sensible people from

Samuel Johnson to Bernard Williams have shown that it is very hard for anyone to believe consistently in the non-existence of a world "out there." As Williams has argued, it is in the realms of ethics and politics that the claims of skepticism and relativism have a more powerful impact, for "justice" is a much more problematic concept than "truth," and it is much harder for people to come to agreement as to what is just than to reconcile their conceptions of what is true.[15] For it is impossible to develop a conception of justice entirely independent of people's prejudices, needs, and desires, and no amount of experimentation or scientific method can convince people to abandon deeply held beliefs and arrive at a purely disinterested perspective on human affairs. This does not mean that we should not attempt to arrive at shared beliefs about justice, but it does mean that we cannot expect ever to achieve a world in which conflicting opinions about what is good or right can be resolved as easily as competing opinions about whether or not the world is flat. For the modernists, however, living in an age in which the moral uncertainty unleashed by varieties of relativism was still new and even more unsettling than it is today, the idea that right and wrong could not be known with objective certainty was terrifying, and the nation-state seemed capable of offering a solution to it.

Fifty years ago, Lionel Trilling saw a tension between liberalism's "great primal act of imagination" of "a general enlargement and freedom and rational direction of human life" and the tendency of institutional forms of liberalism to deny "the emotions and the imagination."[16] He wrote that "the job of criticism would seem to be . . . to recall liberalism to its first essential imagination of variousness and possibility, which implies the awareness of complexity and difficulty" (p. xii). I hope to have shown that the complexity of modernism in the novel responded to the crisis of imagination that the problems of cultural and national difference posed for a weary liberalism. Liberalism has always had a complex relationship to the national idea. In the nation, liberals had found the possibility of overcoming, through the cultivation of sympathy and character, the individualism that Tocqueville criticized as one of the by-products of the condition of equality. The nation offered the possibilities of tempering economic competition and encouraging the virtues of citizenship. However, in this very turn towards national solidarity, liberalism showed the limits of its tolerance of difference and degraded the demand for universal equality to the homogenizing requirement of social similarity. The allure of privatism on the one hand and authoritarianism on the other appeared so strong to the modernists because the institutions of liberty and equality seemed to have failed to establish fraternal and friendly relations either within or among nations. The modernists generally made their claims on behalf of variousness and possibility, but they also saw the appeal of a kind of simplicity that would structure their chaotic worlds into meaningful, mythical patterns. Their desire for a form of authenticity that could transcend their own finitude often led them to look for a type of fetishistic protection to the "magic pronoun 'my'": "to forge in the smithy of my soul the uncreated conscience of my race"; "it was written I should be loyal to the nightmare of my choice"; "in myself, I serve my god."[17] It is Proust, who perhaps has most the reputation of hermeticism and self-absorption, for whom the pronoun "my" is least sufficient: "it seemed to me that they would not be 'my' readers, but the readers of their own selves, my book being merely a sort of magnifying glass like those which the optician at Combray used to offer his customers – it would be my book, but with its help I would furnish them with the means of reading what lay within themselves." Ultimately, it is not in the redemptive fantasies of Stephen Dedalus or of d'Annunzio, nor even in Conrad's resigned faithfulness to the national idea, but in the complexity and difficulty of Proust's attempts to read the book of himself that the liberal ideal of the nation-state may have found its way forward.

Notes

I THE MODERN NOVELIST AS REDEEMER OF THE NATION

1 *Portrait*, pp. 252–253.
2 Seamus Deane, Introduction to *A Portrait of the Artist as a Young Man* (Harmondsworth: Penguin, 1992), p. xli.
3 *Oxford English Dictionary.*
4 Louis Althusser, "Ideology and Ideological State Apparatuses," in *Lenin and Philosophy and Other Essays*, trans. Ben Brewster (London: New Left Books, 1971), pp. 127–186.
5 See John Fletcher and Malcolm Bradbury, "The Introverted Novel," in Malcolm Bradbury and James McFarlane, eds., *Modernism: A Guide to European Literature, 1890–1930* (London: Penguin, 1976), pp. 394–415.
6 See Ian Watt, *The Rise of the Novel* (Berkeley: University of California Press, 1959).
7 Friedrich Nietzsche, *Human, All too Human* (1878), trans. R. J. Hollingdale (Cambridge: Cambridge University Press, 1986), p. 2.
8 Ernest Gellner, *Nations and Nationalism* (Ithaca: Cornell University Press, 1983), p. 56.
9 Eric Hobsbawm, *Nations and Nationalism since 1780* (Cambridge: Cambridge University Press, 1990), p. 102.
10 See R. F. Foster, *Modern Ireland, 1600–1972* (New York: Penguin, 1989), pp. 431–460.
11 See Martin Clark, *Modern Italy 1871–1982* (London: Longman, 1984), pp. 114–117, 150–153.
12 *Origins*, p. 275.
13 Michael Tratner, *Modernism and Mass Politics: Joyce, Woolf, Eliot, Yeats* (Stanford: Stanford University Press, 1995). See also Michael Levenson, *Modernism and the Fate of Individuality: Character and Novelistic Form from Conrad to Woolf* (Cambridge: Cambridge University Press, 1991).
14 Thomas Hobbes, *Leviathan* (1651), ed. C. B. MacPherson (Harmondsworth: Penguin, 1968), Part I, chapter 15.
15 Terry Eagleton, *Exiles and Émigrés* (New York: Schocken Books, 1970).
16 Robert Denoon Cumming, *Human Nature and History: A Study of the Development of Liberal Political Thought* (Chicago: University of Chicago Press, 1969), I, p. 5.

17 See J. W. Burrow, *Whigs and Liberals: Continuity and Change in English Political Thought* (Oxford: Clarendon Press, 1988).

18 See Seyla Benhabib, *Critique, Norm, and Utopia: A Study of the Foundations of Critical Theory* (New York: Columbia University Press, 1986), pp. 1–146.

19 See Tony Judt, "The New Old Nationalism," *New York Review of Books*, May 26, 1994: 44–51.

20 Max Weber, *The Protestant Ethic and the Spirit of Capitalism* (1904–5), trans. Talcott Parsons (London: Routledge, 1992), p. 27.

21 Georg Lukács, *The Theory of the Novel: A Historico-Philosophical Essay on the Epic Forms of Great Literature* (1920), trans. Anna Bostock (Cambridge, Mass.: MIT Press, 1971), p. 112.

22 Honoré de Balzac, *A Harlot High and Low* [*Splendeurs et misères des courtisanes*, 1839–47], trans. Rayner Heppenstall (Harmondsworth: Penguin, 1970). See Richard Ellmann, *James Joyce*, rev. edn (New York: Oxford University Press, 1982), p. 385 and Colin MacCabe, *James Joyce and the Revolution of the Word* (New York: Harper and Row, 1979), pp. 27ff.

23 Georg Lukács, *The Historical Novel* (1937), trans. Hannah and Stanley Mitchell (Lincoln: University of Nebraska Press, 1983), p. 171.

24 Lukács, *Theory of the Novel*, p. 41.

25 See Hans Ulrich Gumbrecht, "Sinnbildung als Sicherung der Lebenswelt: ein Beitrag zur funktionsgeschichtlichen Situierung der realistischen Literatur am Beispiel von Balzacs Erzählung," in Hans Ulrich Gumbrecht, Karlheinz Stiere and Rainer Werning, eds. *Honoré de Balzac* (Munich: Fink, 1980), pp. 339–389.

26 See Roland Barthes, *S/Z: An Essay* (1970), trans. Richard Miller (New York: Hill and Wang, 1974).

27 *LI*, p. 50; *IP*, p. 166.

28 *IP*, p. 256; *LI*, p. 151.

29 "Les Deux Poètes," title of volume I of *Illusions perdues*.

30 *IP*, pp. 707–708. *LI*, pp. 654–655.

31 Erich Auerbach, *Mimesis: The Representation of Reality in Western Literature* (1946), trans. Willard R. Trask (Princeton: Princeton University Press, 1953), p. 480.

32 Honoré de Balzac, Preface (1842) to the *Human Comedy* in *The Works of Balzac*, trans. Katharine Prescott Wormeley (Boston: Little, Brown, 1899), I, pp. vii–viii.

33 *LI*, p. 649; *IP*, p. 703.

34 Preface, pp. x, xvi.

35 Alexis de Tocqueville, *Democracy in America* (1835–40), trans. Henry Reeve and Francis Bowen (New York: Random House, 1945), I, p. 330. Cf. Larry Siedentop, *Tocqueville* (Oxford: Oxford University Press, 1994), p. 59.

36 John Stuart Mill, *Considerations on Representative Government* (1861) (Chicago: Henry Regnery Company, 1962), chapter 2.

37 Catherine Gallagher, *The Industrial Reformation of English Fiction: Social Discourse and Narrative Form, 1832–1867* (Chicago: University of Chicago Press, 1985), p. xii.

38 John Locke, *Two Treatises of Government* (1650), ed. Peter Laslett (Cambridge: Cambridge University Press, 1988), second treatise, chapter 8, paragraph 95.

39 Jean-Jacques Rousseau, *On the Social Contract*, Book I in *The Basic Political Writings*, trans. Donald A. Cress (Indianapolis: Hackett, 1987), p. 141.

40 *LI*, p. 633; *IP*, p. 689.

41 See Burrow, *Whigs and Liberals*, esp. pp. 51–76, and *Evolution and Society: A Study in Victorian Social Theory* (Cambridge: Cambridge University Press, 1966), pp. 260–277.

42 Immanuel Kant, "Foundations for the Metaphysics of Morals" (1797), in *Selections*, ed. Lewis White Beck (New York: Macmillan, 1988).

43 Tocqueville, *Democracy in America*, II, pp. 90–93.

44 Matthew 22:21; Luke 17:21. Cf. Weber, *The Protestant Ethic and the Spirit of Capitalism*.

45 Franco Moretti, *The Way of the World: The Bildungsroman in European Culture* (London: Verso, 1987), pp. 135–142.

46 Martin Heidegger, *Being and Time* (1927), trans. John Macquarrie and Edward Robinson (New York: Harper, 1962), p. 71; Hannah Arendt, *The Human Condition* (Chicago: University of Chicago Press, 1958), pp. 181–188.

47 Preface, p. x.

48 Benedict Anderson, *Imagined Communities: Reflections on the Origin and Spread of Nationalism*, 2nd edn (London: Verso, 1991), p. 30.

49 See John Bishop, *Joyce's Book of the Dark:* Finnegans Wake (Madison: University of Wisconsin Press, 1986), pp. 180–181; Giambattista Vico, *The New Science* (1725), trans. Thomas Bergin and Max Fisch (Ithaca: Cornell University Press, 1984).

50 James Joyce, *Ulysses*, ed. Hans Walter Gabler, Wolfhard Steppe, and Claus Melchior (London: Penguin, 1986), p. 28. Cf. Karl Marx, "The Eighteenth Brumaire of Louis Bonaparte" (1852) in *The Marx-Engels Reader*, ed. Robert C. Tucker, 2nd edn (New York: Norton, 1978), p. 595.

51 See Seyla Benhabib, *Critique, Norm, and Utopia*.

52 Quoted in Conor Cruise O'Brien, "Passion and Cunning: An Essay on the Politics of W. B. Yeats," in *In Excited Reverie*, ed. A. Norman Jeffares and K. G. W. Cross (New York: MacMillan, 1965), p. 216.

53 See Don Gifford, *Joyce Annotated: Notes for* Dubliners *and* A Portrait of the Artist as a Young Man, 2nd ed. (Berkeley: University of California Press, 1982), p. 196; John Milton, *Paradise Lost*, I:44–45, in *Complete Poems and Major Prose*, ed. Merritt Y. Hughes (New York: MacMillan, 1957).

54 See Gifford, *Joyce Annotated*, p. 203.

55 See *Ulysses*, p. 151.

56 See Gifford, *Joyce Annotated*, p. 167.

57 Dominic Manganiello, *Joyce's Politics* (London: Routledge and Kegan Paul, 1980), p. 232.

58 Emer Nolan, *James Joyce and Nationalism* (London: Routledge, 1995), pp. 38, 44.

59 Vincent J. Cheng, *Joyce, Race, and Empire* (Cambridge: Cambridge University Press, 1995), p. 64.

60 James Joyce, *Stephen Hero* (written 1904–5; first published 1955) (New York: New Directions, 1963), p. 54, quoted in Tratner, *Modernism and Mass Politics*, p. 130.

61 James Joyce, "The Day of the Rabblement," in *Critical Writings*, ed. Ellsworth Mason and Richard Ellman (New York: Viking, 1959), p. 70.

62 *Paradise Lost*, II.194–196. See also II.347–349, II.380–385, and X.385.

63 Cheng, *Joyce, Race, and Empire*, p. 27.

64 See George W. Stocking, Jr., *Victorian Anthropology* (New York: MacMillan, 1987), pp. 137–143.

65 Foster, *Modern Ireland*, p. 450.

66 Ellmann, *James Joyce*, p. 200.

67 See St. Anselm, *Proslogium*, chapter 5, in Samuel Enoch Stumpf, ed. *Philosophical Problems: Selected Readings* (New York: McGraw-Hill, 1971), pp. 93–104.

68 Cheng lists the eleven uses in *Joyce, Race, and Empire*, p. 17.

69 *Ulysses*, p. 170.

70 Hugh Kenner, *Joyce's Voices* (Berkeley: University of California Press, 1978), p. 82. Cf. Wayne Booth, *The Rhetoric of Fiction* (1961), 2nd ed. (Chicago: University of Chicago Press, 1983), pp. 323–336.

71 See Gustave Flaubert, letter to Mlle. Leroyer de Chantepie, March 18, 1857, quoted in Gifford, *Joyce Annotated*, p. 256.

72 See Deane's introduction to his edition of *A Portrait*, cited in note 2 above.

73 *Ulysses*, p. 400. See also pp. 272–273, 554–557, and chapter 12, the "Cyclops" episode.

74 Erich Auerbach, "Figura" (1944) in *Scenes from the Drama of European Literature* (Minneapolis: University of Minnesota Press, 1984), p. 72.

75 See Enda Duffy, *The Subaltern Ulysses* (Minneapolis: University of Minnesota Press, 1994).

2 THE CRISIS OF LIBERAL NATIONALISM

1 E. J. Hobsbawm, *Nations and Nationalism Since 1780* (Cambridge: Cambridge University Press, 1990), p. 133.

2 Woodrow Wilson, Speech of July 4, 1918, "The Four Ends," in H. W. V. Temperley, *A History of the Paris Peace Conference* (London: Henry Frowde, 1920), I, p. 444. See also Sharp, *The Versailles Settlement: Peacemaking in Paris, 1919* (New York: St. Martin's Press, 1991), p. 19.

3 Woodrow Wilson, Speech of February 11, 1918, "The Four Principles," in Temperley, *Paris Peace Conference*, vol. I, p. 439.

4 L. T. Hobhouse, *Liberalism and Other Writings*, ed. James Meadowcroft (Cambridge: Cambridge University Press, 1994), p. 65.

5 J. A. Hobson, *Imperialism: A Study*, ed. Philip Siegelman (Ann Arbor: University of Michigan Press, 1965).

6 George Dangerfield, *The Strange Death of Liberal England, 1910–1914* (1935, New York: Perigee, 1980). See Michael Tratner, *Modernism and Mass Politics: Joyce, Woolf, Eliot, Yeats* (Stanford: Stanford University Press, 1995), pp. 48–76.

7 R. K. Webb, *Modern England: From the 18th Century to the Present* (New York: Harper and Row, 1968), pp. 400–402. I draw on Webb's work in the following paragraphs.

8 See Jean-Marie Mayeur and Madeleine Rebérioux, *The Third Republic from its Origins to the Great War, 1871–1914*, trans. J. R. Foster (Cambridge: Cambridge University Press, 1984), pp. 23–25. I draw on the work of Mayeur and Rebérioux in the following paragraphs.

9 Eugen Weber, *France Fin de Siècle* (Cambridge, Mass.: Harvard University Press, 1986), pp. 105–129.

10 See Mayeur and Réberioux, *The Third Republic*, p. 203.

11 Eugen Weber, *The Nationalist Revival in France, 1905–1914* (Berkeley: University of California Press, 1959).

12 See Leo Strauss, *Natural Right and History* (Chicago: University of Chicago Press, 1953).

13 H. Stuart Hughes, *Consciousness and Society: The Reorientation of European Social Thought, 1890–1930*, rev. ed. (New York: Vintage, 1977), p. 37.

14 See George D. Painter, *Marcel Proust* (Harmondsworth: Penguin, 1983), pp. 190–191, 419–423; Richard Ellmann, *James Joyce*, rev. edn (New York: Oxford University Press, 1982), pp. 200, 208.

15 Stefan Collini, *Public Moralists: Political Thought and Intellectual Life in Britain, 1850–1930* (Oxford: Clarendon Press, 1991), p. 315.

16 See C. B. MacPherson, *The Political Theory of Possessive Individualism: Hobbes to Locke* (Oxford: Clarendon Press, 1962).

17 In *Liberalism*, Hobhouse repeats and updates these arguments from Mill's *Considerations on Representative Government*.

18 See Arthur Walworth, *Wilson and His Peacemakers: American Diplomacy at the Paris Peace Conference, 1919* (New York and London: Norton, 1986), pp. 119–120; 310–311.

19 Hannah Arendt, "On Humanity in Dark Times: Thoughts on Lessing," foreword to *"Nathan the Wise," "Minna Von Barnhelm," and Other Plays and Writings*, by Gotthold Ephraim Lessing, ed. Peter Demetz (New York: Continuum, 1991), pp. xi, xv.

20 Seyla Benhabib, *The Reluctant Modernism of Hannah Arendt*, Modernity and Political Thought series (Thousand Oaks, Calif.: Sage, 1996), p. 20. See Aristotle, *Nicomachean Ethics*, trans. David Ross (Oxford: Oxford University Press, 1980), book 5, chapter 11, 1134a and book 8, chapter 8.

21 Aristotle, *Nicomachean Ethics*, book 8, chapter 1, 1155a.

22 See Michael J. Sandel, *Liberalism and the Limits of Justice* (Cambridge: Cambridge University Press, 1982).

23 Bonnie Honig, *Political Theory and the Displacement of Politics* (Ithaca: Cornell University Press, 1993).

24 Georg Lukács, "Reification and the Consciousness of the Proletariat," in

History and Class Consciousness: Studies in Marxist Dialectics (1922; Cambridge, Mass.: MIT Press, 1971), pp. 83–222.

25 Hobson, *Imperialism*, p. 5. John Stuart Mill, *Considerations on Representative Government* (1861; Chicago: Henry Regnery Company, 1962), chapter 16.

26 Ernest Gellner, *Nations and Nationalism* (Ithaca: Cornell University Press, 1983).

27 Immanuel Kant, "Foundations for the Metaphysics of Morals," in *Selections*, ed. Lewis White Beck (New York: Macmillan, 1988), p. 448.

28 Stefan Collini, Donald Winch, and John Burrow, *That Noble Science of Politics: A Study in Nineteenth-Century Intellectual History* (Cambridge: Cambridge University Press, 1983), p. 159.

29 See Yael Tamir, *Liberal Nationalism* (Princeton: Princeton University Press, 1995).

30 See Bernard Williams, *Morality: An Introduction to Ethics* (Cambridge: Cambridge University Press, 1993) and *Ethics and the Limits of Philosophy* (Cambridge, Mass.: Harvard University Press, 1985); Michael J. Sandel, *Liberalism and the Limits of Justice*, and Michael J. Sandel, ed., *Liberalism and its Critics* (Oxford: Blackwell, 1984).

31 See John Rawls, *A Theory of Justice* (Cambridge, Mass.: Harvard University Press, 1972) and "Justice as Fairness: Political not Metaphysical," *Philosophy and Public Affairs* 14 (1985): 223–251; and Jürgen Habermas, *The Structural Transformation of the Public Sphere*, trans. Thomas Burger and Frederick Lawrence (1962; Cambridge, Mass.: MIT Press, 1989) and *The Philosophical Discourse of Modernity: Twelve Lectures*, trans. Frederick Lawrence (Cambridge, Mass.: MIT Press, 1987).

32 See Larry Siedentop, *Tocqueville* (Oxford: Oxford University Press, 1994), p. 58.

33 See Pierre Nora, "Nation," in *Critical Dictionary of the French Revolution*, ed. François Furet and Mona Ozouf, trans. Arthur Goldhammer (Cambridge, Mass.: Harvard University Press, 1989), p. 742; Sandy Petrey, *Realism and Revolution: Balzac, Stendhal, Zola, and the Performances of History* (Ithaca: Cornell University Press, 1988).

34 Edmund Burke, Speech on the Reform of Representation in the House of Commons, May 7, 1782, in *Works*, Bohn's Standard Library Edition (London, 1887), VI, pp. 146–147.

35 See William Doyle, *The Old European Order, 1660–1800*, 2nd edn (Oxford: Oxford University Press, 1992), pp. 310–312.

36 See Avrom Fleishman, *Conrad's Politics: Community and Anarchy in the Fiction of Joseph Conrad* (Baltimore: Johns Hopkins University Press, 1967).

37 John Emerich Edward Dalberg Acton, "Nationality," in *Essays on Freedom and Power*, ed. Gertrude Himmelfarb (Boston: Beacon Press, 1949), p. 183.

38 See Sandel, *Liberalism and its Critics*, pp. 1–11.

39 John Locke, *Two Treatises on Civil Government* (1690), ed. Peter Laslett (Cambridge: Cambridge University Press, 1988), second treatise, chapter viii, paragraph 95.

40 See Peter Laslett, introduction to *ibid.*, p. 85.

41 Jean-Jacques Rousseau, *On the Social Contract* (1761), Book I, in *The Basic Political Writings*, trans. Donald A. Cress (Indianapolis: Hackett, 1987), p. 141.

42 See Sandel, *Liberalism and the Limits of Justice*, pp. 6–7.

43 See L. T. Hobhouse, *The Metaphysical Theory of the State: A Criticism* (London: Routledge/Thoemmes, 1993).

44 *On the Social Contract*, Book IV, Chapter I, in *The Basic Political Writings*, p. 204.

45 See Ernst Cassirer, *Rousseau, Kant, Goethe: Two Essays* (Princeton: Princeton University Press, 1945).

46 See Robert Wokler, *Rousseau* (Oxford: Oxford University Press, 1995).

47 Article VI, in Christine Fauré, ed., *Les déclarations des droits de l'homme en 1789* (Paris: Payot, 1988).

48 Article II.

49 François Furet, *Interpreting the French Revolution*, trans. Elborg Forster (Cambridge: Cambridge University Press, 1981), p. 27.

50 Emmanuel Sieyès, *Qu'est-ce que le Tiers état*, ed. Roberto Zapperi (Geneva: Droz, 1970), p. 124. See Furet, *Interpreting the French Revolution*, p. 44.

51 G. W. F. Hegel, "Absolute Freedom and Terror," in *Phenomenology of Spirit*, trans. A. V. Miller, ed. J. N. Findlay (Oxford: Oxford University Press, 1977), pp. 355–363.

52 Isaiah Berlin, "Two Concepts of Liberty," in Sandel, ed., *Liberalism and its Critics*.

53 Rousseau, *On the Social Contract*, in *Basic Political Writings*, p. 150.

54 Ernest Renan, "What is a Nation?," trans. Martin Thom, in *Nation and Narration*, ed. Homi K. Bhabha (London: Routledge, 1990), p. 19.

55 Joseph-Arthur de Gobineau, *The Inequality of Human Races* (1853), trans. Adrian Collins (New York: Putnam, 1915).

56 Cf. George Armstrong Kelly, *The Humane Comedy: Constant, Tocqueville and French Liberalism* (Cambridge: Cambridge University Press, 1992), pp. 236–245.

57 Kant, "Foundations of the Metaphysics of Morals," in *Selections*, p. 276.

58 Ernest Renan, letter to Arthur de Gobineau of June 26, 1856, in *Oeuvres Complètes*, ed. Henriette Psichari (Paris: Calmann-Lévy, 1947–1961), X, p. 204.

59 Renan, "What is a Nation?," p. 34.

60 Maurice Barrès, *Scènes et doctrines du nationalisme* in *Oeuvres*, ed. Philippe Barrès (Paris: Club de l'Honnête Homme, 1965), V, p. 72.

61 See Wokler, *Rousseau*, p. 112.

62 Edmund Burke, *Reflections on the Revolution in France*, in *Writings and Speeches*, ed. L. G. Mitchell (Oxford: Clarendon Press, 1989), VIII, p. 76.

63 Edmund Burke, "Appeal from the New to the Old Whigs," in *Works*, III, pp. 44–45.

64 Edmund Burke, Speech on the Reform of Representation in the House of Commons, May 7, 1782, in *Works*, VI, pp. 146–147. See H. T.

Dickinson, *Liberty and Property: Political Ideology in Eighteenth-Century Britain* (New York: Holmes and Meier, 1977), p. 300.

65 *Origins*, p. 176.

66 Herbert Butterfield, *The Whig Interpretation of History* (London: Bell, 1959).

67 See H. T. Dickinson, *Liberty and Property*, p. 68.

68 See Conor Cruise O'Brien, *The Great Melody: A Thematic Biography and Commented Anthology of Edmund Burke* (London: Sinclair-Stevenson, 1992), pp. 596 and *passim*.

69 J. W. Burrow, *Whigs and Liberals: Continuity and Change in English Political Thought* (Oxford: Clarendon Press, 1988).

70 Burke, *Works*, I, pp. 447–448.

71 See Burrow, *Whigs and Liberals*, p. 35.

72 Leslie Stephen, *English Thought in the Eighteenth Century*, quoted in Burrow, *Whigs and Liberals*, p. 9; John Stuart Mill, *A System of Logic*, book 6, chapter 9, section 4, in *Collected Works* (Toronto: University of Toronto Press, 1963–1991), VIII, p. 904.

73 George W. Stocking, Jr., *Victorian Anthropology* (New York: MacMillan, 1987); and J. W. Burrow, *Evolution and Society: A Study in Victorian Social Theory* (Cambridge: Cambridge University Press, 1966).

74 "Anthropology A Practical Science," *Popular Magazine of Anthropology* 1 (1866): 7–8, quoted in Stocking, *Victorian Anthropology*, p. 251.

75 See Burrow, *Evolution and Society*, pp. 93ff.

76 See Stocking, *Victorian Anthropology*, pp. 314–324, and more generally Burrow, *Evolution and Society*, pp. 228–259.

77 Burrow, *Evolution and Society*, p. 268.

78 Mill, *System of Logic*, book 6, chapter 5, section 4, in *Collected Works*, VIII, p. 869.

79 Leslie Stephen, *The Science of Ethics*, 2nd edn (New York: Putnam, 1907), p. 91.

80 See Noel Annan, *Leslie Stephen: The Godless Victorian* (London: Weidenfeld and Nicolson, 1984).

81 Rousseau, *Discourse on the Origins of Inequality*, in *Basic Political Writings*, p. 77.

82 Rawls, *A Theory of Justice*, p. 27.

83 Tamir, *Liberal Nationalism*.

84 Samuel Beer, "Liberalism and the National Idea," *The Public Interest* 5 (1966): 70–82.

85 Walter Benjamin, "The Storyteller" (1936), in *Illuminations*, ed. Hannah Arendt, trans. Harry Zohn (New York: Schocken, 1969), p. 87.

3 CONRAD AND THE DISCOURSE OF NATIONAL CHARACTER

1 Joseph Conrad, "Youth," in *Youth, Heart of Darkness and The End of the Tether*, ed. C. B. Cox (London: Dent, 1974), p. 3.

2 *HD*, pp. 16, 12.

3 See Eloise Knapp Hay, *The Political Novels of Joseph Conrad* (Chicago:

University of Chicago Press, 1963), p. 154; Benita Parry, "Conrad and England," in *Patriotism: The Making and Unmaking of British Character*, ed. Raphael Samuel (London: Routledge, 1989), p. 196.

4 *HD*, p. 10; Conrad, letter to Aniela Zagórska, December 25, 1899, *The Collected Letters of Joseph Conrad*, ed. Frederick R. Karl and Laurence Davies (Cambridge: Cambridge University Press, 1983–), II, p. 230; Conrad, quoted in Frances B. Singh, "The Colonialistic Bias of *Heart of Darkness*," in *HD*, p. 279; Conrad, letter to Roger Casement, December 21, 1903, *Collected Letters*, III, p. 97.

5 See Ian Watt, *Conrad in the Nineteenth Century* (Berkeley: University of California Press, 1979).

6 Heracleitus, fragment 119 DK, quoted in Bernard Williams, *Shame and Necessity* (Berkeley: University of California Press, 1993), p. 136.

7 *Ibid.*

8 See Edward Said, "Two Visions in *Heart of Darkness*," in *Culture and Imperialism* (New York: Alfred A. Knopf, 1993), pp. 19–31.

9 "Youth," p. 22.

10 Avrom Fleishman, *Conrad's Politics: Community and Anarchy in the Fiction of Joseph Conrad* (Baltimore: Johns Hopkins University Press, 1967), p. 10.

11 Watt, *Conrad*, p. 110. Professor Watt first drew my attention to Fleishman's book and discussed these objections to it with me.

12 Conrad, letter to George W. Keating, December 14, 1922, reprinted in *The Portable Conrad*, ed. Morton Dauwen Zabel (New York: Penguin Books, 1976), pp. 751–753.

13 Conrad, letter to R. B. Cunninghame Graham, February 8, 1899, *Collected Letters*, II, pp. 157–161. Translations from the French parts of the letter are based on the translation offered by the editors of the *Collected Letters*. See also the notes in *Collected Letters* and in *Joseph Conrad's Letters to Cunninghame Graham*, ed. Cedric Watts (Cambridge: Cambridge University Press, 1969).

14 Conrad, Author's note to "Youth."

15 See Fleishman, *Conrad's Politics*, pp. 49ff.

16 Quoted in *HD*, p. 142.

17 See J. W. Burrow, *Whigs and Liberals: Continuity and Change in English Political Thought* (Oxford: Clarendon Press, 1988); and Stefan Collini, *Public Moralists: Political Thought and Intellectual Life in Britain, 1850–1930* (Oxford: Clarendon Press, 1991) and "Liberalism and the Legacy of Mill," *Historical Journal* 20 (1977): 237–254.

18 See Collini, *Public Moralists*.

19 George W. Stocking, Jr., *Victorian Anthropology* (New York: Macmillan, 1987).

20 Charles Adderley, quoted in Walter E. Houghton, *The Victorian Frame of Mind, 1830–1870* (New Haven: Yale University Press, 1957), p. 47.

21 Conrad, letter to Aniela Zagórska, December 25, 1899, *Collected Letters*, II, p. 230.

22 Karl Pearson, *National Life from the Standpoint of Science* (London: Adam and Charles Black, 1901), pp. 27–28.

23 T. H. Huxley, *"Evolution and Ethics" and Other Essays* (New York, 1894), pp. 37–38.

24 See Watt, *Conrad*, p. 168.

25 See H. Stuart Hughes, *Consciousness and Society: The Reorientation of European Social Thought, 1890–1930*, revised edn. (New York: Vintage, 1977).

26 See Watt, *Conrad*, pp. 147–168.

27 Conrad, *Notes on Life and Letters*, quoted in Fleishman, *Conrad's Politics*, pp. 34, 57.

28 Edmund Burke, Speech on the Reform of Representation in the House of Commons, May 7, 1782, *Works*, Bohn's Standard Library Edition (London, 1887), VI, p. 147.

29 Fleishman, *Conrad's Politics*, pp. 49ff.

30 Jean-Jacques Rousseau, *Émile*, trans. Allan Bloom (New York: Basic Books, 1979), p. 67.

31 See Watt, *Conrad*, p. 168.

32 See Stocking, *Victorian Anthropology*, pp. 66–67.

33 Hunt Hawkins, "Conrad's Idea of Englishness," paper presented at the Joseph Conrad Society meeting, Washington, D.C., December 29, 1996.

34 See John Batchelor, *The Life of Joseph Conrad: A Critical Biography* (Oxford: Blackwell, 1994), pp. 34–36; Watt, *Conrad*, p. 92.

35 Knapp Hay, *Political Novels*, p. 128.

36 Conrad, *The Nigger of the "Narcissus" and Typhoon and Other Stories*, ed. Norman Sherry (London: Dent, 1974), p. 163.

37 See Homi K. Bhabha, *The Location of Culture* (London: Routledge, 1994).

38 Edmund Burke, *Reflections on the Revolution in France*, in *Writings and Speeches*, ed. L. G. Mitchell (Oxford: Clarendon Press, 1989), VIII, p. 138.

39 Conrad, "Youth," p. 22.

40 Arendt, *Origins*, p. 159.

41 Conrad, "Author's Note," 1919, *A Personal Record*, in *Collected Works* (New York: Doubleday, 1925), VI, p. v–vii.

42 Conrad, *Nostromo* (1904; Harmondsworth: Penguin, 1963), p. 423.

4 PROUST AND THE DISCOURSE OF NATIONAL WILL

1 *Remembrance*, III, pp. 913–914. The roman numeral preceding the page number refers to the volume number.

2 *Ibid*; *Recherche*, IV, p. 458.

3 Maurice Barrès, *Scènes et doctrines du nationalisme* in *Oeuvres*, ed. Philippe Barrès (Paris: Club de l'Honnête Homme, 1965), V, p. 25. See Michael Curtis, *Three Against the Third Republic: Sorel, Barrès, and Maurras* (Princeton: Princeton University Press, 1959), pp. 253–254.

4 Alexis de Tocqueville, letter to Gobineau of November 17, 1853, in *"The European Revolution" and Correspondence with Gobineau*, ed. and trans. John Lukacs (Gloucester, Mass.: Peter Smith, 1968), p. 226.

5 See Michael J. Sandel, *Liberalism and the Limits of Justice* (Cambridge:

Cambridge University Press, 1982); Seyla Benhabib, Judith Butler, Drucilla Cornell, and Nancy Fraser, *Feminist Contentions: A Philosophical Exchange* (London: Routledge, 1995).

6 Ernest Renan, "What is a Nation?," trans. Martin Thom, in *Nation and Narration*, ed. Homi K. Bhabha (London: Routledge, 1990), p. 19.

7 Sandel, *Liberalism and the Limits of Justice*, p. 58.

8 See *Remembrance*, I, p. 1021, n. 6; *Recherche*, I, p. 1052.

9 See Alison Winton, *Proust's Additions: The Making of "A la recherche du temps perdu"* (Cambridge: Cambridge University Press, 1977), I, p. 26 and *passim*.

10 Leo Bersani, *Homos* (Cambridge, Mass.: Harvard University Press, 1995), p. 7. See also pp. 129–151.

11 Alexis de Tocqueville, *Democracy in America*, trans. Henry Reeve and Francis Bowen (New York: Random House, 1945), II, p. 216 and *passim*.

12 George D. Painter, *Marcel Proust* (Harmondsworth: Penguin, 1983), p. 455. See Marcel Proust, *Le Carnet de 1908*, ed. Philip Kolb, Cahiers Marcel Proust, n.s., number 8 (Paris: Gallimard, 1976), p. 48 and *passim*.

13 See P.-V. Zima, *Le désir du mythe: Une lecture sociologique de Marcel Proust* (Paris: Nizet, 1973), pp. 252–306.

14 The editors of the Pléiade edition note the probable allusion to Mignet at *Recherche*, I, p. 1086, n. 2. See François Mignet, *La Rivalité de François Ier et de Charles-Quint*, 3rd ed. (Paris, 1886), II, pp. 440–464, especially pp. 462–463.

15 Renan, "What is a Nation?," p. 19.

16 René Girard, *Deceit, Desire, and the Novel: Self and Other in Literary Structure*, trans. Yvonne Freccero (Baltimore: Johns Hopkins University Press, 1965).

17 Wordsworth, "Lines Composed a Few Miles above Tintern Abbey," line 106.

18 *Remembrance*, III, pp. 913–914; *Recherche*, IV, p. 457.

19 René Descartes, *Meditations on First Philosophy, With Selections from the Objections and Replies*, trans. and ed. John Cottingham (Cambridge: Cambridge University Press, 1996), p. 18.

20 Georges Poulet, *Studies in Human Time*, trans. Elliott Coleman (Baltimore: Johns Hopkins University Press, 1956), p. 291.

21 In a recent series of lectures, Judith Butler has traced the relevance of the *Meditations* to the works of Kafka and Borges, and I draw here on her analysis of Descartes. The lectures were delivered in a course on "philosophical fictions" at the University of California at Berkeley in the fall of 1996. They are cited here with permission. See also Jacques Derrida, "Cogito and the History of Madness," in *Writing and Difference*, trans. Alan Bass (Chicago: University of Chicago Press, 1978).

22 René Descartes, *Méditations métaphysiques* (Paris: Vrin, 1976), p. 4; *Meditations on First Philosophy*, p. 12. The French quotation is from the translation into French from Latin that was published with Descartes's approval during his lifetime. The English is my own translation from the French, adapted from John Cottingham's translation from the Latin. See Cottingham, "Note on the text and translation," in René Descartes, *Meditations on First Philosophy*, pp. xliii–xlvi.

23 *Recherche*, I, p. 3; *Remembrance*, I, p. 3.
24 Frederick J. Copleston, S.J., *A History of Philosophy* (Garden City, N.Y.: Doubleday, 1944–1974), IV, p. 77.
25 *Meditations*, 13; *Méditations métaphysiques*, 6.
26 "Esquisse IV," in *Recherche*, I, p. 653.
27 *Recherche*, I, p. 3; *Remembrance*, I, p. 3. See Gérard Genette, "Time and Narrative in *A la recherche*," in Harold Bloom, ed., *Marcel Proust: Modern Critical Views* (New York: Chelsea House, 1987), pp. 145–164.
28 Butler, lecture of September 5, 1996.
29 See Edmund Husserl, *Cartesian Meditations: An Introduction to Phenomenology*, trans. Dorion Cairns (Dordrecht: Kluwer, 1991).
30 See Jean de Pierrefeu, "Le cas de M. Proust" and Ramon Fernandez, "La Garantie des sentiments" in Leigh Hodson, ed., *Marcel Proust: The Critical Heritage* (London: Routledge, 1989), pp. 133–136 and 337–344; Richard Terdiman, *The Dialectics of Isolation: Self and Society in the French Novel from the Realists to Proust* (New Haven: Yale University Press, 1976); Michael Sprinker, *History and Ideology in Proust:* A la recherche du temps perdu *and the Third French Republic* (Cambridge: Cambridge University Press, 1994).
31 See Terdiman, *Dialectics of Isolation*, p. 235.
32 Paul de Man, *Allegories of Reading: Figural Language in Rousseau, Nietzsche, Rilke, and Proust* (New Haven: Yale University Press, 1979).
33 See Paul de Man, *Blindness and Insight: Essays in the Rhetoric of Contemporary Criticism* (Minneapolis: University of Minnesota Press, 1983).
34 René Descartes, *A Discourse on Method*, trans. F. E. Sutcliffe (Harmondsworth: Penguin, 1968), part I. *Remembrance*, III, p. 353; *Recherche*, III, p. 848 and 1774n.
35 See *Remembrance*, I, pp. 416–427.
36 Jean-Jacques Rousseau, *On the Social Contract*, Book IV, Chapter I, in *The Basic Political Writings*, trans. Donald A. Cress (Indianapolis: Hackett, 1987), p. 204.
37 See Judith Butler, *Gender Trouble: Feminism and the Subversion of Identity* (London: Routledge, 1993).
38 Morris B. Kaplan, "Refiguring the Jewish Question: Arendt, Proust, and the Politics of Sexuality," in *Feminist Interpretations of Hannah Arendt*, ed. Bonnie Honig (University Park: Pennsylvania State Press, 1995), pp. 135–166.
39 Eugen Weber, *Peasants into Frenchmen* (Stanford: Stanford University Press, 1976).
40 See especially Eve Kosofsky Sedgwick, *The Epistemology of the Closet* (Berkeley: University of California Press, 1990), pp. 67–90 and 213–251.
41 "Refiguring," p. 123.
42 "Exclusive identification" is Judith Butler's phrase, quoted in Kaplan, "Refiguring."
43 "What is a Nation?," pp. 14, 15.
44 Quoted in Painter, *Marcel Proust*, p. 210.

45 Sprinker makes this mistaken claim in *History and Ideology in Proust.*
46 *Remembrance*, II, p. 240. See Painter's discussion of the affair in *Marcel Proust.*
47 J. Rivers in *Proust and the Art of Love* criticizes Proust's internalized homophobia, a simplification and misreading of the gay and lesbian themes in *A la recherche* that Sedgwick criticizes very effectively in her *The Epistemology of the Closet.*
48 See Judith Butler, *Bodies that Matter: On the Discursive Limitations of "Sex"* (London: Routledge, 1993), pp. 167–186.
49 *Remembrance*, I, pp. 98–99. "[C]e n'était pas d'habitude parmi les meilleurs que je le choisissais." *Recherche*, I, pp. 90–91.
50 Walter Benjamin, "The Image of Proust," in *Illuminations*, ed. Hannah Arendt, trans. Harry Zohn (New York: Schocken, 1969), p. 203.
51 Marcel Proust, *Selected Letters*, trans. Terence Kilmartin, ed. Philip Kolb (New York: Oxford University Press, 1983–   ), I, pp. 343–344.
52 Painter, *Marcel Proust*, p. 344.
53 Proust, *Selected Letters*, II, p. 188.

5 D'ANNUNZIO AND THE DISCOURSE OF EMBODIMENT

1 Gabriele d'Annunzio, letter of July 15, 1897 to Luigi Lodi, quoted in Alatri, p. 193. I draw extensively on Alatri's magisterial biography in what follows.
2 For the allusion to Dante, see Paolo Valesio, *D'Annunzio: The Dark Flame*, trans. Marilyn Migiel (New Haven: Yale University Press, 1992), p. 88 and Dante, *Paradiso*, 33.65–66, in *The Divine Comedy: A Verse Translation*, trans. Allen Mandelbaum (New York: Bantam, 1982).
3 See Christopher Seton-Watson, *Italy from Liberalism to Fascism, 1870–1925* (London: Methuen, 1967), pp. 580, 676.
4 Valesio, *D'Annunzio*, p. xviii.
5 Michael Tratner, *Modernism and Mass Politics: Joyce, Woolf, Eliot, Yeats* (Stanford: Stanford University Press, 1995), pp. 116–131.
6 Seton-Watson, *Italy from Liberalism to Fascism*, p. 596.
7 D'Annunzio, letter of January 20, 1933 to G. Rizzo, quoted in Alatri, p. 490.
8 Alfredo Bonadeo, *D'Annunzio and the Great War* (Madison: Farleigh Dickinson University Press, 1995), p. 162.
9 See Renzo de Felice, *D'Annunzio politico, 1918–1938* (Rome: Laterza, 1978); and Michael Ledeen, *The First Duce: D'Annunzio at Fiume* (Baltimore: Johns Hopkins University Press, 1977).
10 See Alatri, pp. 485–490.
11 See Seton-Watson, *Italy from Liberalism to Fascism*, pp. 612–629; De Felice, *D'Annunzio politico*, pp. 141–223; Alatri, *D'Annunzio*, pp. 491 ff.
12 Hans Ulrich Gumbrecht, "I Redentori della Vittoria: On Fiume's Place in the Genealogy of Fascism," *Journal of Contemporary History* 31 (1996): 255. See also Jared Becker, *Nationalism and Culture: Gabriele D'Annunzio and Italy after the Risorgimento*, Studies in Italian Culture, Literature in History (New York: Lang, 1994).

13 Quoted in Seton-Watson, *Italy from Liberalism to Fascism*, p. 13.
14 Emilio Gentile, *The Sacralization of Politics in Fascist Italy*, trans. Keith Botsford (Cambridge, Mass.: Harvard University Press, 1996).
15 D'Annunzio, "La très amère Adriatique," article of April 25, 1915, quoted in Alatri, p. 349.
16 D'Annunzio, "Orazione di Quarto," trans. Michael Ledeen, quoted in Ledeen, *The First Duce*, p. 9.
17 *Notturno*, p. 55.
18 Charles Klopp, *Gabriele d'Annunzio* (Boston: Twayne-Hall, 1988), p. III.
19 Gentile, *The Sacralization of Politics*, p. 17.
20 Bonadeo, *D'Annunzio and the Great War*, p. 88.
21 Jeffrey Schnapp, "Nietzsche's Italian Style: Gabriele D'Annunzio," in *Nietzsche in Italy*, ed. Thomas Harrison (Saratoga, Calif.: Anma Libri, 1988), pp. 251–253, 262–263. On the competing images of d'Annunzio, see also Barbara Spackman, *Decadent Genealogies: The Rhetoric of Sickness from Baudelaire to D'Annunzio* (Ithaca: Cornell University Press, 1989).
22 Jeffrey Schnapp, *Staging Fascism: 18BL and the Theater of Masses for Masses* (Stanford: Stanford University Press, 1996), p. 103.
23 Valesio, *D'Annunzio*, p. 94.
24 See Carla Riccardi, "L'elaborazione del 'Notturno': il delirio lirico organiz-zato," in *D'Annunzio Notturno* (Pescara: Centro Nazionale di Studi Dannunziani, 1986), p. 41.
25 See Erich Auerbach, "Figura," in *Scenes from the Drama of European Literature* (Minneapolis: University of Minnesota Press, 1984), pp. 11–76; Dante, Letter to Can Grande in *Critical Theory since Plato*, ed. Hazard Adams (San Diego: Harcourt Brace Jovanovitch, 1971).
26 *Notturno*, p. 49; *Nocturne*, p. 217.
27 De Voto, Oli, *Dizionario della lingua italiana*.
28 Giorgio Bárberi Squarotti, *La scrittura verso il nulla: D'Annunzio* (Turin: Genesi, 1992), p. 314.
29 Bonadeo, *D'Annunzio and the Great War*, pp. 96–101.
30 Dante, *Inferno*, 34.22–25.
31 See Riccardi, "L'elaborazione del 'Notturno,'" p. 43. See also Riccardi, "Autografi inediti del 'Notturno': 'I giorni funebri' e 'L'apparizione,'" *Autografo: Quadrimestrale del Centro di Ricerca sulla Tradizione Manoscritta di Autori Contemporanei* 3.7 (February 1986): 14–26; "Modelli di edizione critica per il 'Notturno,'" in *Studi su D'Annunzio* (Genoa: Marietti, 1991) 127–144; "La prima forma del 'Notturno,'" *Paragone Letteratura* 464 (October 1988): 24–31; and Carla Riccardi, ed., "Gabriele D'Annunzio: Taccuini, diari, lettere: Nuovi documenti sulla genesi del 'Notturno,'" *Strumenti critici* n. s. 55 (1987): 371–389.
32 See Riccardi, "L'elaborazione del 'Notturno,'" p. 46.
33 *Ibid.*, p. 52.
34 *Notturno*, p. 121.
35 Riccardi, "Le forme del racconto notturno."

36 See *Oxford English Dictionary* and De Voto, *Dizionario della lingua italiana*.
37 Bonadeo, *D'Annunzio and the Great War*, p. 101.
38 Gumbrecht, "I redentori della vittoria," p. 268.
39 *New Grove Dictionary of Music*, pp. 258–259.
40 *Notturno*, p. 240.
41 Robert Pogue Harrison, *The Body of Beatrice* (Baltimore: Johns Hopkins University Press, 1988), p. 94.
42 See Fredi Chiappelli's notes to his edition of the *Vita Nuova* (Milan: Mursia, 1983), section 3.
43 Renato Barilli, *D'Annunzio in Prosa* (Milan: Mursia, 1993), p. 238.
44 Niva Lorenzini, *Il segno del corpo: saggio su d'Annunzio* (Rome: Bulzoni, 1984), pp. 12–13.
45 Gabriele d'Annunzio,*The Child of Pleasure*, trans. Georgina Harding (London: Dedalus, 1991), p. 24. See also *Il Piacere* in *Prose di romanzi*, ed. Ezio Raimondi, Annamaria Andreoli, and Niva Lorenzini (Milan: Mondadori, 1988–1989), I, p. 36.
46 See the poem on *The Child of Pleasure*, pp. 104–106; *Il Piacere*, pp. 149–151.
47 Erich Auerbach, *Mimesis: The Representation of Reality in Western Literature*, trans. Willard R. Trask (Princeton: Princeton University Press, 1953), p. 536.
48 Matthew 22:21.

CONCLUSION

1 On the agonistic element in modernism, see Renato Poggioli, *Theory of the Avant-Garde*, trans. Gerald Fitzgerald (Cambridge, Mass.: Harvard University Press, 1968).
2 Georg Lukács, *The Theory of the Novel: A historico-philosophical essay on the epic forms of great literature*, trans. Anna Bostock (Cambridge, Mass.: MIT Press, 1971), p. 112.
3 *Remembrance*, III, p. 917; *Recherche*, IV, p. 467.
4 Walter Benjamin, "The Storyteller," in *Illuminations*, ed. Hannah Arendt, trans. Harry Zohn (New York: Schocken, 1969), p. 101.
5 Georg Lukács, *History and Class Consciousness: Studies in Marxist Dialectics*, trans. Rodney Livingstone (Cambridge, Mass.: MIT Press, 1971), p. 145.
6 Hannah Arendt, *The Human Condition* (Chicago: University of Chicago Press, 1958), p. 184.
7 See Max Weber, *The Protestant Ethic and the Spirit of Capitalism*, trans. Talcott Parsons (London: Routledge, 1992).
8 Immanuel Kant, preface to second edition, *Critique of Pure Reason*, trans. Norman Kemp Smith (New York: St. Martin's Press, 1965), p. 22.
9 See Bernard Williams, *Ethics and the Limits of Philosophy* (Cambridge, Mass.: Harvard University Press, 1985); Seyla Benhabib, *Critique, Norm, and Utopia: A Study of the Foundations of Critical Theory* (New York: Columbia University Press, 1986).
10 Stefan Collini, Donald Winch, and John Burrow, *That Noble Science of Politics:*

A Study in Nineteenth-Century Intellectual History (Cambridge: Cambridge University Press, 1983).

11 Erich Auerbach, *Mimesis: The Representation of Reality in Western Literature*, trans. Willard R. Trask (Princeton: Princeton University Press, 1953), pp. 541–542.

12 Virginia Woolf, "Mr. Bennett and Mrs. Brown," quoted in Raymond Williams, *The English Novel* (New York: Oxford University Press, 1970), p. 189.

13 Ian Watt, *The Rise of the Novel* (Berkeley: University of California Press, 1959).

14 See Max Horkheimer and Theodor W. Adorno, *Dialectic of Enlightenment*, trans. John Cumming (New York: Continuum, 1988).

15 Williams, *Ethics and the Limits of Philosophy*, pp. 93–119.

16 Lionel Trilling, *The Liberal Imagination* (Garden City, NY: Doubleday, 1953), p. xi.

17 Yael Tamir, *Liberal Nationalism* (Princeton: Princeton University Press, 1995); *Portrait*, pp. 252–253; *HD*, p. 64; *Notturno*, p. 180; *Remembrance*, III, p. 1089. Some of the conclusions of these final paragraphs were stimulated by Elizabeth Fox-Genovese's talk at a conference on "The Broken Middle" at Yale University in September 1998 and by conversations I had afterwards with Tyrus Miller, who organized the conference.

Select bibliography

Alatri, Paolo. *Gabriele D'Annunzio*. Turin: Unione Tipografico-Editrice Torinese, 1983.

Althusser, Louis. "Ideology and Ideological State Apparatuses." *Lenin and Philosophy and Other Essays*. Trans. Ben Brewster. London: New Left Books, 1971.

Anderson, Benedict. *Imagined Communities: Reflections on the Origin and Spread of Nationalism*. 2nd edn London: Verso, 1991.

Arendt, Hannah. *The Human Condition*. Chicago: University of Chicago Press, 1958.

The Origins of Totalitarianism. New ed. San Diego, New York, and London: Harcourt Brace, 1979.

"On Humanity in Dark Times: Thoughts on Lessing." Foreword to *"Nathan the Wise," "Minna Von Barnhelm," and Other Plays and Writings* by Gotthold Ephraim Lessing. Ed. Peter Demetz. New York: Continuum, 1991. vii–xx.

Auerbach, Erich. *Mimesis: The Representation of Reality in Western Literature*. Trans. Willard R. Trask. Princeton: Princeton University Press, 1953.

"Figura." *Scenes from the Drama of European Literature*. Minneapolis: University of Minnesota Press, 1984. 11–76.

Barthes, Roland. *S/Z: An Essay*. Trans. Richard Miller. New York: Hill and Wang, 1974.

Beer, Samuel H. "Liberalism and the National Idea." *The Public Interest* 5 (1966): 70–82.

Benhabib, Seyla. *Critique, Norm, and Utopia: A Study of the Foundations of Critical Theory*. New York: Columbia University Press, 1986.

The Reluctant Modernism of Hannah Arendt. Modernity and Political Thought, vol. 10. Thousand Oaks: Sage, 1996.

Benjamin, Walter. *Illuminations*. Ed. Hannah Arendt. Trans. Harry Zohn. New York: Schocken, 1969.

Berlin, Isaiah. *The Crooked Timber of Humanity: Chapters in the History of Ideas*. Ed. Henry Hardy. New York: Vintage-Random House, 1992.

Bersani, Leo. *Homos*. Cambridge, Massachusetts: Harvard University Press, 1995.

Marcel Proust: The Fictions of Life and Art. New York: Oxford University Press, 1965.

Bhabha, Homi K., ed. *Nation and Narration*. London: Routledge, 1990.

Bloom, Harold, ed. *Marcel Proust: Modern Critical Views*. New York: Chelsea House, 1987.

Burrow, J. W. *Evolution and Society: A Study in Victorian Social Theory*, Cambridge: Cambridge University Press, 1966.

    Whigs and Liberals: Continuity and Change in English Political Thought. Oxford: Clarendon Press, 1988.

Butler, Judith. *Bodies that Matter: On the Discursive Limitations of "Sex."* London: Routledge, 1993.

Cassirer, Ernst. *Rousseau, Kant, Goethe: Two Essays*. Princeton: Princeton University Press, 1945.

Cheng, Vincent. *Joyce, Race, and Empire*. Cambridge: Cambridge University Press, 1995.

Clark, Martin, *Modern Italy 1871–1982*. London: Longman, 1984.

Collini, Stefan. "Liberalism and the Legacy of Mill." *Historical Journal* 20 (1977): 237–254.

    Public Moralists: Political Thought and Intellectual Life in Britain, 1850–1930. Oxford: Clarendon Press, 1991.

Collini, Stefan, Donald Winch, and John Burrow. *That Noble Science of Politics: A Study in Nineteenth-Century Intellectual History*. Cambridge: Cambridge University Press, 1983.

Cumming, Robert Denoon. *Human Nature and History: A Study of the Development of Liberal Political Thought*. 2 volumes. Chicago: University of Chicago Press, 1969.

Curtius, Ernst Robert. *Marcel Proust*. 1925. Translated into French (from the German) by Armand Pierhal. Paris: Éditions de la Révue Nouvelle, 1928.

Deane, Seamus. *Celtic Revivals: Essays in Modern Irish Literature, 1880–1980*. London: Faber and Faber, 1985.

Deane, Seamus, ed. *A Portrait of the Artist as a Young Man* by James Joyce. Harmondsworth: Penguin, 1992.

De Felice, Renzo. *D'Annunzio politico, 1918–1938*. Rome: Laterza, 1978.

De Man, Paul. *Allegories of Reading: Figural Language in Rousseau, Nietzsche, Rilke, and Proust*. New Haven: Yale University Press, 1979.

Ellmann, Richard. *James Joyce*. Revised edn New York: Oxford University Press, 1982.

Fleishman, Avrom. *Conrad's Politics: Community and Anarchy in the Fiction of Joseph Conrad*. Baltimore: Johns Hopkins University Press, 1967.

Foster, R. F. *Modern Ireland, 1600–1972*. New York: Penguin, 1989.

Furet, François. *Interpreting the French Revolution*. Trans. Elborg Forster. Cambridge: Cambridge University Press, 1981.

Gallagher, Catherine. *The Industrial Reformation of English Fiction: Social Discourse and Narrative Form, 1832–1867*. Chicago: University of Chicago Press, 1985.

Gellner, Ernest. *Nations and Nationalism*. Ithaca: Cornell University Press, 1983.

Gentile, Emilio. *The Sacralization of Politics in Fascist Italy*. Trans. Keith Botsford. Cambridge: Harvard University Press, 1996.

Gifford, Don. *Joyce Annotated: Notes for* Dubliners *and* A Portrait of the Artist as a Young Man. 2nd edn Berkeley: University of California Press, 1982.

Girard, René. *Deceit, Desire, and the Novel: Self and Other in Literary Structure*. Trans. Yvonne Freccero. Baltimore: Johns Hopkins University Press, 1965.

Gumbrecht, Hans Ulrich. *Making Sense in Life and Literature*. Trans. Glen Burns. Minneapolis: University of Minnesota Press, 1992.

"I Redentori della Vittoria: On Fiume's Place in the Genealogy of Fascism." *Journal of Contemporary History* 31 (1996): 253–272.

Harrison, Robert Pogue. *The Body of Beatrice*. Baltimore: Johns Hopkins University Press, 1988.

Hobhouse, Leonard T. *Liberalism and Other Writings*. Ed. James Meadowcroft. Cambridge: Cambridge University Press, 1994.

Hobsbawm, E. J. *Nations and Nationalism since 1780*. Cambridge: Cambridge University Press, 1990.

Hobson, J. A. *Imperialism: A Study*. 1902. Ed. Philip Siegelman. Ann Arbor: University of Michigan Press, 1965.

Honig, Bonnie. *Political Theory and the Displacement of Politics*. Ithaca: Cornell University Press, 1993.

Horkheimer, Max, and Theodor W. Adorno. *Dialectic of Enlightenment*. Trans. John Cumming. New York: Continuum, 1988.

Hughes, H. Stuart. *Consciousness and Society: The Reorientation of European Social Thought, 1890–1930*. Revised edition. New York: Vintage, 1977.

Huxley, Thomas H. *"Evolution and Ethics" and Other Essays*. New York. 1894.

Jameson, Fredric. *The Political Unconscious: Narrative as a Socially Symbolic Art*. Ithaca: Cornell University Press, 1981.

Kaplan, Morris B. "Refiguring the Jewish Question: Arendt, Proust, and the Politics of Sexuality." *Feminist Interpretations of Hannah Arendt*. Ed. Bonnie Honig. University Park: Pennsylvania State Press, 1995. 135–166.

Kelly, George Armstrong. *The Humane Comedy: Constant, Tocqueville and French Liberalism*. Cambridge: Cambridge University Press, 1992.

Knapp Hay, Eloise. *The Political Novels of Joseph Conrad: A Critical Study*. Chicago: University of Chicago Press, 1963.

Ledeen, Michael. *The First Duce: D'Annunzio at Fiume*. Baltimore: Johns Hopkins University Press, 1977.

Levenson, Michael. *Modernism and the Fate of Individuality: Character and Novelistic Form from Conrad to Woolf*. Cambridge: Cambridge University Press, 1991.

Lloyd, David. *Anomalous States: Irish Writing and the Post-Colonial Moment*. Durham: Duke University Press, 1993.

Lorenzini, Niva. *Il Segno del corpo: saggio su d'Annunzio*. Rome: Bulzoni, 1984.

Lukács, Georg. *History and Class Consciousness: Studies in Marxist Dialectics*. Cambridge, Massachusetts: MIT Press, 1971.

The Theory of the Novel: A Historico-Philosophical Essay on the Epic Forms of Great Literature. 1916. Trans. Anna Bostock. Cambridge, Massachusetts: MIT Press, 1971.

MacCabe, Colin. *James Joyce and the Revolution of the World*. New York: Harper and Row, 1979.

Manganiello, Dominic. *Joyce's Politics*. London: Routledge and Kegan Paul, 1980.

Mayeur, Jean-Marie, and Madeleine Rebérioux. *The Third Republic from its Origins to the Great War, 1871–1914*. Trans. J. R. Foster. Cambridge: Cambridge University Press, 1984.

Moretti, Franco. *The Way of the World: The Bildungsroman in European Culture*. London: Verso, 1987.

Nolan, Emer. *James Joyce and Nationalism*. London: Routledge, 1995.

O'Brien, Conor Cruise. "Passion and Cunning: An Essay on the Politics of W. B. Yeats." *In Excited Reverie*. Ed. A. Norman Jeffares and K. G. W. Cross. New York: Macmillan, 1965. 207–278.

Painter, George D. *Marcel Proust*. Harmondsworth: Penguin, 1983.

Parry, Benita. "Conrad and England." *Patriotism: The Making and Unmaking of British Character*. Ed. Raphael Samuel. London and New York: Routledge, 1989. Vol. 3. 189–198.

Petrey, Sandy. *Realism and Revolution: Balzac, Stendhal, Zola, and the Performances of History*. Ithaca: Cornell University Press, 1988.

Rawls, John. *A Theory of Justice*. Cambridge, Massachusetts: Harvard University Press, 1972.

  "Justice as Fairness: Political not Metaphysical." *Philosophy and Public Affairs* 14 (1985): 223–251.

Riccardi, Carla. "L'elaborazione del 'Notturno': il delirio lirico organizzato." *D'Annunzio Notturno*. Pescara: Centro Nazionale di Studi Dannunziani, 1986. 37–61.

Said, Edward. *Joseph Conrad and the Fiction of Autobiography*. Cambridge, Massachusetts: Harvard University Press, 1966.

  Culture and Imperialism. New York: Knopf, 1993.

Sandel, Michael J. *Liberalism and the Limits of Justice*. Cambridge: Cambridge University Press, 1982.

Sandel, Michael J., ed. *Liberalism and Its Critics*. Oxford: Blackwell, 1984.

Schnapp, Jeffrey T. "Nietzsche's Italian Style: Gabriele D'Annunzio." *Nietzsche in Italy*. Ed. Thomas Harrison. Saratoga, California: Anma Libri, 1988. 247–264.

Sedgwick, Eve Kosofsky. *Epistemology of the Closet*. Berkeley: University of California Press, 1990.

Seton-Watson, Christopher. *Italy from Liberalism to Fascism, 1870–1925*. London: Methuen, 1967.

Siedentop, Larry. *Tocqueville*. Oxford: Oxford University Press, 1994.

Spackman, Barbara. *Decadent Genealogies: The Rhetoric of Sickness from Baudelaire to D'Annunzio*. Ithaca: Cornell University Press, 1989.

Sprinker, Michael. *History and Ideology in Proust: A la recherche du temps perdu and the Third French Republic*. Cambridge: Cambridge University Press, 1994.

Sternhell, Zeev. *Maurice Barrés et le nationalisme français*. Cahiers de la fondation nationale des sciences politiques 182. Paris: Colin, 1972.

Stocking, George W., Jr. *Victorian Anthropology*. New York: Macmillan, 1987.

Strauss, Leo. *Natural Right and History*. Chicago: University of Chicago Press, 1953.

Tamir, Yael. *Liberal Nationalism*. First paperback printing with new preface. Princeton: Princeton University Press, 1995.

Taylor, Charles. *Hegel*. Cambridge: Cambridge University Press, 1975.

Terdiman, Richard. *The Dialectics of Isolation: Self and Society in the French Novel from the Realists to Proust*. New Haven: Yale University Press, 1976.

Tratner, Michael. *Modernism and Mass Politics: Joyce, Woolf, Eliot, Yeats*. Stanford: Stanford University Press, 1995.

Valesio, Paolo. *D'Annunzio: The Dark Flame*. Trans. Marilyn Migiel. New Haven: Yale University Press, 1992.

Watt, Ian. *The Rise of the Novel*. Berkeley. University of California Press, 1959.
Conrad in the Nineteenth Century. Berkeley: University of California Press, 1979.

Webb, R. K. *Modern England: From the 18th Century to the Present*. New York: Harper and Row, 1968.

Weber, Eugen. *The Nationalist Revival in France, 1905–1914*. Berkeley: University of California Press, 1959.
France Fin de Siècle. Cambridge, Massachusetts: Harvard University Press, 1986.

Weber Max. "The Meaning of 'Ethical Neutrality' in Sociology and Economics." *The Methodology of the Social Sciences*. Trans. and ed. Edward A. Shils and Henry A. Finch. Glencoe, Illinois: Free Press, 1949. 1–47.
The Protestant Ethic and the Spirit of Capitalism. Trans. Talcott Parsons. London: Routledge, 1992.

White, Hayden. *Metahistory: The Historical Imagination in Nineteenth-Century Europe*. Baltimore: Johns Hopkins University Press, 1973.

Williams, Bernard. *Ethics and the Limits of Philosophy*. Cambridge, Massachusetts: Harvard University Press, 1985.
Shame and Necessity. Berkeley: University of California Press, 1993.

Williams, Raymond. *The English Novel from Dickens to Lawrence*. New York: Oxford University Press, 1970.
Culture and Society: 1780–1950. 2nd edn New York: Columbia University Press, 1983.

Wilson, Edmund. *Axel's Castle: A Study in the Imaginative Literature of 1870–1930*. New York: Charles Scribner's Sons, 1931.

Winton, Alison. *Proust's Additions: The Making of "A la recherche du temps perdu."* 2 volumes. Cambridge: Cambridge University Press, 1977.

Index